HISTORIC HAMPTON ROADS

Where America Began

By Paul Clancy

Commissioned by the Hampton Roads Chamber of Commerce,
the Virginia Peninsula Chamber of Commerce, and
the Williamsburg Area Chamber of Commerce

Historical Publishing Network
A division of Lammert Incorporated
San Antonio, Texas

A scene at Norfolk Harbor, 1856.

COURTESY OF THE SARGEANT MEMORIAL ROOM,
NORFOLK PUBLIC LIBRARY.

ISBN: 9781893619654

Library of Congress Card Catalog Number: 2006933624

Historic Hampton Roads: Where America Began

author:	Paul Clancy
cover artist:	Claiborne D. Gregory, Jr.
contributing writers for "Sharing the Heritage":	Joe Goodpasture and Scott Williams

Historical Publishing Network

president:	Ron Lammert
project managers:	Lou Ann Murphy, Joe Neely, and Robin Neely
director of operations:	Charles A. Newton III
administration:	Angela Lake, Donna M. Mata, and Diane Perez
book sales:	Dee Steidle
production:	Colin Hart, Evelyn Hart, and Craig Mitchell

PRINTED IN SINGAPORE

CONTENTS

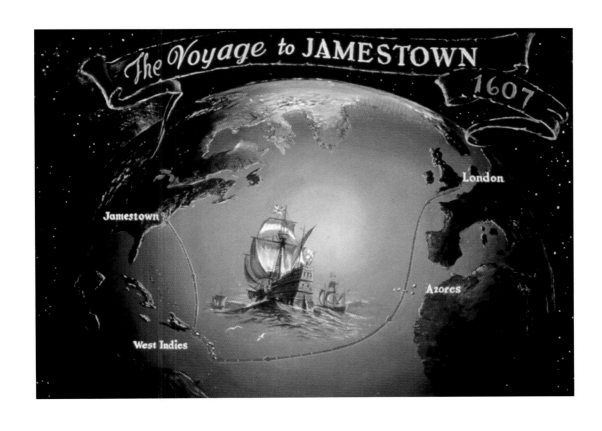

The Jamestown journey followed the traditional route to the West Indies, then northward to Virginia.

COURTESY OF THE NATIONAL PARK SERVICE, COLONIAL NATIONAL HISTORICAL PARK.

PROLOGUE

On days stormy or fair you can stand at an overlook on the high dunes at Cape Henry, where pelicans patrol the shoreline, where sea grasses wave in the breeze, and imagine what native people must felt when they saw three small ships, flying flags of a strange country, making for the entrance of the great bay. And you can sense, perhaps, the relief and wonder among the passengers and crew upon sighting journey's end and imagining a new beginning.

The first English settlers could not have foreseen what was in store for them or the nation they were about to create, but the waters they had entered would run wide and deep. They would leave Hampton Roads, as the region would become known, saturated with history, an almost-mind-boggling parade of events that shaped a region and the nation. The evidence is everywhere, and the exciting thing is that you can find it just about any place you look, from artifacts to museums, historic houses, monuments, and sweeping overlooks. You can wander across Hampton Roads and find yourself caught in the midst of it all.

At Cape Henry one may stand and listen to the timeless roar of the ocean and imagine the scene four hundred years ago, or at other places on Hampton Roads and the James River, where the settlers briefly stopped, and then of course Jamestown where exhibits and archaeological digs vividly tell the story of the first permanent English settlement in America. You can wander through historic homes in Norfolk, Portsmouth and Suffolk, tour museums in Hampton and Newport News, walk through restorations and reenactments of America's colonial past in Williamsburg and tour the battlefield at Yorktown where the nation's independence was secured. The history of Hampton Roads comes at you with open arms.

The story does not, of course, begin with April 26, 1607, the day the English colonists arrived in the new world.

The landing of the English settlers at Jamestown Island. Their ships were, from left, the Discovery, Susan Constant, *and* Godspeed. *It took the colonists four and a half months to make the voyage. New replicas of the* Godspeed *and* Discovery *were under construction, with the completed* Godspeed *expected to take part in the 2007 celebration. From a painting by Griffith Baily Coale, 1890-1950.*
COURTESY OF THE LIBRARY OF VIRGINIA.

CHAPTER I

BEGINNINGS

They came gradually, small bands of hunter-gatherers who crossed the land bridge over the Bering Sea during the last great ice age, and then moved, generation by generation, clear across the continent. These Paleo-Indians migrated eastward in search of game and arable land. About sixteen thousand years ago, people we now call Native Americans settled along the fertile flood plains of Virginia's rivers, enjoying a plentiful harvest of fish and oysters and clams, hunting big game, gathering wild fruit and marsh tubers. At the same time the Chesapeake Bay and its tributaries filled in as the sea level rose. It was a goodly place.

It is one thing to celebrate the founding of a nation 400 years ago in a place called Jamestown, and quite another to realize that native people had lived and endured in this land for 160 centuries. The Virginia Algonquians did not build permanent villages or settlements, but lived as foragers, moving from one place to another because they lacked the fertilizer to keep crop land productive. They camped along what has become known as the Suffolk Scarp, the edge of a crater formed by a meteor impact millions of years before. As recently as ten thousand years ago, it was the dune line of the ocean.

During the pre-Jamestown era they spent several months each year in their settlements, but went out for lengthy foraging trips. They made their dwellings by bending and lashing together the tops of saplings, covering them with bark or reed mats. The huts were rounded, making them somewhat wind resistant. And they were flimsy, but not meant to be permanent anyway. Instead, over hundreds of years, new dwellings sometimes were constructed right on top of the remains of previous ones. Each one housed anywhere from 6 to 20 people, with a small entrance and a smoke hole on top. In winter, the villages would be bathed in smoke and the living quarters chokingly close.

Nevertheless the Algonquians were a sturdy lot. The women managed all the farming and household chores, planting and harvesting, cooking, curing hides, tending fires, making baskets, mats, pots and utensils. They even built the huts. This freed the men for equally rigorous work. From early childhood they were taught to hunt and fight. Whether from chasing a foe or running from one, or pursuing a wounded animal, the more accomplished of them were robust and fit.

Giovanni da Verrazano, who landed first to the south and then the north of the Chesapeake region in 1524, described the natives as russet-hued, with hair that was black and straight. They ate fish, game and wild peas, he said, and used reed arrows tipped with stone. They made canoes from whole tree trunks, charring them and hollowing them out with shells. They used tobacco not for pleasure but ceremony, burning it as sacrifice to various gods to ensure good weather or safe passage. They smoked pipes of peace with former enemies and, literally, buried hatchets to signal the end of hostilities.

Instead of months they divided a year into five seasons for the budding of corn, the earing of corn, the highest sun, the gathering of corn, and the call of the goose.

There appear to have been few major conflicts between tribes in the southeastern part of Virginia. Mostly, the fights were territorial skirmishes. They often shared foraging grounds, so the chances of running into each other were good. One reason for the relative harmony among the native peoples was the extraordinary power of one paramount "weroance," or chief, known as Powhatan. This man, born around 1540, inherited the leadership of six tribes when he came to power, but by the time the colonists arrived he had, either by intimidation or outright force, established a confederacy of about thirty tribes. Some, like the Chickahominy, were more independent than others. Some believe that Powhatan, acting on the prophesy of a dream, completely wiped out another tribe, the Chesapeakes, or Chesapeians, living in what is today South Hampton Roads. It was this tribe with

⚓

Secoton, a village of unknown location, was depicted by John White during his pre-Jamestown forays into Carolina and Virginia. Soon after, Flemish engraver Theodor de Bry copied and embellished the drawings. The scene depicts several plots of corn in various stages, with Indians at lower right doing a ceremonial dance.

whom the remnants of the Lost Colony in
North Carolina may have intermingled. But
these conflicts were nothing like the all-out
warfare that was to visit these shores in the
decades to come after white sails materialized
out of the seas.

ARRIVAL

It was just before dawn on Saturday, April
26, 1607, when the watch on board one of
three small ships spotted a long stretch of
beach and sand dunes off to port and cried

out that land, almost certainly the coast of Virginia, had been spotted. It was a most welcome sight for the 144 passengers and crew of the storm-battered *Susan Constant*, *Godspeed*, and *Discovery*. After five days and nights in the teeth of a "vehement tempest," as one put it, they were desperate to learn their position and depth. And now the coastline, brooding at first light, crept into sight.

The three square-rigged ships carried the hopes and dreams of investors in the Virginia Company, who expected the men to find a coveted passage to the Orient and shores flecked with gold. At the helm of the largest of the vessels was Captain Christopher Newport, an accomplished mariner who had made his name as a privateer in the Caribbean, capturing or destroying a score or more of Spanish cargo ships. Imprisoned in the hold of his ship, the *Susan Constant*, was an equally strong personality, John Smith. This head-strong soldier of fortune was opinionated, cocky, and almost certainly irritating. A commoner, he had infuriated the blueblood Edward-Maria Wingfield and gotten himself accused—falsely, as it turned out—of plotting treason. For this, he was almost hanged during a stopover in the Caribbean. His journey to the New World must have been humiliating, and yet he would one day emerge as savior of the whole enterprise.

Hours after sighting land, with fair winds at last filling their sails, the crews entered the Chesapeake Bay. They anchored just beyond a point they would call Cape Henry after Henry, Prince of Wales, the young first son of King James. Newport and thirty in his party—not Smith—went ashore. They discovered fair meadows and tall trees, with fresh streams running through the woods. They might have been near the present Broad Bay, an area that is now, and certainly was then, teeming with marshes, streams, and wildlife. George Percy, a young gentleman who was among the company of adventurers, said he was "almost ravished at the first sight thereof."

⚓

The first party of Englishmen came ashore at a spot just inside the entrance to the Chesapeake Bay, which they would call Cape Henry. The painting was done by Sidney King around 1950 for the 350th celebration of the arrival. The area is now First Landing State Park.

COURTESY OF THE NATIONAL PARK SERVICE, COLONIAL NATIONAL HISTORICAL PARK.

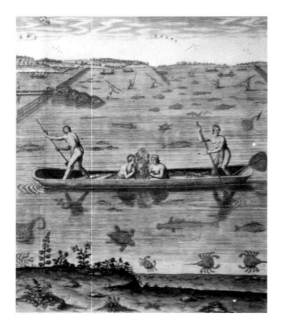

Top, left: "Their manner of fishing," is de Bry's depiction of Indians using fishing poles with hooks of hollowed fish bones.
COURTESY OF THE JAMESTOWN-YORKTOWN FOUNDATION COLLECTION.

Top, right: Typical Indian foods, by Robert Llewellyn.
COURTESY OF VIRTUAL JAMESTOWN, VIRGINIA TECH UNIVERSITY.

Below: In 1606, King James I granted a charter to a group of London entrepreneurs to establish a settlement in America. James, the son of Mary Queen of Scots, was an intellectual who had many other things on his mind, including the authorization of a new version of the Bible and an intense dislike for tobacco. The portrait is by Adrian Vanson, c. 1995.
COURTESY OF THE JAMESTOWN-YORKTOWN FOUNDATION COLLECTION.

What they didn't suspect was that a small band of warriors watched and followed, creeping through the woods on all fours with arrows in their teeth. As the visitors made their way to the boats that were to return them to their ships, the Indians attacked. They "charged us very desperately in the faces," Percy related, wounding Captain Gabriel Archer in both hands and one of the sailors in parts unmentioned. The Englishmen returned fire with their muskets and the attackers, their arrows spent anyway, turned and fled. These may have been warlike allies of Powhatan who had only recently routed the Chesapeakes from this seaside real estate. Regardless of who they were, the English settlers' first contact was hardly auspicious.

They were not the first white men to come with designs on setting up outposts on the Indians' ancestral lands. In August 1570, Spanish Jesuits established a mission on the shores of what was to be named the York River, expecting to civilize and Christianize the natives. The Spanish, who already had a strong presence in Florida, were actively engaged in exploring the Chesapeake Bay and in fact had named it *Bahia de Santa Maria*. But six months later, a war party crept into the small village and wiped out the mission. There would be bloody retribution, and although further attempts at a permanent Spanish settlement were abandoned, the long-time residents of this tidewater region were anything but thrilled or

awed at the sight of sailing vessels approaching from the sea.

On board the *Susan Constant*, the captains of the three ships—Newport, Bartholomew Gosnold of the *Godspeed*, and John Ratcliffe, of the *Discovery*—gathered to open the sealed orders from the Virginia Company of London, and received a slap in the face. Among the seven leaders selected to sit on the colony's ruling council were not only the predictable ones like Newport and Wingfield, but that irksome fellow down below, John Smith. They must have gritted their teeth even while they continued to hold him captive for a few more days. Nevertheless, Smith never seemed to lose heart. "Heaven and earth never agreed better to frame a place for man's habitat," he would later declare.

Besides the lineup of leaders, there were detailed instructions about where and how the party should locate their village. The orders were based not so much on fear of the Indians but on England's old adversaries, the Spanish. Place your settlement far from the

sea, the colonists were told, far enough that a warning might be given in the event that a foe approached. In fact, they were advised, make it at least a hundred miles from the mouth of the bay. It should also be at a narrow place on the river so that enemy ships would be within musket range of both shores and, most importantly, be "the strongest, most

wholesome and fertile place" they could find. Finally, the would-be intruders were urged to "have great care not to offend the naturals."

The colonists may have set out to follow these instructions, but it is remarkable how many of them would ultimately be ignored or simply forgotten.

The next day, April 28, they began assembling, from parts they had brought with them from England, a small boat called a shallop, a sailing/rowing vessel that would allow them to explore places they would not be able to reach in deep-draft vessels. They did quite a bit of exploring with their shallop, noting the shallow depths in the nearby river to the south and then crossing the bay to its westernmost shore. There they took soundings that revealed a deep channel and were so comforted by this that they named it Point Comfort. It was an inviting place and the following day they recrossed in their ships and went ashore. Seeing natives backing away, trembling with fear, Newport gestured to them, laying his hand over his heart in a sign of friendship. The warriors at last signaled for the visitors to follow them to their town, which they called Kecoughtan.

Above: This most famous likeness of Smith was intended to promote the sale of his account of a voyage to what would be the Maine and Massachusetts coasts in 1614. He surveyed the coastline, drawing a map as he went along and gave it a name: New England. From an engraving by Simon van de Passe.
COURTESY OF THE VIRGINIA HISTORICAL SOCIETY.

Left: Smith's richly illustrated map of Virginia shows Cape Henry at the mouth of the Chesapeake Bay and, just across, Point Comfort. It demonstrates how familiar Smith was with much of the Bay region through his own explorations.
COURTESY OF THE JAMESTOWN-YORKTOWN FOUNDATION COLLECTION.

they renamed it the James. On May 12, they stopped at a point of land where a creek empties into the main river. Some of the men, especially Gabriel Archer, liked this as a possible settlement. The soil was good, with plenty of trees, thick vines, squirrels and birds. They were enchanted by the sound of redwing blackbirds. But the main river was too shallow off this point, a majority of the party felt, and not particularly defensible. Besides, Newport argued, a more remote stretch of land would be less objectionable to the natives. They left, but not before naming the spot Archer's Hope.

On May 13, five miles further upriver, they anchored off a low-lying peninsula.

The water here was deep enough that the ships could stand right off the shore, moored to trees on land. They spent the night on board, and the next morning, May 14, brought their provisions ashore and began building crude fortifications. There were uninvited visitors that night, Indians from across the river who paddled over to check on this new development. The next day, a delegation of Paspaheghs from the local village arrived. Their chief would come, they indicated, bearing gifts.

The "weroance" did come but it was warriors, not gifts, that he brought: a hundred or so, armed and threatening:

> [He] made great signes to us to lay our Armes away. But we would not trust him so far: he seeing he could not have convenient time to worke his will, at length made signes that he would give us as much land as we could desire to take.

But it was not that friendly a first meeting. One of the "savages" stole a hatchet from one of the settlers, only to have it ripped from his hand. Another "came fiercely at our man with a wooden sword, thinking to beat out his brains." When the settlers braced for a fight, the chief stormed off angrily with all his company.

It seemed the settlers would have taken the trouble to prepare a stout defense, but their only fortification was a flimsy fence. And so conscientious were they about not offending

The Kecoughtans received the white men enthusiastically, bringing out mats from their houses and sitting down to share bread, corn and tobacco, which they smoked in clay pipes. After the feast, the hosts, naked except for leather briefs, heads half shaved, bodies painted red and black, danced, chanted and clapped, stomping and carrying on like wolves and devils, it seemed to the Englishmen. After their performance, Newport gave the dancers "Beades and other trifling Jewells," the sort of gifts that went a long way, at least at first.

There were similar receptions as the colonists scouted up and down what was known then as the Powhatan River—until

the natives, they left most of their guns in shipping crates. There the guns remained, even when Newport and several others, including a now-freed Smith, went off to explore the river. The party sailed and rowed all the way to the falls at present-day Richmond. It was only after they returned a week later, finding more than a dozen wounded and at least one dying from a ferocious attack, that they decided to erect a fort and defend it with weapons. A three-sided fort with guard stations on each corner was hurriedly built, even as Indians lurked in the woods, shooting and killing some of the men as they went to the woods to relieve themselves.

But it turned out that hostile attacks were not the worst of the settler's problems. For one thing, instructions to the contrary, the site they chose was anything but a "wholesome and fertile place." It was neither. Almost half of the island was a swamp, with standing water that bred swarms of mosquitoes. The rest was covered with a thin layer of topsoil over clay and sand. The men seemed far too lazy to dig wells and the water they drank was a brackish, vermin-filled stew. And although there were craftsmen and artisans among the colonists, many who thought of themselves as "gentlemen," rather than workers, hardly managed to lift a finger to fend for themselves, neither hunting nor fishing nor planting.

When Christopher Newport departed on June 22, returning to England with the *Susan Constant* and *Godspeed*, the men had barely thirteen weeks worth of provisions on hand—mostly barley and wheat—and even though Newport would not be back for six months at the earliest, they seemed content to wait. Even when they began dying. Percy's journal is extraordinary.

The fifteenth day, there died Edward Browne and Stephen Galthorpe. The sixteenth day, there died Thomas Gower Gentleman. The seventeenth day, there died Thomas Mounslic. The eighteenth say, there died Robert Pennington, and John Martine Gentleman. The nineteenth day, there died Drue Pigasse Gentleman…

The litany went on and on. John Smith supposed that "God (being angry with us) plagued us with such famin and sicknes, that the living were scarce able to bury the dead." By September 10, about 46 men, including Bartholomew Gosnold, had perished. They fell, Percy related, to "cruel diseases as Swellings, Fluxes, Burning Feavers, and by warres, and some departed suddenly, but for the most part they died of meere famine."

Percy's lament is salted with bitterness. "There were never Englishmen left in a forreigne Countrey in such miserie as wee were in this new discovered Virginia."

Instead of fighting for their lives, John Smith related, the men were in such despair "as they would rather starve and rot

James Fort
Built in the period of
May 14 to June 15, 1607.

with idleness, than be persuaded to do any thing for their owne reliefe..." Smith had had enough of this and began a series of relief missions, setting off for Kecoughtan and other villages to trade with the natives for corn, fish, oysters, deer and bread, learning enough of the Algonquian language to get by and knowing when to apply flattery or pressure. Over the next several months, he almost single-handedly saved the settlement from starvation.

The resourceful and restless Smith soon embarked on a journey that has rung down through the ages as one of the great romances of American history, but the romance part is almost certainly untrue. It was his exploration of the Chickahominy River, or as he mangled the spelling, the "Checka Hamania." Smith and his comrades, sailing and rowing their trusty shallop, explored several miles up the wide and deep and breathtakingly beautiful river. He left behind some of the men, who were lured ashore by natives and slaughtered. He went ashore himself on a small island and came under attack, "struck with an arrow on the right thigh, but without harm." He scared off his attackers with his pistol but then, much to his embarrassment, backed up into a marsh and fell in.

"Thus surprised, I resolved to trie their mercies," he wrote shortly after the incident.

This is where two versions of the story diverge. In the first, written in 1608—just a year later—he is captured and escorted all over the region but generally treated well. He is taken before the great chief Powhatan, at his main village, Werowocomoco, on the north side of the present-day York River, and the two seem to hit it off. He dazzles the old man with a compass and a discourse on the stars and planets. He is surfeited with platters of bread and venison, then escorted through a series of villages, and eventually makes his way back to the fort. No one threatens to smash his brains in—until, in his memory, 16 years later.

The second version, written in England long after his explorer days were over, is completely different. That's where Powhatan condemns him to death and Pocahontas, "the king's dearest daughter, when no intreaty could prevaile, got his head in her armes, and laid her owne upon his to save him from

Ætatis suæ 21. Aᵒ. 1616.

...toaks als Rebecka daughter to the mighty Prince ...whatan Emperour of Attanoughkomouck als Virginia ...nverted and baptized in the Christian faith, and ...Wife to the wor." Mr. Tho: Rolff

death." The story has been embellished and Disneyfied ever since, practically painting the two as lovers. No matter that Pocahontas was a mere child of about 10 or 11 at the time, or that she later married tobacco planter John Rolfe.

Some have suggested that the rescue was invented to justify the later all-out warfare against head-crushing "salvages," as Smith called them, or just to make it a better story. He was, after all, selectively self-serving in his writing. There is also recent speculation that Smith may have misinterpreted an elaborate Indian ritual in which a favored visitor is threatened with death and then saved by a young princess. It is probably true that Pocahontas took a liking to Smith and may have again saved him by warning of a planned attack. But this story, too, is from Smith's later writings.

In any case her loyalty was not to be rewarded. After Smith's departure, she was to be tricked into going on board one of the colonists' boats and kidnapped, then held in hopes of gaining, among other things, "a great quantity of corn."

Smith, who had been imprisoned, plotted against and almost executed, had the satisfaction of being elected president of the council in the fall of 1608. He immediately set out to shape things up, drilling the men, setting up watches and, generally, laying down the law. He declared that colonists who refused to work "shall not eate" and that the labors of 30 or 40 industrious men "shall not be consumed to maintaine an hundred and fiftie idle loyterers."

In what seems almost a distraction rather than relief, Christopher Newport returned in January and then again the following September with seventy more colonists, including two women: a Mistress Forrest, along with her gentleman husband, Thomas, and Anne Burras, her maid. As the only single woman among long-abstaining men, Burras must have received much attention and had her pick of the lot. She quickly married one of the original colonists, John Layton, and the two went on to bear the first English babies in the New World. Newport led a largely unsuccessful mission to secure more

food and then, with winter coming on, promptly departed.

With the cupboard almost bare, Smith went on some desperate food hunting missions, cajoling and bullying natives into turning over supplies of corn. But his tenure

at Jamestown was not to last. The following year, on a long, lazy trip from the falls at Richmond, he dozed off and a spark or cinder ignited the contents of a powder bag with a flash that burned him badly and brought his days in Virginia to a premature close. After one year in office he boarded a ship returning to England. The glue that had held the fledgling colony together was now gone.

Sensing this, Powhatan began turning the screws on the starving white men, scrimping on promised deliveries of food and launching attacks on the outposts that had been more successful at raising food. The survivors fled to the fort where they now faced the winter of 1609-1610 and what was to be remembered as "the starving time." Afraid of crossing over to "Hog Isle," where Smith had established an emergency supply of hogs for food—Powhatan later had the hogs slaughtered—the residents of the fort turned to horses, dogs and cats, and then eventually mice and shoe leather. Some dug up graves and consumed corpses. One killed his pregnant wife, salted her and ate her—before being condemned to death and burned at the stake. It was a time of unspeakable horror. By March 1610, 60 of the 500 colonists who had come to Jamestown were left. And these sad survivors were ready to go home.

Jamestown almost took its place as another of the long series of unsuccessful attempts at European settlement of America. In June, when relief ships, stalled by storms that left them stranded in Bermuda, finally arrived, the colony seemed so devastated, so pathetic, the decision was made to return home. The survivors actually pulled up stakes and sailed down the James toward the Atlantic, only to be met at Hampton Roads by a substantial relief fleet under the command of Thomas West, third Baron De La Warr. It was back to the fort they went, and there De La Warr shaped them up with strict orders to get to work.

The Jamestown settlers rebuilt their fort and hunkered down in an uneasy truce with the natives. There were constant skirmishes as hunting parties fought for and stole corn. Relations seemed to improve after Pocahontas, having been taken hostage at one point, took a liking to tobacco planter John Rolfe and married him. They sailed to England where she was briefly celebrated, but she took ill before their ship could leave London and died.

In 1619 the Jamestown settlers, by now well on their feet, created the first general assembly in the new world, patterned after the English Parliament. Consisting of two burgesses from each of four shires and seven private plantations, the members met for the first time in the choir of their church. They promptly fell into a dispute about membership, gave Captain John Martin a sort of wrist-slap for an "outrage" against the Indians—he stole some corn from

others in the new land, as indentured servants, and some of them were later set free and given land. But the fact was there was no cheap labor to be had—they dared not try to enslave the natives—and the shackles began to tighten, at first on those who were non-Christian. By 1640, Virginia courts sentenced at least one black servant to "serve his said master or his assigns for the time of his natural life here or elsewhere." In 1705, the General Assembly made it official.

"All servants imported and brought into the Country...who were not Christians in their native Country...shall be accounted and be slaves," the Assembly declared, furthermore deeming them "real estate" and exempting slaveholders from punishment for killing them for insubordination—"as if such accident never happened." For minor offences, such as association with whites, slaves could be whipped, branded or maimed. Slavery was to spread throughout the new nation, but it was the burgeoning tobacco and cotton farms that eventually brought overwhelming numbers to the

Above: Slaves arriving at Jamestown, 1619. The first slaves were from the kingdom of Ndongo in Angola.

COURTESY OF THE MARINERS' MUSEUM.

Right: This bronze plaque is of an official of the royal court of Benin in West Africa where Portuguese, French and Dutch mariners traded weapons for slaves.

COURTESY OF THE JAMESTOWN-YORKTOWN FOUNDATION COLLECTION.

their canoe—and pledged "no injury or oppression be wrought by the English against the Indians whereby the present peace might be disturbed."

In the same year that the first representative government was created, a dark cloud formed over the fledgling country. In late summer, sailing out of a violent storm, a Dutch warship put in at Point Comfort with a cargo of twenty or so Africans who had been stolen from a Portuguese ship. Being short of food, the captain and crew traded their human cargo for provisions and sailed off. These new arrivals were treated, like so many

plantation South. It would take sixteen decades for these laws to be stricken from the books.

As for the colonists and the natives, there would be ferocious assaults in succeeding years and the Indians, sensing that the colonists were gaining ground, attempted to wipe them out. All-out war ensued, with horrific uprisings and brutal reprisals in 1622 and 1644 but the colonists held their ground and the first English settlement in the New World was there to stay.

John Smith, whose likeness on a statue looks out at the James where the settlers first landed. The sculptor was William Cooper, c. 1907.

CHAPTER II

LIFE & LIBERTY

When the Englishmen first arrived in America, the land they set foot on was unlike anything they had ever seen. A short distance inland, they found, in the words of that faithful chronicler George Percy, "faire meddowes and goodly tall Trees," and "Fresh-waters running through the woods." The next day, a party of eight "gentlemen and soldiers" struck out on an eight-mile trek inland. They didn't see any more "savages," but the Indians apparently saw or heard them, because the party stumbled across an abandoned fire with oysters still simmering on it. They couldn't resist sampling. They were, said George Percy, "very large and delicate in taste." The nearby Lynnhaven River would one day be renowned for its plump, succulent oysters. And Percy's account would be remembered as the first recorded description of a Lynnhaven oyster roast.

They launched their trusty shallop with Newport and some of the others on board, sailing and paddling along the shoreline, and found the entrance to the Lynnhaven. They were disappointed that it was too shallow. Further along, heading toward what would become Little Creek, they went ashore at a flat, low place where they found a huge log canoe, but no one to claim it. They also found oysters and mussels "which lay on the ground as thicke as stones." Undaunted by their brush with natives a few days before, they marched right into the brush, covering three or four miles, discovering smoky fires where grass had been burned.

"We past through excellent ground full of Flowers of divers kinds and coulors, and as goodly trees as I have ever seen," including cypress and cedar, and then, further on, "a little plat of ground full of fine and beautifull Strawberries, foure times bigger and better than ours in England."

On April 29, they marched to a spot overlooking the bay and erected a cross, probably of English oak that had already been fashioned for that purpose and offered a prayer of thanksgiving for their arrival. The place where they stood would eventually be called Virginia Beach, but it was a vast wilderness then. In spite of the earlier brush with the natives, there were no further contacts. The history of the region might explain why.

Some of that history is shrouded in a mystery that began in 1584 when the first of several expeditions was launched by Sir Walter Raleigh to Roanoke Island on the lee side of what is now North Carolina's Outer Banks. A party led by Philip Amadas and Arthur Barlowe set out on a six-day journey northward and may have happened upon Skicoak, the native village that is present-day Norfolk. The next year a party that included Governor John Lane and artist John White again trekked north to see if a more suitable settlement could be found. White drew a map of the region that shows the site of "Chesepioc," apparently near the present London Bridge in Virginia Beach. Lane wrote that the "Territore and soyle of the Chesepions," was "not to be excelled by any other whatsoever." Subsequent parties were instructed to plant a colony at this excellent place, but it is not known whether they ever made it there, only that they disappeared with barely a trace. Some speculate that the lost colonists may have migrated to the land of the Chesapeakes and become interspersed with them, finally meeting with the same fate as the tribe. In any event, one of the instructions given to the Jamestown settlers was to search for signs of their predecessors. They never found any.

The "Territore" of the Chesapeake tribe was vast at one point: the Chesepians were spread out over the area that now includes Norfolk, Portsmouth, Chesapeake, and Virginia Beach. The main settlement, known as Skicoak, probably occupied land north of the present Fort Norfolk, with two other villages near the Chesapeake Bay in present-day Virginia Beach. All three of these towns were palisaded with stakes driven into the ground. But that did not stop Powhatan's warriors. The powerful chief, who controlled almost every tribe in the region, did not like the Chesepians' independence. And when his priests warned in the 1590s that another nation would arise and destroy his empire,

The Bruton Parish churchyard and George Wythe House. Watercolor by Dwight Williams. The house served as General Washington's headquarters during the Revolutionary War.

COURTESY OF THE COLONIAL WILLIAMSBURG FOUNDATION. GIFT OF MR. AND MRS. WILLIAM G. PERRY.

he responded with brute force, virtually annihilating his rivals and leveling their towns. He then sent some of his trusted warriors to take control, and these may have been the fighters the Englishmen encountered.

It is surprising that it took twenty more years for the colonists, who had begun spreading to other New World territories, to reach the broad fertile plains of future Princess Anne County and Virginia Beach. It may have been the prospect of encountering hostile Indians, an annoying inconvenience that Ensign Thomas Willoughby removed when, after the Indian uprising of 1622, he headed a militia force that either completely wiped out what remained of the Chesapians or forced them to flee. The land suddenly became open to settlement and one truly energetic entrepreneur jumped into the breach.

Adam Thoroughgood was the son of a minister in County Norfolk, England, who seized on the chance to make his fortune in the New World. In 1621, at age 18, he signed on as an indentured servant, sailed to Virginia and landed at Kecoughtan where he learned all he could about growing tobacco. He returned to England six years later, married Sarah Offley, daughter of the former lord mayor of London, and set sail again with thirty-five passengers and a dozen more to follow. For recruiting the would-be settlers, Thoroughgood was entitled to a land grant of fifty acres per head. By the time he was through, he had recruited enough "headright" emigrants to qualify for one of the largest landholdings in the history of the young colony. The payoff came in June 1635 when the Virginia government awarded him 5,320 acres on the west side of the mouth of what was then the Chesopean River. It was changed to the Lynnhaven in honor of his birthplace, King's Lynn. Adam served as commissioner of the Elizabeth City County court and member of the House of Burgesses in 1629-32. He also established a ferry across the Elizabeth River near the junction of the eastern and southern branches. It is not clear what sort of person he was, except that he apparently went to great lengths to shield his reputation. In 1637, Anne Fowler was ordered to receive twenty lashes for scandalous remarks about him. The

This portrait of Queen Anne was painted in 1710, eight years after she took the throne upon the death of King William. In 1691, when Lynnhaven Parish was carved out of Norfolk County, it was named for the then-Princess Anne.

COURTESY OF THE LOCAL HISTORY COLLECTION, VIRGINIA WESLEYAN COLLEGE.

outspoken Fowler had also called Thomas Keeling, Adam's servant, a "Jackanape" and told him that if he did not get out of her sight she would break his head.

Thoroughgood died at thirty-five, leaving Sarah to remarry twice, each time with wealthy, powerful men. One of them was Daniel Gookin, the son of one of the original settlers at Newport News Point.

Things were moving fast now with shires, or counties, divided into manageable sizes as more settlers poured in. In 1636-37, that part of Elizabeth City County on the south side of Hampton Roads became New Norfolk County, only to be divided again into Upper Norfolk County and Lower Norfolk County. Then in 1691, Upper Norfolk became Nansemond County and Lower Norfolk was split into Norfolk County and Princess Anne County. Ten years later, George Kemp received a grant of 400 acres on the Eastern Branch of the Elizabeth River, and there established Kemp's Landing as a trading post and tobacco port.

NAKED IN THE MOONLIGHT

Lower Norfolk was the site of a religious struggle between the official Church of England and a band of Puritans who had come from New England with an abiding belief that the forces of evil, including those they believed to be witches, must be confronted. There was not a lot of sympathy in this region for this movement. Courts were loath to entertain charges of witchcraft, slapping heavy fines for libel on false accusers. But a strong puritanical strain—with or without a capital "P"—nonetheless survived. And even though most of the Puritans had left by this time, Grace Sherwood, it seemed, was just too tempting a target.

Grace, who lived with her husband on Muddy Creek Road near Pungo, was independent, pretty, and flirtatious. What's more, neighbors claimed, she danced naked in the moonlight, bewitched their cows and slipped though cracks in the door like a black cat. Once, they imagined, she sailed off to England in an eggshell and brought back wild lupine and rosemary. She accused several neighbors of slander and one of assaulting her, collecting a token 20 shillings for her pains. But in February 1706, a judge bowed to all the pressure brought by her accusers and ordered a trial. First, a panel of women was instructed to examine her for suspicious marks on her body. No matter that one of the women had been one of her accusers. And

sure enough they found blue stains and other signs of trafficking with the Devil. Grace's only response was to laugh at her accusers.

Finally, after the case had been back and forth in the courts, she was ordered to stand a "trial by water" in which she would be thrown overboard with hands and feet tied to each other. In the rather convoluted rules of the trial, if she survived the ducking, she was guilty; only if she drowned was her innocence proven. She was having none of that, and on July 10, while spectators lined the shore of the Lynnhaven River, at a place that would forever be called Witch Duck, she was rowed out and, naked, dumped into the water.

What her accusers did not know was that Grace was apparently a good swimmer and as handy with knots as she was with insults, for she easily freed herself, even after a heavy Bible was placed around her neck and she was pushed under. Not only did Grace surface, but she proceeded to swim about the cove, singing and laughing at her accusers, all the more evidence of her guilt. Grace Sherwood was sent to prison, then released in 1715 after witch-hunting had gone out of favor. On July 10, 2006, three centuries after her trial by

"Kempe's Landing," sketch by

Emily Whaley.

water, Sherwood finally became witch no more as Governor Timothy M. Kaine officially cleared "her good name."

NEWPORT'S NEWS

It was apparently at what is now Newport News Point that the Spanish missionaries had stopped in 1570 to say mass before proceeding up the James River. They disembarked at the entrance to a creek, either Mulberry Island or College Run, only a few miles from what was to be the Jamestown settlement. From there the Jesuits traveled across the peninsula to what awaited them on the shores of the York River. Four decades later, the ship *Sea Venture*, a year late after being driven ashore on

Boat building at Kecoughtan. By Sidney King.

COURTESY OF THE NATIONAL PARK SERVICE, COLONIAL NATIONAL HISTORICAL PARK.

Bermuda by a hurricane, showed up and nearly left with the starving Jamestown survivors. Near Mulberry Island, they spotted the relief expedition commanded by Lord De La Warr and decided to stay after all. The man credited with bringing them the news of their rescue was none other than Christopher Newport. So "Newport's News," as they called it, was the name that stuck. Or so the story goes. Another version calls it "New Port Newce," after brothers of that name who came here from Ireland, and still another holds that "News" came from the Old English word "Ness," for headland or point.

At any rate, several of the *Sea Venture's* passengers became the first white men to lay claim to the land. They included Lieutenant

Edward Waters, who settled land near today's Lake Maury, Lieutenant William Pierce and John Rolfe who received land grants on Mulberry Island. In 1621, Daniel Gookin, Sr., arrived with about 80 settlers and received a kingly grant of more than 2,000 acres on land that would eventually become downtown Newport News. Then it was called Marie's Mount in honor of his wife. It was not a good time to be setting up lodgings in Virginia. A year later, the Indians attacked in force, but Gookin and dozens of his men survived behind palisades they had erected. It was a favored spot for mariners who came ashore to take on fresh water from "a fine spring," as one Dutch sailor noted.

More and more settlers led the House of Burgesses in 1634 to establish eight shires in Virginia, among them Warwick Shire, soon to achieve even greater status as Warwick County. The area that embraces the present Virginia Beach, Norfolk, Portsmouth, Chesapeake, and Hampton became part of Elizabeth City County. Thus began a series of name changes and mergers that would go on for centuries.

OYSTERS

The village of Kecoughtan, first visited by the English right after their arrival, might have been the best place for a permanent fort. No, it wasn't far enough from the ocean, at least by the lights of the Virginia Company, but it had a lot of other things going for it, including a vantage point. According to a map drawn by Smith, the site of the Indian village was approximately where the Veteran's Hospital now sits. It had 2,000 to 3,000 acres, with garden plots following the course of streams and the Hampton Roads waterfront. Instead of being low-lying and surrounded by hostile Indians, the future Hampton was far more healthful, with a magnificent view of the bay and the ocean beyond. And the natives were, at least initially, friendly, viewing the newcomers as gods, or perhaps devils. But when the white men became persistent in their quest for handouts, the natives were not so welcoming.

In September 1607, when Captain Smith visited Kecoughtan, "sixty or seventy of them...came in a square order, singing and

dancing out of the woods, with their Okee (an idol made of skins) borne before them." The English repelled the attack and the Indians sought peace and swapped food for trade goods. The following year, Smith returned and this time, because of inclement weather, he and his men spent Christmas week with the natives and were "never more merry, not fed on more plenty of good oysters, fish, flesh, wild fowl, and good bread, nor never had better fires in England than in the dry, warm, smoky houses of Kecoughtan."

In 1609, George Percy, by now president of the Jamestown council, sent Captain John Ratcliffe and a detachment of men to set up a fort there, named Fort Algernourne. Ratcliffe, on a later expedition, was captured and tortured to death, but the fort endured and those who guarded it never experienced the "starving time," thanks in part to a ready supply of oysters.

The following year, Thomas Gates, using the excuse of a murdered member of the Jamestown settlement—even though the deed had apparently not been done by the Kecoughtans—attacked their village, killing or driving the natives away. Soon after, the English began planting in those same garden plots. They built two forts, Henry and Charles, and a settlement, evolving near the forts, would gain the title of the oldest continuous English settlement in America. In 1706, in honor of Henry Wriothesly, earl of Southampton—and treasurer of the Virginia Company—the town was given its present name of Hampton. The body of water immediately adjacent was dubbed Hampton Roads. "Roads" derives from "Roadstead," a place where ships may ride at anchor. Kecoughtan ("kik-o-tan"), one of the "heathen" names the English decided to abolish, survives throughout the region in school, street and scout pack names.

The settlers also established the oldest Anglican parish in America, St. John's Church. There were four churches, the first built in 1610. After the population moved closer to Hampton Creek, the present structure was built in 1728 in the shape of a Latin cross. Its communion silver bears the date 1618 and has been termed "the most precious relic in the Anglican Church in America." To the right of the altar today is a stained glass window depicting the baptism of Pocahontas. Besides erecting a church, the settlers laid out a crossroads town, with King Street running north-south and Queen Street east-west.

The floodgates to settlement of the new land were wide open. By 1634, just 27 years after the first ships sailed up the James River, there were 859 inhabitants of Elizabeth City. Even though most of the region was made up of small farms, harvesting mostly tobacco and corn, there were signs of community. In 1639, a license was granted for "a common ale house and victualizing house," so long as the licensees did not allow "any unlawful games to be used in this house nor any evil rule or order to be kept within the same." Another enterprising fellow erected a windmill on the west side of Hampton River and a third began a ferry near the mouth of the river, agreeing not to charge more than one penny per passenger. There was a jail and a court by 1640.

As tobacco became valuable, pirates began preying on ships leaving port with the addicting commodity. The briefly notorious Edward Teach, better-known as Blackbeard, was so vexing to the colonists that Governor Alexander Spotswood fitted out two sloops at his own expense and sent them after him. The ships, commanded by Lieutenant Robert Maynard of the Royal Navy, set out from Hampton in 1718 and found the dastardly pirate at Okracoke, North Carolina. After a furious gun battle, and then hand-to-hand combat, Teach was overwhelmed, falling with no less than five pistol and twenty sword wounds. The slain pirate's head was dispatched and returned to Hampton where it was displayed at the entrance to Hampton Creek for all would-be

Above: Adam Thoroughgood arrived in America in 1621. This house was built by one of his grandsons in 1680. The photograph shows the house, oldest in Virginia Beach, after it was restored in 1957. It is now open as a museum.
COURTESY OF THE LIBRARY OF CONGRESS.

Below: The Francis Land House, built by the third Francis Land in 1732.
COURTESY OF THE VIRGINIA BEACH PUBLIC LIBRARY.

blackguards to see. Today, there's a grizzly replica of the famous head to greet visitors to the new Hampton History Museum.

GARDEN PLOTS

Captain Smith, it seems, never met a river he didn't want to explore, and the Elizabeth was one of these. During the summer of 1608, on his way back down the bay with twelve other colonists, he ran into a violent nighttime storm and only found Point Comfort with the help of lightning flashes. After a stopover, they set sail for the southern shore of Hampton Roads and headed up the river, which

> …hath a good channel, but many shoules about the entrance. By that we had sayled six or seaven myles, we saw two or three little garden plots with their houses, the shore overgrowne with the greatest Pyne and Firre trees we ever saw in the Country. But not seeing nor hearing any people, and the river very narrow, we returned to the great river, to see if we could finde any of them.

It is clear that the once-great town of Skicoak, the future Norfolk, was by then no more. It is possible, historians believe, that the people who dwelt there were the ones wiped out by Chief Powhatan in his spur-of-the moment reaction to a perceived threat.

By the time of the first Indian uprising, those garden plots had been turned into small farms and waterfront enterprises. In 1622, Nicholas Wise, a shipwright bought two hundred acres of land from Lewis Vandermill. The property spilled down to the Elizabeth River and included what would soon become a thriving village. Two years later, Thomas Willoughby—who had helped put down the uprising—was granted five hundred acres of magnificent dune-fringed land on the Chesapeake Bay at a site that would one day become Ocean View.

Even though no towns were officially established, it is clear that thriving commercial ports were growing along what would become Norfolk and Portsmouth. In fact, in 1636, the ever-enterprising Adam Thoroughgood established a small ferry—six rowboats and three scows—between the two communities. The General Assembly clearly felt the burgeoning villages needed protection, and in 1673 authorized the construction of a fort at Four Farthing Point, at what would become Town Point Park. It was called Half Moon Fort. Norfolk was almost an island then, jutting out into the river, with a wide, marshy creek to its back. It was bristling with wharves that whiskered out into the Elizabeth, and wide-bottomed schooners were loaded with building material, livestock and salted meat, tobacco, wheat, corn and all the other crops that, by 1691, began flooding in from Princess Anne County and the swampy forests south of town.

Most travel was still by water, although a few oyster shell roads and pathways bisected the waterfront. One of them, identified on a plat in 1680 as "the street leading out of town," would one day bear the name of Saint Paul. In 1637, the first court for Lower Norfolk County was held—as it would be for twenty-four years—in a private home. In 1661, the first courthouse was built on Broad Creek. (This was before Lower Norfolk was split into Norfolk and Princess Anne counties in 1691.)

It seems almost a "by the way" instruction, but in 1679 the colonists were advised to "build towns upon every river, and especially one at least on every great river, as tending very much to their security and profit." The assembly responded promptly, decreeing in 1680 that 20 fifty-acre towns be built, the land paid for with 10,000 pounds of tobacco. As a result, part of the Nicholas Wise tract was purchased on August 16, 1682—and this date is now celebrated as the Norfolk's birthday.

POWER STRUGGLE

It is certain that Smith, in his exploration of the river, also noticed what is now Portsmouth and considered it a possible source of food. But his relationship with the people who ranged throughout the area bounded by the Elizabeth and Nansemond Rivers had gotten off to a rocky start. Nevertheless, the territory became part of the sprawling Elizabeth City County.

In 1657, William Carver, master mariner and merchant, arrived on the scene. He was granted more than six hundred acres of land and quickly established himself as a member of the House of Burgesses and as high sheriff of Lower Norfolk County, which by then had become one of the fast-growing shires of the new colony. But his story is interwoven with what became a dark power struggle between Governor William Berkeley and Nathaniel Bacon, a troublemaker and schemer who in 1676 seized control of Jamestown but then abruptly died of dysentery and a severe case of lice. Twenty-three of his co-conspirators, including Carver, who had command of Bacon's tiny navy, were strung up as Berkeley again seized power. Carver's lands reverted to the crown.

In 1716 this land, along with additional parcels, was granted to Lieutenant Colonel William Crawford, a prosperous merchant and ship owner, presiding judge of Norfolk County Court and lieutenant colonel in the local militia. In 1752, the General Assembly authorized the surveying of lots for what was to become a town and named it for Crawford's hometown in England, Portsmouth. Crawford built his home near the Elizabeth River on

what was to become High Street. It was the part of this land, projecting into the Western Branch of the Elizabeth River, that became known as Crawford's Point and the location for the Portsmouth Naval Hospital.

The lots were quickly subscribed and a prosperous village sprang up, peopled largely at first by Scots who were fiercely loyal to the crown. A "hotbed of Toryism," it was called. Among the most prominent of these Scots was Andrew Sprowle, who bought three lots at the intersection of Crawford and King streets. His property grew and jumped over Crab Creek on the south where a small Village named Gosport—after the famous English naval shipyard (meaning God's Port)—was formed. Sprowle stuck to the script, building a shipyard of his own that was to serve not only merchant ships but also the British Navy. Large warehouses were erected and giant cranes were imported from London for the great American facility that would become Gosport Navy Yard, and eventually, Norfolk Naval Shipyard.

In one of the many interesting—and to come, confusing—name changes of the early period, Portsmouth citizens pulled off a coup in December 1800, gaining authority to erect a new Norfolk County Courthouse in their city. The General Assembly approved, and the new building, complete with stocks, whipping post, "necessary" and well, was built on the corner of High and

⚓

Nathaniel Bacon and his rebels seized control of Jamestown in 1676 and burned much of the village to the ground. Painting by Sidney King

Court streets. Norfolk County's new official seat was open for public business in May 1803. But Norfolk County, once occupying nearly the entire area of South Hampton Roads, would continue to be subdivided until it eventually vanished, leaving only municipalities across the region.

Portsmouth would continue to draw its life's breath from the shipyard. The huge naval facility, largest in the nation, would become a prize when the North and South went to war.

King William and Queen Mary assumed the throne jointly in 1689. In 1693, a charter for "a place of universal study" was granted and the College of William and Mary, the second oldest in America (behind Harvard) was begun.

A MUSKET VOLLEY

Nearly every city in Hampton Roads begins its modern history with John Smith, and Suffolk is no exception. In 1608, when Smith and twelve others explored the Nansemond River, they at first received a warm reception from the "proud and warlike" people who inhabited its shores. Near the present-day Reid's Ferry, the Nansemonds lived close to the riverbank where they farmed, hunted, fished and foraged. It was a complex society, where corn, pumpkins, beans, melons and tobacco grew, and pottery was made of clay and crushed shell.

But when Smith and his companions approached Dumpling Island, where the Indians kept a cache of corn, his boat was attacked by a group of Nansemonds in canoes. A musket volley so frightened the Indians that they jumped overboard and swam to safety. Seizing his opportunity, Smith made signs as if to destroy their canoes—the hollowed-out log canoes were built by back-breaking labor—and they quickly agreed to his terms: four hundred bushels of corn. Later, when the settlers were threatened with starvation, Smith ordered that a farm be established on the Nansemond. The problem was that he sent Captain John Martin to run it, along with a hundred colonists. Martin, however, had his own ideas about cooperation with the Indians and seized a local chief and settlement and helped himself to the corn on Dumpling Island. A surprise counterattack sent Martin and his men, many of them wounded, stumbling back to Jamestown.

After the great Indian uprising of 1622, Sir George Yeardley entered the Nansemond territory with three hundred soldiers. He destroyed the settlement at Reid's Ferry, wasting the farmland and killing many warriors. Later attacks by the English decimated the Nansemonds and forced them off their ancestral lands. What was bad for the Indians was good for the colonists and by 1630, many had settled along the waterways in what was to become Nansemond County.

Richard Bennett, one of the new settlers, was awarded 2,000 acres of land at what is now Bennett's Creek after bringing over 40 settlers. After the Virginia legislature approved the town acts of 1680, 1691, and 1705, Nansemond Town was formed at Bennett's creek landing. The town didn't survive, but what was to become Suffolk certainly did.

KISKIAK

The beginnings of another city, Yorktown, are draped in sorrow. After landing near Newport News Point in 1570, Spanish missionaries—with the lad Paquiquino, who had been educated in Spanish Schools and converted, they thought, to Christianity— traveled across the Peninsula to a new location at the mouth of King's Creek, where it flows into the York, and here they set about building their mission. But Paquiquino, who

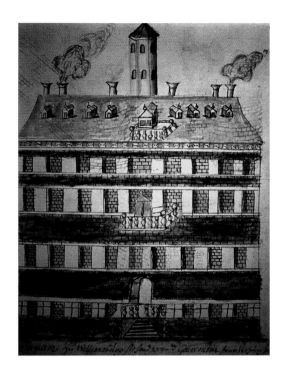

had run off and rejoined his warriors, now led an attack on the mission. All were slain. Later, a Spanish warship nearly annihilated a crowd of Indians who had come down to the shore.

John Smith's first map of the Chesapeake region includes the name of "Kiskiak" in the area now known as Yorktown. It was the name of a tribe of Indians who generally resisted attempts by the English to move onto their land. But, beginning in 1630 after the Indian uprising was squashed, the first English settlers arrived, gradually pushing the native people across the river. It retained the name Kiskiak, but in 1691, when the colonial government established it as a town, it was renamed in honor of the Duke of York. Fifty acres of land along the York River were purchased from Benjamin Read of Gloucester County for ten thousand pounds of tobacco. This land, on a bluff overlooking the river, was subdivided into eighty-five lots and offered for sale. The "under-the-hill" waterfront was designated a "common shore." By the time of the American Revolution, Yorktown had a well-developed waterfront, with wharves, docks, storehouses and waterfront businesses. On the bluff above, stately homes lined the streets, with taverns, shops and a church serving the town's nearly two thousand residents. But declining tobacco prices and then the ravages of war were to change everything.

NEW BEGINNING

In a fledgling nation a seemingly secondary development can suddenly change its destiny. Bacon's rebellion nearly destroyed it. The roots

Above: The Wren Building, said to have been designed by famed British architect Sir Christopher Wren, was begun in 1695, and remains the oldest academic building in continuous use in America. This is a view by Franz Ludwig Michel in 1702.
COURTESY OF THE COLLEGE OF WILLIAM & MARY.

Left: This plate found in the Bodleian Library in England is the only known eighteenth century drawing of the main buildings in the colonial capital. They are, top row, the Brafferton, the Wren Building and the President's House; middle row, the Capitol, the back of the Wren Building and the Governor's Palace; and, bottom, flora and fauna and Indians native to Virginia.
COURTESY OF THE COLONIAL WILLIAMSBURG FOUNDATION. GIFT OF THE BODLEIAN LIBRARY.

of this bizarre conflict are intertwined with the cash crop that had become the colony's salvation, tobacco. Discontent among farmers over a drop in tobacco prices, as well as limits imposed on new settlements to keep peace with the Indians, led to open revolt against Governor Berkeley. In the summer of 1676, Bacon and his rebels marched on Jamestown, forced Berkeley to flee to the Eastern Shore and set fire to the town. The rebellion was finally suppressed, but the capital lay in ruins. The next year, the governing assembly met at a place further inland that had come to be called Middle Plantation, but the love affair with the bog-dominated island wasn't over. The long-established Jamestown offered easy access to ships bringing supplies from England and taking on tobacco bound for overseas markets. But when fire again destroyed the statehouse in 1698, the time to move had arrived.

This time the desire to place the government at a more central and healthful location made Middle Plantation, less than ten miles inland, far more appealing. It was already populated by several prominent planters. Moreover, it was home to Bruton Parish Church, built in 1683, the College of William and Mary, chartered in 1693, several ordinaries, a blacksmith shop and a malt house. It already had the look and feel of a central town, and in June 1699 the General Assembly made it official, renaming the town "Williamsburgh," "in Honour of the most gracious and glorious King William." In this new capital, the seeds of independence would find fertile soil.

FREE & INDEPENDENT

Williamsburg entered a period of prosperity that was nurtured by several popular royal governors. It was a place where rising stars like Thomas Jefferson and Patrick Henry would flourish. But when Parliament passed the Stamp Act in 1765, relations with the mother country began to deteriorate. Henry denounced the act from the floor of the House of Burgesses and introduced a resolution asserting Virginia's right of self-government. The act was repealed, but later tax levies stirred the pot again. When Lord

Botetourt, the governor, adjourned the house, the burgesses repaired to Raleigh Tavern and resolved not to import British goods. The legislator who introduced the non-importation resolution was 37-year-old George Washington, at this point a 10-year veteran of colonial governance. Things went from bad to worse when Virginia's last royal governor, John Murray, fourth Earl of Dunmore, arrived.

Among other failings, the puffed-up Dunmore declined to meet with his subjects and discontent continued to build. Jefferson, Henry and others called for a committee of correspondence to keep abreast of what was going on elsewhere in the colonies. Word soon reached them that the British had closed the port of Boston in retaliation for the "Boston Tea Party," and the burgesses set aside a day for fasting, humiliation and prayer. When Dunmore dissolved the assembly, the burgesses repaired again to Raleigh Tavern and proposed a gathering among representatives from all the colonies. The idea met with great favor and soon the Continental Congress assembled in Philadelphia. In April 1775, after Dunmore had troops seize the colony's store of gunpowder, Henry led a band of armed volunteers to the capital and demanded its return. Dunmore reimbursed the colony, but his days were numbered. Finally, on June 8, he and his family fled and boarded a warship lying in the York River.

Now liberated, the Virginia Convention of Delegates, meeting in Williamsburg in May 1776, called on the Continental Congress to declare the colonies free and independent states. In June, a constitutional convention approved a document that Jefferson drew upon for the opening paragraphs of the Declaration of Independence. The Virginia Declaration of Rights, written by George Mason, declares:

That all men are by nature equally free and independent and have certain inherent rights, of which, when they enter into a state of society, they cannot, by any compact, deprive or divest their posterity: namely, the enjoyment of life and liberty, with the means of acquiring and possessing property, and pursuing and obtaining happiness and safety.

The declaration further asserts that if a government goes against the wishes of its citizens, a majority has an inalienable right to "reform, alter or abolish it." It also foreshadows separate legislative and judicial branches, the right to vote, speedy trials, freedom of the press, a well-regulated militia, and several other constitutional bulwarks.

With the nation at war to secure these rights, Patrick Henry became the first post-colonial governor of Virginia. He served in Williamsburg from 1776 to 1779 when he was succeeded by Jefferson. With questions now raised about the continued safety of the capital and its accessibility to other parts of the growing state, Jefferson agreed that it should be moved to Richmond. Early in 1780, Williamsburg's remarkable first chapter came to a close.

BLOOD & VICTORY

Lord Dunmore had fled to Portsmouth where he became the guest of loyalist Andrew Sprowle. He was there said to be entertained lavishly. From Sprowle's shipyard he commanded his navy and earned Gosport the brief title of royal capital of Virginia—what was left of it. All the while, the erstwhile royal governor held out for what would surely, he thought, be relief ships from the homeland. They never arrived. Incensed at the treasonous conduct of the rebels, Dunmore vowed to teach them a lesson, pillaging their farms, winning slaves over to his side and seizing printing presses. "I really believe we should reduce this colony to a proper sense of their duty," he fumed in November 1775. He and a force of British regulars and loyalists won a minor skirmish with Virginia patriots at Kemps Landing. He then proceeded to Great Bridge, then part of Norfolk County, to cut off commerce coming to Norfolk from the Carolinas and build a makeshift fort, which he armed with cannons. The soldiers of the crown were in a perfect spot to halt traffic across a causeway and bridge through the swampy section of what is now Chesapeake.

General Washington was not happy with these developments and felt that Dunmore

Patrick Henry in the House of Burgesses, from a painting by P. H. Rothermal.

John Murray, fourth earl of Dunmore, in regimental tartans, copied from original by Joshua Reynolds.

"should be instantly crushed" lest his forces grow. He told the Continental Congress that "the fate of America a good deal depends on his being obligated to evacuate Norfolk this winter or not."

On Saturday, December 2, Colonel William Woodford arrived at Great Bridge with the Second Virginia Regiment and five companies of Culpeper Minutemen. Not yet having any cannons, they set up a breastwork opposite the British fort and waited. There were frequent exchanges of gunfire, but neither force could be persuaded to attack until Dunmore took the bait. He was convinced the rebels were then weak but would soon be reinforced.

On the raw morning of December 9, Dunmore's forces marched six abreast across the causeway, approaching within 15 feet of the breastworks when Woodford's riflemen opened fire. The result was a bloody slaughter, with dozens of British soldiers killed or wounded. The only Virginia casualty was a slight wound to the hand. The scene was appalling. "From the vast effusion of blood on the bridge, and in the fort, from the accounts of sentries who saw many bodies carried out of the fort to be entered," Woodford wrote the next day, "I conceive their losses to be much greater than I thought it yesterday, and the victory to be complete."

As Washington had urged, Dunmore had been crushed. He abandoned Norfolk and, along with numerous Tories, including Sprowle, fled to the safety of his ships in Norfolk Harbor. There ensued a standoff that was to end with Dunmore, cold and faced with growing complaints of hunger on board, deciding on revenge. On the afternoon of New Year's Day 1776 he ordered the ships to bombard the city and then, under cover of the cannonade, sent landing parties ashore to set fire to warehouses on the waterfront. One lasting memento was a cannon ball that lodged high up on one wall of St. Paul's Episcopal Church, where it can be seen today.

But his forces were not the only ones to bring destruction to the city. American troops seized the opportunity to plunder. Breaking into rum shops and warehouses, then going door to door, they dragged out supplies and put houses and shops to the torch. Most of the city now lay in ashes.

At least one thing that was no longer in doubt was who was in charge of the Commonwealth. Although he briefly encamped at what was to become Hospital Point in Portsmouth, Dunmore soon fled to Gwynn's Island on the Chesapeake Bay and then to New York. It was clear that his defeat and departure left Virginia in the hands of Virginians. Sprowle, once Portsmouth's biggest mover and shaker, died on

that remote island in the Chesapeake and was buried in an unmarked grave.

The bombardment of Norfolk was a battle cry of the new republic, part of a litany of offenses laid at the feet of King George III. "He has plundered our seas, ravaged our coasts, burnt our towns, and destroyed the lives of our people," said the Declaration of Independence, drafted by Thomas Jefferson and approved by the convention in Philadelphia on July 4, 1776.

The British did not forget the drubbing they had received at Great Bridge in 1775. Six years later, after another invasion of Virginia, the traitor Benedict Arnold, who had set up his headquarters in Portsmouth, sent Lieutenant Colonel John Simcoe to Great Bridge to establish a post, and he promptly tore down much of the village to build his

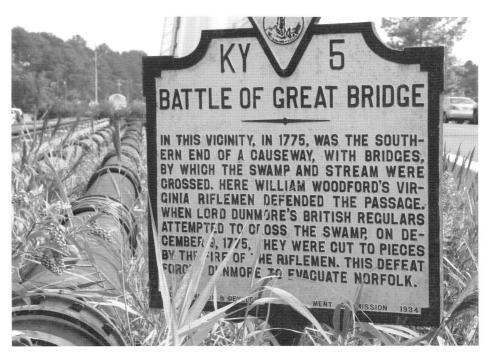

Top: Great Bridge, photograph around 1895.
COURTESY OF THE SARGEANT MEMORIAL ROOM, NORFOLK PUBLIC LIBRARY.

Middle: Modern highway sign near the bridge at Great Bridge.
PHOTO BY PAUL CLANCY.

Bottom: Ball-in-the wall. A cannon ball lodged high up in the wall of St. Paul's Church, said to have been fired by Lord Dunmore's ships, January 1, 1776.
PHOTO BY PAUL CLANCY.

fortifications and then left it a mass of charred rubble upon departing. As it turned out the little village of Great Bridge was to have played roles at the beginning and the end of the American Revolution.

Norfolk was best described as "Chimney Town" after the fires. Barely a building stood. But it eventually would, Thomas Jefferson predicted, outstrip New York, Boston, Philadelphia and Baltimore as a port city. The city would, "rise like a Phoenix out of the ashes to that importance to which the laws of nature destine it." And it did, although the rebuilding that went on furiously after the war was not terribly well planned. Benjamin Latrobe, the architect, who arrived in the city in 1796, called it an "ill-built" and "unhealthy" town, with filthy, narrow streets, with numerous uninhabited houses coexisting with newer ones, and a prevailing nastiness and stench. The warehouses were so crowded together, many of them stacked up on stilts, that one could barely see the water. What was not crowded with wharves was packed with shipyards.

One of Jefferson's proudest accomplishments, the Statute for Religious Freedom, was a prelude to an important development in Norfolk's future. His 1779 draft of a bill was finally passed in 1786 through the skillful leadership of James Madison. It held that, in Virginia, "no man shall be compelled to frequent or support any religious worship, place or ministry whatsoever." The law was to become a model for other states and the basis for the Constitution's freedom of religion clause. It also sent a signal to the nation that Virginia's cities were places of open worship.

In the late 1780s, Moses Myers, an ambitious businessman who imported and exported goods all over the world, was looking for a port city that would suit his needs and one that would fully accept him as a Jew. He and his wife, Eliza, moved to the city in 1787 and began work on a splendid home on Freemason and Catherine streets that would accommodate their growing family and befit their increasing wealth. They would raise twelve children there, and the family name would be linked to Norfolk's future for several generations. So prominent were Moses and Eliza that they both sat for portraits by

Moses and Eliza Myers, oil on poplar, portraits by Gilbert Stuart , c. 1808.

famed artist Gilbert Stuart. They lived and socialized among a couple dozen established families, with names like Plume, Boush, and Tazewell. The Myers descendants kept the house in the family for almost a century and a half, so that original furnishings would one day grace a downtown museum.

INFERNO

The burning of Norfolk turned the spotlight briefly on a sister city to the west. Suffolk by then was a thriving town, with

tobacco the economic engine that spurred its colonization. By 1728, John Constant had built a warehouse and wharf for exporting tobacco, grain and salt. Continuing prosperity led to a request to the colonial legislature in Williamsburg to establish a town, which was approved in 1742. At the same time, the name Constant's Wharf was changed to Suffolk Town, in honor of Governor William Gooch's home in Suffolk County, England.

Refugees streamed into Suffolk and the city became a storehouse for food and military supplies for the rebels, and the Nansemond River served as a hiding place for their ships. A number of ships that were built in Suffolk staged raids on the enemy. The British blockade of the Chesapeake also shifted some commerce from Norfolk.

It was only a matter of time before the British turned their attention to troublesome Suffolk. Fearing an attack, the Suffolk militia sent Josiah Riddick, Thomas Granbury, and Thomas Brittle out to reconnoiter. All three were taken prisoner and sent to New York. Then, on May 13, the hammer came down as some six hundred British troops overcame light resistance and marched into Suffolk. What had happened to Norfolk now reoccurred in Suffolk. The town, including the courthouse and clerk's office, was burned

and all records destroyed. The government stores were captured and wharves and warehouses put to the torch. Eight thousand barrels of tar, pitch, and turpentine went up in an inferno of flame.

THE TRAP IS SPRUNG

While Hampton Roads played a key role in the start of the Revolutionary War, it played an even greater one in its conclusion.

Although no one knew it at the time, the endgame began with the decision by Lord Charles Cornwallis to march from North Carolina to Virginia. He and his force disembarked at Portsmouth in the summer of 1781 and prepared to sail for New York. But before he could leave, he received orders to "take a post and hold it" in Virginia. He briefly toyed with the idea of staying in Portsmouth, or possibly moving to Point Comfort in Hampton, but then chose the old tobacco port of Little York or Yorktown. There, he could be easily resupplied by British ships sailing down from New York. Or so he thought.

Now enter Admiral Francois de Grasse, commander of a huge fleet of French warships riding at anchor in the West Indies. He was ready and willing to offer the Americans help, and both General Jean-Baptiste de

⚓

In May 1779 the British marched into Suffolk and set fire to the town. Stores of tar, pitch and turpentine in waterfront warehouses turned the town into an inferno. Sketch by Judith Whitney Godwin.
COURTESY OF JUDITH WHITNEY GODWIN.

Above: A view of Yorktown from the York River, c. 1781. British flags fly from a ship on the river and from the town.
COURTESY OF THE MARINERS' MUSEUM.

Below: Swan Tavern, built in 1722, was considered the most prominent in Yorktown. One critic claimed that the many taverns of the town were evidence of an "unbounded licentiousness" that seemed to "taint the morals of the young gentlemen of this place." By Albert S. Burns, 1937.
COURTESY OF THE LIBRARY OF CONGRESS.

Rochambeau and General Washington had just the mission for him. Could he sail to the entrance of the Chesapeake Bay, they wanted to know, and cut off a possible retreat by Cornwallis? On August 5, when twenty-eight French ships of the line and their supporting fleet raised anchor at St. Domingo, the stage was set. On hearing news that de Grasse was on the way, the combined French and American troops began an arduous 450-mile march from New York to Yorktown.

By August 30 the Frenchman and his fleet had anchored in Lynnhaven Bay, just inside the Virginia Capes. It was incredibly delicious news for Washington. While his troops were marching through Philadelphia early in September, the usually stoic general practically jumped for joy when he heard the news. Embracing Rochambeau, he shouted over and over, "He's here! He's arrived."

At that very moment, British Vice Admiral Thomas Graves and an armada of nineteen ships approached the Capes. They discovered de Grasse's superior force already inside the bay. The Frenchman was forced to wait for a favorable tide to come out to meet the enemy, and might have been vulnerable if Graves had attacked then and there, but the British elected to form a long, formal battle line. This gave the French an opportunity to form their own. And so, on the afternoon of September 5, as the two great fleets opened fire on each other, the Battle off the Capes, one of the greatest and most important

naval engagements in history, began within sight of the bluffs where the Jamestown colonists had arrived.

When the smoke cleared two hours later, the British had suffered 336 casualties and several ships were so badly damaged, with much of their rigging shot away, they were useless for further battle. Reluctantly, Graves turned his fleet north and limped back to New York, all the while unaware that Washington and Rochambeau were at that moment on their way south. With de Grasse and his fleet now totally in control of the Chesapeake, Cornwallis was trapped.

The American and French armies converged on Williamsburg. It was now no longer the capital of Virginia, but a fitting place to prepare for what could be a decisive victory in the long and bitter war. When Washington spotted his dashing young French friend, Gen. Marquis de Lafayette, who had led harassing moves against Cornwallis, the tall American spread his arms in welcome, then hugged and kissed him from ear to ear.

Washington likely took a sentimental journey through the town he had known so well, past the College of William and Mary, Bruton Parish Church, the Capitol and Governor's Palace, stopping at the home of his friend George Whythe, now his headquarters. He would spend two weeks there, making final preparations for the march to Yorktown, urging other generals who were on their way

to help, to fly with utmost speed. Gen. George Lincoln and his regiments landed at College Landing on the James River, near the city. Another detachment was sent to guard against a possible escape across the York River to Gloucester. In all, seventeen thousand troops were assembled.

On September 17, Washington and Rochambeau sailed down the James to Hampton Roads and the mouth of the bay where they went aboard de Grasse's flagship, the formidable 104-gun *Ville de Paris*, and they dined and conferred with the admiral. De Grasse agreed to sail up the York River and assist the siege of the town. While the generals were on board, a storm came up that delayed their departure for several days, finally relenting enough for Washington to be rowed up the James and return to his headquarters. A visitor to Williamsburg today might see an actor portraying Washington, conferring with "Rochambeau" and then, on the commons outside the courthouse, addressing his troops with stirring words about the great battle that is to come.

It was at daybreak on September 28 that the combined American and French troops began the seven-mile trek over sandy roads toward Yorktown.

THE BATTLE THAT WON AMERICA

If you stand near the visitor center and look out over the fields, you can see flags flying where American and French batteries were set up, and you can imagine how the British soldiers must have felt when they saw thousands of enemy troops assembling. If you walk out to the siege lines, you can see the deep, wide York River behind the town and imagine the French warships slowly closing the trap. And you can stand on the reconstructed breastworks and just about

⚓

Top, left; Lord Charles Cornwallis, lieutenant general of the British Army, from painting by S. W. Beechey.
COURTESY OF THE NATIONAL ARCHIVES.

Top, right: George Washington at Dorchester Heights. Painting by Gilbert Stuart.
COURTESY OF THE NATIONAL ARCHIVES.

Below: Comte de Rochambeau. From painting by J. D. Court.
COURTESY OF THE NATIONAL ARCHIVES.

hear the roar of the cannons that would begin to tear the town to pieces.

It took several days for the French and American soldiers to bring up their big guns, their howitzers, their mortars. There was no hurry. The allies were delighted when they found that the British forward line had retreated, making it possible to move in even closer. There was furious artillery fire from behind the fortifications in the town, but nothing, it seemed, could stop the methodical preparations. And at last, on the morning of October 9, the French guns opened up the barrage. Shortly afterward, according to one witness, General Washington himself "put the match to the first gun," and then a continuous thunder of American cannon fire ensued. The bombardment went on without pause throughout the night, making it difficult for the British to make repairs. Their fortifications quickly splintered and hundreds of soldiers lost their lives. As for the grand old homes that made up the town, most of them were reduced to dust. Conwallis and his staff hunkered down in a bunker beneath the garden of the once-elegant home owned by Thomas Nelson, the uncle of Thomas Nelson Jr., one of the signers of the Declaration of Independence. Nor was the younger Nelson's home spared. In fact, the owner made sure, instructing the gunners to aim for his house. The gunners also directed their aim at British

warships lying just off the town, striking some with hot shot and setting them afire.

The relentless siege continued for eight days. Cornwallis made a desperate attempt to escape across the York River at night, only to be thrown back by a sudden storm. The last hope was gone. Now the defenders were staring at heavy guns brought to within point blank range. There was no use. Holding out any longer would simply mean more deaths. It would have been "wanton and inhuman," he concluded, to continue.

At about 9 a.m. on October 17, as shells continued to rain on the doomed British fortifications, a lone drummer boy, his heart surely thumping as furiously as his drum, stepped upon the parapet and an officer holding a white flag over his head fell in with the lad. As they stepped forward, the guns at last fell silent.

After two days of negotiations and preparations, what remained of Cornwallis's army marched out of the town and down the road to what would one day be called Surrender Field, and regiment by regiment, laid down their arms. To the British, who had grown weary of the war, it was an unthinkable calamity. Upon hearing the news, Prime Minister Frederick North is said to have cried, "Oh, God! It's all over!"

Today, captured British guns line a walkway leading to a platform overlooking the place where the war all but ended. "Surrendered by the capitulation of Yorktown

October 19, 1781," says an engraving on one of the 17 mortars and four cannons. You can stand and look over the field, push a button and listen to sounds of fifes and drums and realize that this, as much as any other place, is where the country was born. You can also imagine a little more of what life was like "under the hill," the waterfront village that sparked its economy. Riverwalk Landing, a recreated community of shops and restaurants and a new pier that welcomes visitors by water, opened in 2005.

Above: The Battle off the Capes.
COURTESY OF THE HAMPTON ROADS NAVAL MUSEUM.

Below: The capture of Yorktown. Lithograph by Turgis.
COURTESY OF THE NATIONAL ARCHIVES.

Above: The surrender of Cornwallis. The British commander, complaining of illness, actually sent one of his generals to the formal surrender. Painting by Trumbull.
COURTESY OF THE NATIONAL ARCHIVES.

Below: A hundred years after the surrender, Yorktown held a major celebration, inviting ships from around the world to participate.
COURTESY OF THE MARINERS' MUSEUM.

UNDISCOVERED JEWEL

Meanwhile, in Princess Anne County, Kemps Landing had become a center of population, and court was conducted in a former store. In 1778, the county seat was moved here from Newtown and in 1783 the town of Kempsville was created. That year, the population of Princess Anne included 3,999 whites and 2,656 blacks. A few of the blacks had been freed during the Revolution, and some owned land, but many migrated to Norfolk where they could adopt a trade or ship out to cities in the North.

Kempsville was flourishing and vying to become a major port. An act was passed in 1783 to dredge out a navigable canal from the Elizabeth River to the North Landing River. This would have brought ship traffic from North Carolina, but apparently not enough subscribers could be found and the project was abandoned. Instead, the focus would shift to the Dismal Swamp Canal, connecting Norfolk and Elizabeth City and, finally, in 1852, to the Albemarle and Chesapeake Canal, which was dug through Great Bridge, bypassing Kempsville.

The largely rural Princess Anne County remained an undiscovered jewel. Although farms sent produce to market in Norfolk, it was isolated from the outside world. Neither the Revolution nor the War of 1812 had much of an impact, except that the embargoes and depressions that accompanied the wars left much of the region in poverty. One of the hottest issues ever to dawn on the county had to do not with who would run the nation, but where the county seat ought to be.

The county was briefly touched by the war and demonstrated a bit of tenacity. The British made an amphibious landing near Chesapeake Beach, but when they landed south of Cape Henry to forage for supplies they were promptly driven back by local militia. The area, part of present day Virginia Beach, became known as Seatack, for "sea attack."

With the Kempsville courthouse falling into disrepair and farms spreading over a wide territory that stretched clear to Back Bay, a strong movement was initiated to move the

courthouse to the village of Princess Anne. Against bitter opposition from Kempsville, the legislature approved the move in 1820. The shift did little to change the center of population, however. In fact, as people moved out to lands further west, the population of Princess Anne shrank, dropping from 9,102 residents in 1830 to 7,285 in 1840.

THE BEACON

One of the first acts of the new Congress, meeting in 1789, was the creation of the United States Lighthouse Service, which in turn opened the door for creation of a lighthouse at Cape Henry. Virginia authorities had long desired a lighthouse at the sprawling entrance to the Chesapeake Bay, so when President Washington forwarded a copy of the new act to Governor Beverly Randolph, they acted promptly. In November, the General Assembly authorized the conveyance of two acres of land "to the United States for the purpose of building a light-house." Washington passed along the authorization to

Secretary of the Treasury Alexander Hamilton and, on March 31, 1791, a contract was signed by John McComb, Jr., a prominent builder who designed the Government House, the planned residence for the president in New York City.

The contract called for "a Light House of Stone, Faced with hewn or hammer dressed Stone" rising seventy-two feet from the water table to the top of the stone work. It was to be in the shape of an octagon, with three windows on the east side and four on the west. The foundation would have to be twenty feet below the water table because of the sandy soil. The price: $17,700. Finished in October 1792, it became the first completed public works project of the new government. Washington again took an interest, personally reviewing the list of applicants for keeper. That same month, the light that was to direct thousands of mariners safely between the Virginia Capes blazed out over the Atlantic. The Cape Henry Light, still standing, still accessible to the public, is now the symbol of the City of Virginia Beach.

The first Cape Henry Lighthouse, completed in 1792, was the first built and operated by the new federal government. It was replaced by the second, cast iron light in 1881. The photo was taken to be included in the Virginia Room exhibit at the 1919 World's Fair in New York.

COURTESY OF THE LIBRARY OF VIRGINIA.

CHAPTER III

BROADSIDES

Hampton Roads went marching confidently into the nineteenth century. Portsmouth, a half-century after incorporating as a town, was sending thousands of workers daily to Gosport Navy Yard to build and repair ships. But the giddy pace of growth began to stumble as the nation's uneasy relationship with England worsened. One affair that almost led to war originated in Norfolk waters. On June 22, 1807, the USS *Chesapeake*, a Gosport-built frigate, weighed anchor and headed out to sea to relieve the USS *Constitution* in the Mediterranean. Before she could clear the capes, a British warship, the HMS *Leopard*, began shadowing her. About forty miles out to sea, an officer on board the *Leopard* hailed her and came aboard, demanding to be allowed to inspect the ship for deserters. When the *Chesapeake's* captain, James Barron, refused, the *Leopard* responded with a succession of broadsides that killed three crew members and injured 18 others. Ill-prepared and poorly trained, the *Chesapeake* had no option but to strike her colors and allow a boarding party to search and depart with four suspected deserters.

As the riddled *Chesapeake* limped into port, citizens reacted with outrage and war fever swept the region. The two nations patched up their differences diplomatically and the British squadron withdrew from local waters, but not before Norfolk and Portsmouth declared an embargo on trade with Britain.

If the embargo severely crimped the local economy, the War of 1812, "the second war for independence," nearly destroyed it. The Brits, still possessing a far more powerful navy, blockaded the Elizabeth River and probed for ways to attack. But fortunately, Norfolk was prepared and, luckily, the U.S. Frigate *Constellation* was around. The thirty-eight-gun *Constellation*, built in Baltimore in 1797, earned the nickname "Yankee Racehorse" because of her clipper-like speed. But the ship was unable to leave the Elizabeth River after British Rear Admiral George Cockburn arrived with a powerful squadron and blockaded the Chesapeake Bay. Bottled up in the river, the *Constellation's* crew helped set up fortifications at Craney Island at the mouth of the river and man the guns. Other defenses at Fort Norfolk and Fort Nelson in Portsmouth were also beefed up. Cockburn, hoping to take Norfolk and destroy the *Constellation*, made his move. At dawn on June 22, 1813, about two thousand British troops landed ashore on the western side of Craney Island and several gunboats approached from the east. The defenders, including gunners from the *Constellation* and local militia, opened fire with devastating effect, mowing down the attackers and sinking the boats. The Battle of Craney Island was over quickly, with two hundred enemy dead and not a single American loss.

Hampton was not so fortunate. Three days later, a force of twenty-five hundred British infantry landed at Indian River, marched on the town and brushed aside the far-smaller defending force. The invaders were quite brutal. "Every horror was committed with impunity—rape, murder, pillage and not a man punished," a British officer later admitted. The sacking of Hampton helped galvanize American public opinion against the enemy.

DISMAL TALE

With commerce severely throttled during the war, one development that held out hope for the local economy arose from the depths of the swamp—The Great Dismal Swamp, that is. George Washington, in his entrepreneurial days, was part of a group of "adventurers" who bought thousands of acres of pristine wetland for the purpose of extracting timber, especially cedar, which they cut into shingles and shakes for house construction. The swamp also inspired the notion of one day bisecting it with a canal connecting the great waterways of the two states and in

HMS Leopard *(left) rakes the USS* Chesapeake *in an affair that shocked Hampton Roads and almost led to war with Britain in 1807.*
COURTESY OF THE MARINERS' MUSEUM.

1797 Congress authorized the ambitious dredging project.

The grueling, brutal job of digging the twenty-two-mile-long Dismal Swamp Canal was performed by slaves. Some, on loan from their owners, were paid and were able to purchase their freedom by the sweat of their brows. Funding was slow in coming and digging even slower, so the project stretched on for years. One version, aided by several locks, was completed in 1805, permitting passage of poled, shallow-draft lighters carrying shingles. With renewed labor, a wider, deeper canal opened in 1814, and the first canal boat, bearing bacon and brandy from North Carolina, arrived in Norfolk. The blockade was still on, but this, at least, was one defense against economic strangulation.

So vast was the Great Dismal, so impenetrable, it generated its own legends that spider-webbed it with intrigue for generations. But it also had true stories to tell,

stories of lost and desperate and frightened people that trumped the legends by far.

In 1856, Harriet Beecher Stowe followed her *Uncle Tom's Cabin* with *Dred, A Tale of the Dismal Swamp*. In forays from his island in the swamp, fictional Dred—inspired by the real-life Nat Turner—preached against slavery. The book, panned by critics, sold three hundred thousand copies anyway. The swamp apparently drew the young Robert Frost to thoughts of suicide, according to a Frost biographer who says the poet, disheartened because his beloved Elinor White spurned his offer of marriage, decided to end it all by plunging into the swamp and—he'd show her—letting it destroy him. The account has it that Frost arrived in Norfolk in November 1894, made his way to Deep Creek, crossed a drawbridge and walked along a wagon road in the swamp. Despite a morbid fear of the dark, he wandered through the night. The next morning, apparently cured of his misery, he boarded a boat bound for the Outer Banks. He returned to New England and later married his once-reluctant love.

But the dark secret of the swamp was the connection with slavery. Many took advantage of its vast wilderness to make their way to a kind of dismal freedom. Historians speculate that the Great Dismal supported thousands of runaways. But others were hounded mercilessly by bounty hunters. Stories of runaways inspired Henry Wadsworth Longfellow in 1842 to pen "The Slave in the Dismal Swamp." Not only was the swamp a hiding place for runaway slaves, it also was a conduit in the Underground Railroad, which spirited them out of the South.

Another development that brought prosperity to Hampton Roads was the decision by Congress in 1827 to authorize construction of facilities for building and repairing ships. One was to be at Charlestown near Boston and the other at Gosport. "Drydock Number One" began as a 40-foot hole in the ground, with a foundation of brick and stone and then blocks of granite shipped from Massachusetts. Finally, in June 1833, with President Andrew Jackson looking on, the drydock, 340 feet long by 100 feet wide, became the first in the nation to serve the overhaul and repair of warships. There was much ceremony as the *Delaware*, a 74-gun ship-of-the-line that had been built at Gosport in 1817, now came in for repairs. In 1860, just before the nation was to be fractured by war, the yard reigned as the largest in the nation, spurring the growth of Portsmouth, tripling its population to about 9,500 and generating business throughout the region. A year later, still brimming with warships and armaments, it would become a tempting spoil of war.

There was another proud federal presence in Portsmouth. Responding to the need to treat sick and wounded sailors, Congress approved funds for construction of the nation's first naval hospital. The land at Hospital Point, once purchased by Captain Thomas Willoughby and used as a colonial fort, was now to play host to the Navy's first hospital. Portsmouth Naval Hospital, opened in July 1830, would eventually sprawl over 135 acres on the banks of the Elizabeth River, with a capacity of more than 2,000 patients. Those beds would be needed.

CONTAGION

The devastating years that were to rain down on the South were not far off, but there was one more tragedy to be played out before that curtain rose. On the morning of June 6, 1855, the steamer *Ben Franklin* arrived in Hampton Roads from St. Thomas with several

Hotel at Lake Drummond — Suffolk, Va.

This photo, taken in 1895, shows a hotel on the Suffolk side of Lake Drummond, considerably less lavish than the original.
COURTESY OF THE *VIRGINIAN-PILOT*.

victims of yellow fever aboard. After 12 days in quarantine, during which the captain hid evidence of the disease, the ship was allowed to proceed to the Page and Allen Shipyard next to the Navy Yard for repairs. No one knew at the time that the disease was spread by mosquitoes, an insect with which Hampton Roads has long been familiar in the summer. There was good reason to fear the implacable disease. Just three years before, more than fifty people had succumbed to yellow fever. And now, in late June, when the first victims began to appear near the shipyard, the ship was sent back to quarantine and police barricaded the shipyard entrance. But it was too late.

Irish Row, a slum near the shipyard, now festered with the disease and residents began dying faster than they could be buried. The city had become almost a ghost town as panic set in. And now, in late July, the disease leaped across the Elizabeth River to Norfolk's Barry Row, a squalid tenement near the waterfront. Mayor Lamb had declared that the neighborhood "is a perfect cesspool of pestilence. The Irish living there are almost in as degraded a state as they are in the half-starved districts of Ireland." The contagion spread wildly. The disease usually claimed its victims within a few days of its onset, and dozens were dying every day. Mass graves with as many as eighty bodies were dug. There was no time even for funerals and many victims shared coffins and went to their graves in blankets.

Hampton, Suffolk and Smithfield took severely restrictive measures, forbidding all contact with Portsmouth and Norfolk residents. The waterfronts of those cities were deserted. Nearly all shipping ceased and warehouses were closed. Barry's Row was put to the torch, but it did not stop the fever's rampage. *The New York Times* reported on August 11 that seven thousand had fled Norfolk and Portsmouth and others were leaving as rapidly as possible. Almost two-thirds of Norfolk's residents fled the city. Of those who stayed, some forty percent died. And it was not just slum dwellers who were infected. The city's new mayor, Hunter Woodis,

The Gosport Navy Yard welcomes the first visitor to Drydock # 1, the Gosport-built USS Delaware, *in June 1833.*

who helped tend to the sick, was carried off by the fever, as were several doctors from Philadelphia who had come to treat victims. It wasn't until the first frosts of October killed the mosquitoes that one of the worst epidemics to ever visit an American population, killing 2,300 in Norfolk and 900 in Portsmouth, was over. The following year, in one of the most solemn parades the city would ever see, Norfolk firemen led a procession of the living to honor those who died. Among them were orphans and gravediggers.

Still back on its heels, Hampton Roads was about to suffer a near-knockout at a jam-packed intersection of time and place.

RUNAWAYS

Even though the first slaves in America came to Jamestown, Hampton Roads did not become a major slave-holding area. But slave-trading region it was. Slave ships from the West Indies and Africa unloaded their human cargo at Annapolis, Alexandria, Yorktown, and Norfolk, and from these ports the slaves were exported to states in the Deep South. Even though international slave trading was outlawed, Maryland and Virginia continued to ship slaves to other domestic markets.

After the Revolution, Virginia approved laws that allowed masters to free their slaves. In many cases, the slaves were allowed to work on the side as skilled artisans, shopkeepers, laborers and domestics, earning enough money to buy their freedom and that of their loved ones. In urban areas like Norfolk, Portsmouth and Williamsburg, free blacks were very much a part of the local economy. The waterfront was a strong, steady place of employment for both free blacks and slaves. And when war came, many would serve the Union. Five regiments of black troops were raised in Norfolk, Portsmouth and Hampton, and many served bravely and honorably, a few earning the Congressional Medal of Honor.

Up until the early 1800s, many free blacks coexisted with whites, but hard times followed 1831 when Nat Turner's rebellion in nearby Southampton County kindled white fears of a slave uprising. A noose of repressive laws began to tighten, prohibiting blacks from congregating in the streets, from working in many trades and even from defending their rights. There were many reasons to flee to more hospitable places, and Norfolk proved to be a perfect springboard. There were so many merchant ships leaving the city's waterfront, it was relatively easy to stow

⚓

A view from the Portsmouth side of the Elizabeth, with the new Navy Hospital, first in the nation, in the foreground. From a lithograph by A. Sachse.

aboard or hire on as crew. Thus, the conveyor belt of goods leaving local piers became a station stop on the Underground Railroad. The city attracted runaway slaves from all over the compass. And many free blacks, living in neighborhoods the authorities were loath to enter, were more than happy to hide them and spirit them on board friendly vessels.

Norfolk newspapers often carried runaway slave notices.

Aug. 6, 1806. Lucy, 25. Smart, free-spoken, likely girl. When questioned, claims that she is being hired out.

May 17, 1786. Fanny. Mulatto, artful in conversation. Has passed as free in Richmond, suspect she is in Norfolk or some other city.

May 29, 1790. Francis, 25. Mulatto man, Writes a pretty good hand, plays fife extremely well. Good house servant, large wardrobe, 6 shirts. Intends to ship himself for Europe.

Oct. 3, 1806. Charles, 25. Very black, plays violin well, complaisant & smiling when spoken to, saying yes to every word spoken to him. Worked on a craft. Good farmer. Believed to have been harbored by persons in the vicinity.

Even so, Hampton Roads was still strongly pro-Union, especially Norfolk and Portsmouth, which relied on nationwide commerce and federal shipbuilding for much of their prosperity. In February 1861 when delegates were elected to the state convention that would consider secession, Norfolk and Portsmouth were opposed. But that was before Confederate forces opened fire on Fort Sumter in Charleston Harbor. One day after, a group of Norfolk men sailed to Craney Island and raised the rebel flag from an old blockhouse. On April 15, newly elected President Lincoln called for seventy-five thousand volunteers to "cause the laws to be duly executed." Three days later, the Virginia Convention voted 85 to 55 to secede and the capital of the Confederacy soon was moved from Montgomery, Alabama, to Richmond. With little choice now, Hampton Roads fell in line.

TOE TO TOE

The Civil War in Hampton Roads was rough on the economy, but the actual fighting was mercifully brief and largely centered around a single phenomenon. It began with a tense standoff at the gates of what had become

ESCAPING FROM NORFOLK IN CAPT. LEE'S SKIFF.

the oldest and most important shipyard in America, Gosport, brimming with ships and armaments. On April 20, fearful that local militia were about to storm the gates, the commandant of the yard sank several vessels and set fire to the yard. The result was a raging, exploding inferno that a correspondent for *The New York Times* described as the "day of judgment." Among the vessels scuttled was one of the prides of Portsmouth, the USS *Delaware*. Then again, there was the five-year-old Union steam frigate *Merrimack* that was then in the yard for repairs to her balky engines. The *Merrimack* was to have another brief existence, this time as a fearsome "dark monster" that forever changed naval warfare.

Under direction of Confederate Navy Secretary Stephen Mallory, workers at the yard raised the sunken ship, removed the upper decking and erected a roof-like wooden casemate that they covered with four inches of iron. There were many months of delays as the South, lacking the industrial base of its northern foe, tore up trolley tracks and melted them down for the iron plates. Re-commissioned the following February as the CSS *Virginia*, the ten-gun battery with a lethal iron ram, had one mission and one alone: destruction of the federal blockade of obsolete wooden ships waiting out on Hampton Roads.

Meanwhile, the Union command was anxious to launch a bold attempt to capture Richmond and bring a swift conclusion to the war. The Peninsula campaign, led by General George B. McClellan, was to land more than 120,000 troops at Fort Monroe and march on the Confederate capital, supported by warships on the James River. Now, the presence of the rebel ironclad would throw a formidable wrench into these plans. Furthermore, what was to prevent the menacing new warrior from steaming up the Potomac and laying siege to Washington, Lincoln's advisors demanded to know.

Hastily, in October 1861, the Union commissioned Swedish-born inventor John Ericsson and a group of New York investors to build a radically different floating battery with a revolving gun turret, and send it to Hampton Roads to challenge the confederate menace. It took something like one hundred days for the contractors to build the USS *Monitor* in Brooklyn, New York, and, about five minutes after launching her in the East River, to prove that what many were calling "Ericsson's Folly" would even float. Her immediate orders were to make haste to Hampton Roads, proceed up the Elizabeth River to the Navy Yard and blast the *Virginia* out of the water before she could be completed. But a Union spy informed Secretary of the Navy Gideon Welles that the rebel ship was about to be launched.

On the morning of March 6, 1862, the *Monitor* stood out from her berth at the Brooklyn Navy Yard and headed for Hampton Roads. If she had begun her journey half a day earlier, one of the bloodiest days in naval history might have been altogether different.

The largely untrained crew on the *Virginia* assumed they were going out for sea trials on

Left: This was the first burning of the Gosport Navy Yard, this time by federal troops; they abandoned the yard in April 1861 as Virginia joined the Confederacy. The spectators appear to be watching from Hospital Point.
COURTESY OF THE WILSON MEMORIAL HISTORY ROOM, PORTSMOUTH PUBLIC LIBRARY.

Below: The USS Merrimack, *first of a class of new steam frigates—built in 1855 at the Boston Navy Yard—was under repair at the Gosport Navy Yard when war broke out and put to the torch.*
COURTESY OF THE U.S. NAVY HISTORICAL CENTER.

the morning of March 8, but flag officer Franklin Buchanan had other ideas. The *Virginia* was to have her baptism by fire, heading straight down the river to where the federal fleet waited like sitting ducks. With slanting roof and belching smokestack, with sides greased with pig fat to help deflect enemy shot, the *Virginia* looked like a stealthy black beast as she slowly approached the fleet off Newport News Point. Her first target was to be the USS *Cumberland*, but as she slid past another wooden warship, the USS *Congress*, the Confederate gunners let loose a devastating broadside that left their adversary grievously wounded. Then, without a moment's hesitation, the *Virginia* went straight for the *Cumberland* and plunged her huge ram into the wooden adversary's starboard side.

All the while, the *Cumberland*'s gunners and shore batteries bombarded the *Virginia*, but with about as much effect as peashooters. The *Virginia* reversed engines, leaving the ram in the wounded *Cumberland*'s side. After she did, the Yankee ship went straight to the bottom of Hampton Roads. Next, it was the *Congress*'s turn. Executing a slow turn, the Confederate ironclad brought the awesome firepower of her ten guns on the stricken ship and just

about blew it out of the water. The *Congress* sent up a white flag of surrender, but shore batteries kept firing and an enraged Buchanan, wounded in the action, ordered the ship burned with hot shot. There would have been more victims that day, but the tide was falling

and the *Virginia* retired for the night to an anchorage off Sewell's Point. With two ships destroyed and more than 360 sailors killed, that day would stand as the worst bloodbath in U.S. naval history until Pearl Harbor.

The *Monitor* almost didn't make it to Hampton Roads. Bad weather and a general lack of seaworthiness conspired to almost sink her several times during the three-hundred-mile journey from New York. But she made it, late in the afternoon of March 8. Just as she passed Cape Charles and turned into the bay, the officer at the helm heard the sound of heavy gunfire from the direction of Hampton Roads. It was the *Monitor's* lethal adversary at work.

There was every reason to expect that the little pigmy of a ship, as some Union officers viewed the *Monitor*, would have no chance against the Confederate goliath. But the second day of the Battle of Hampton Roads would prove differently.

FREEDOM FORT

Fort Monroe remained a Union stronghold throughout the Civil War, and it didn't take long for next-door Hampton to fall, but not before local soldiers put the entire downtown to the torch in order to deny use of the buildings for Yankee purposes. And this for a town that had been burned down five decades before by the British. A century and a half later, visitors to the Hampton History Museum would learn that it was reduced to "a heap of ashes and scorched brick." A section of the museum resembles burned-out walls and chimneys. *The Philadelphia Enquirer* on August 8, 1861 described "a forest of bleak sided chimneys and walls of brick houses tottering and cooling in the wind. A more desolate sight cannot be imagined than is Hampton today." Ironically, the burned-out village became an instant slum as hundreds of refugees from slavery settled among the ruins. Along with the fire went all the court records of Elizabeth City.

Construction of "Fortress Monroe," as it was once called, was begun after the War of 1812 exposed the weakness of its coastal defenses, especially the entrances to the Chesapeake Bay and Hampton Roads. Among the most famous soldiers garrisoned there was Edgar Allan Poe, writer of the macabre, who enlisted in the Army in 1827 to help pay off gambling debts, a fault for which his foster father, John Allan of Richmond, shunned him. In a letter to Allan on December 22, 1828, he begged for help in getting out of the military. He also pleaded for understanding.

Ambition. If it has not taken the channel you wished it, it is not the less certain of its object. Richmond & the U. States were too narrow a sphere & the world shall be my theater.

The fort, encircled by a moat, fairly bristled with 32-pounder guns, the most powerful artillery of its time, with a range of over one mile. At the same time, Fort Calhoun—or as many called it, the Rip Raps—was built on a manmade island directly opposite, subjecting possible intruders to a murderous crossfire. Both fortifications remained in Union hands throughout the Civil War. And, much to the displeasure of Southern authorities, Major General Benjamin F. Butler welcomed escaped slaves, declaring them "contrabands" of war. It would become known as "Freedom Fort," where several black cavalry and light infantry units were formed to help the fight for freedom. A number of former slaves were taken on board the *Monitor* as crew.

After the war, the fort would have the distinction of briefly being the home of Jefferson Davis, the former president of the Confederacy. Davis was imprisoned in a casemate, changed to a prison cell just for him. He was briefly placed in irons and charged with taking part in the plot to assassinate President Lincoln. He demanded a trial, but never got one and spent two years in the small, damp— and occasionally cold -- cell before being released. Later, in 1951, a casemate museum was established to display the famous prison cell. It has since been expanded to display other Army artifacts and interpret the history of Fort Monroe.

The *Monitor* arrived amid the shattered fleet at 9 p.m. just in time to see the *Congress*, as the fire reached her magazines, go up in a monstrous explosion. "It went right to the marrow of our bones," reported young Executive Officer Dana Greene. Nevertheless, the *Monitor* anchored out for the night beside the USS *Minnesota*, the next most likely rebel target, lying aground on shoals at Middle Ground. (The abandoned Middle Ground Light now sits just off the present-day Monitor-Merrimac Bridge-Tunnel.) As dawn ended a jumpy, sleepless night, the watch on the little Union ship noticed the *Virginia* weighing anchor and heading right for her prey. Just as she did, the plucky ironclad

turret revolved and the first of her two eleven-inch Dahlgren guns was run out and fired. The *Virginia* ignored the insult at first, but when the second gun rattled the iron plates on her side, her attention was fully engaged.

It was 8 a.m. For nearly four hours, the two ironclads slugged it out. Because the Monitor was far more nimble than the *Virginia* and did not have to take up a broadside position to fire, she dogged her opponent through a series of wide circles out on the Roads, ranging from Fort Monroe to Newport News. The ships often seemed to touch each other as they blasted away, with no noticeable effect—other than the shock of having shot bounce off their iron armor. Frustrated, the officers on the *Virginia* attempted to ram the *Monitor*, succeeding only in delivering a glancing blow. Then it was the *Monitor*'s turn. But the attempt to disable the *Virginia*'s rudder backfired. A Confederate gunner fired an exploding shell at the *Monitor*'s pilothouse and Worden, just then peering through the viewing slit, was temporarily blinded.

The *Monitor* withdrew to deal with Worden's injury, then attempted to re-engage. But the *Virginia*'s officers, assuming the *Monitor* was out of action and realizing that their ship was vulnerable because it was now floating higher, was then steaming away. The battle of the ironclads was over without a decisive winner. But as the two withdrew, never to meet again, it was clear that the age of wooden warships was over. It was also clear that the balance of power that was rudely upset by the *Virginia*'s one-sided victories on March 8 was suddenly restored on March 9.

THE VIRGINIA CREEPER

On Monday, March 17, 1862, one of the largest armies ever assembled, with 121,500 men, 25,000 horses, 3,600 wagons, 300 artillery pieces, and all the equipment and provisions needed for a vast assault, sailed down the Chesapeake Bay to Fortress Monroe. McClellan's army began its march up the Peninsula but the next day found its path blocked by Confederate Major General

⚓

Federal troops disembark in Hampton after the town was gutted by fire. Sketched by an officer of the Topographical Engineers.
COURTESY OF THE SARGEANT MEMORIAL ROOM, NORFOLK PUBLIC LIBRARY.

steamed out from beside the *Minnesota* and headed straight for her.

At first, the *Virginia*'s crew seemed not to notice the strange-looking vessel in their path, and they opened fire on the *Minnesota*, sending those still on the *Monitor*'s turret scurrying for cover. Slowly, with Lieutenant John Worden in command, the *Monitor*'s

John B. Magruder's thirteen-thousand-strong "Army of the Peninsula." Magruder had constructed three defensive lines across the Peninsula, the most formidable of which began where the nation had once secured its independence, Yorktown. Magruder improved and strengthened the existing Revolutionary War fortifications, then added earthworks southward to the Warwick River, continuing along the river and angling westward to the James.

Even though his forces vastly outnumbered the Confederates, McClellan, derided as "the Virginia Creeper," hesitated, calling for siege artillery and seeking support from Union gunboats. To defeat a weaker foe, he summoned the largest assemblage of siege weapons in history. The battery of 101 guns and mortar, brought by land and barge, was called by one writer "hell's own arsenal." But the delay gave the opposition plenty of time to make its move. On the night of May 3, rebel artillery fire was unusually strong, but Union forces noticed the following morning an almost eerie quiet. It was the day before McClellan's monster barrage was to begin, and what they soon realized was that the Confederates had abandoned their fortifications and slipped away.

The Union Army raced off in hot pursuit until reaching another set of fortifications a mile east of Williamsburg. It was here that Confederate General Joseph E. Johnston, in

charge of the retreating troops, elected to slow the pursuers down. That afternoon, in what became known as the Battle of Williamsburg, the two forces clashed. In two days of bloody fighting, the Confederates suffered 1,600 casualties to the Union's 2,300. Then on May 6, Johnston resumed his retreat. The Union forces were again slowed down in boggy swamps near the Chickahominy River, and by now, with almost a month gained, and with General Robert E. Lee sending more troops to defend Richmond, the southern forces beat McClellan back and forced him to abandon his campaign.

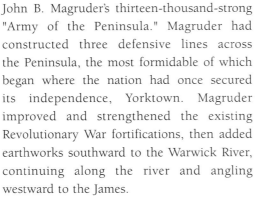

Above: Robert Hudgins Sr. of Hampton, one of the Confederate soldiers who set the town ablaze to deny its use by Union troops. By Christopher Cheney.

COURTESY OF THE HAMPTON HISTORY MUSEUM.

Below: After the Confederates abandoned Norfolk, Union troops boarded waiting vessels near Fort Monroe under General John E. Wool and crossed over to Ocean View. They landed and marched into the city unopposed. In the middle foreground in stovepipe hat is President Lincoln who supervised the operation. Watercolor by G. Kaiser

COURTESY OF THE MARINERS' MUSEUM.

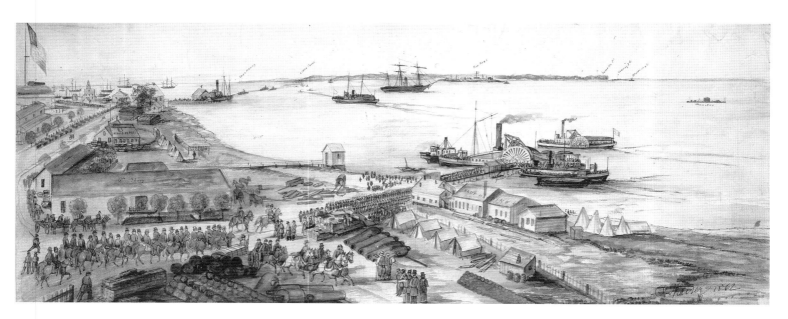

The Peninsula provided the bottleneck that choked Lincoln's hopes for a quick end to the war and left in its wake three more years of bloody conflict.

One thing the Confederate pullback accomplished was to leave Norfolk undefended. Lincoln himself arrived at Fort Monroe on May 8, paid a visit to the crew of the *Monitor* and then supervised an attack against Norfolk. On the night of May 9, 6,000 Union troops, with General John E. Wool in command, were landed at Ocean View. They encountered no resistance as Confederate forces evacuated the city. The Union soldiers were met at Princess Anne Road by Mayor William Lamb and other members of the Norfolk Council bearing a flag of truce. The loquacious Lamb read a long and tiresome proclamation, allowing the Confederate troops to flee across to Portsmouth and put the torch to the shipyard. When Union forces again seized what was left of the shipyard, the name was changed from Gosport to Norfolk Naval Shipyard.

Control of Hampton Roads was now permanently in the hands of the Union. With Norfolk and Portsmouth secured, the South's

Above: Lee Hall Mansion, Italianate house built in 1858 by planter Richard Decauter Lee. Confederate generals Magruder and Johnston used the mansion as headquarters during the Peninsula campaign.
PHOTO BY PAUL CLANCY.

Below: Endview Plantation, built in 1769 by Colonel William Howard, Jr., one of the signers of the Virginia Resolves. It was used by both sides during the Peninsula Campaign.
PHOTO BY PAUL CLANCY.

Above: General McClellan's troops set up camp at Yorktown, erecting fortifications on top of those left by British defenders 81 years before.

COURTESY OF THE NATIONAL ARCHIVES.

Below: General Benjamin F. Butler interviews "contrabands," former slaves who were given freedom and, in some cases, inducted into the Union Army, after the federal takeover of the Peninsula.

COURTESY OF THE HAMPTON HISTORY MUSEUM.

ironclad champion was suddenly without a home. The *Virginia's* seaworthiness was in doubt, in spite of some lofty notions of sending her off to terrorize northern cities. First, she'd have to sneak past the big guns at Fort Monroe and the Rip Raps. The best alternative seemed to be to send the *Virginia* up the James to help defend Richmond, but the ship's deep draft would not allow passage over the shoals at the river's mouth. She would have to be scuttled.

On the early morning of May 10, as they lay at anchor near Fort Monroe, the *Monitor's* sailors could see a bright light in the southwest. At 4 a.m., there was a sudden flash, followed by a dull, heavy explosion. Their old nemesis had been run aground at Craney Island and put to the torch. Though they cheered, there was a note of sadness that the once-dreaded ironclad had died by her own hand and not in a fair fight.

Later that morning, orders came to move to Norfolk, and the *Monitor* crew witnessed the now-silent guns at Sewell's Point. A squad of sailors went ashore, Paymaster William Keeler recounted, marched over the earthworks, and hoisted the Stars and Stripes over the rebel fort. Another Union flag now

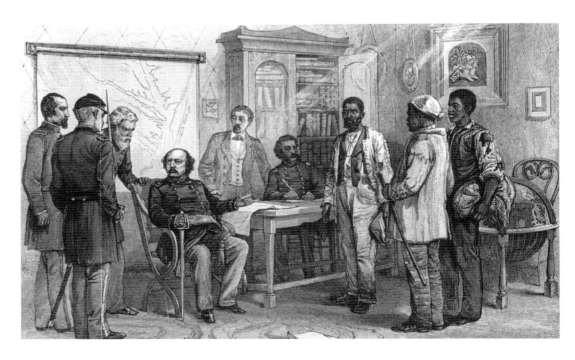

flew from Craney Island, where, as Keeler recounted, "a blackened sunken wreck was pointed out as all that remained of our old foe." The *Monitor* would remain on station in Hampton Roads through the summer and fall of 1862, then receive orders to head to Beaufort, North Carolina, and then to Charleston. But she would not make it past treacherous Cape Hatteras. Just after midnight, on December 31, she would find the bottom of the sea and remain a mystery for more than a century.

SIEGE

Suffolk had revived after the British put it to the torch. It did so again after another disastrous fire swept through town in 1837, burning down the courthouse a second time. That same year, lumber magnate Mills Riddick began building a house on Main Street for his growing family of twelve children. The four-floor, 21-room Greek revival home was considered so outlandish by local citizens that some referred to it as "Riddick's Folly," and the name stuck. It contained about 8,000 square feet of living

space, with 16 fireplaces. By 1850 there were 1,200 residents in town, four hotels, a newspaper, five lawyers and eight doctors.

Surrounding Nansemond County resumed its widespread farm-based economy, with slavery—which had spread throughout the colony and then the commonwealth—one of the keys to its economy. By 1860, Nansemond

⚓

Riddick's Folly was used as Union headquarters after federal troops occupied Suffolk.
PHOTO BY PAUL CLANCY.

AN ARDENT DESIRE

For troops quartered at Suffolk, the end of the war was relatively pleasant. On at least one occasion, Riddick's Folly played host to a grand social that lasted until sunrise. Recently, the Riddick's Folly museum obtained a copy of a letter written by Captain Samuel C. Pierce to his fiancé in Rochester, New York. It is dated April 29, 1865, the very day that generals Grant and Lee met at Appomattox to discuss terms of surrender. Lincoln had been assassinated, Richmond deserted and burned. The long letter is full of musings about the captain's return.

"I can not close this without once more telling you how my love for you increased with each day," he wrote on thin, tissue-like paper. "Morning and night you are in my thoughts and my most ardent desire is to return to you once more."

Another letter, this one to Riddick by Signal Officer A. M. Thayer, compliments him on the house and landscaping, but there is a clearly stated disapproval of his cause.

Dear Sir: Whilst you were away from home striving to subvert this Government the necessities of war made me an inmate of your office— I have great respect for your evident desire to promote the agricultural interest of the Eastern Virginia—great respect for the taste displayed in ornamenting your grounds and I've no doubt a better acquaintance would make me a more admirer of the talents which you evidently possess— But whilst I am no abolitionist I must confess that I believe the cause in which you engaged decidedly wrong—We shall see however—I hope to meet you on friendly terms in more peaceful times and enjoy you socially.

The house served as school board headquarters from 1968 to 1978, during which time several examples of Civil War graffiti were scrubbed from the walls, but one remains, the signature of Henry Van Weeck, from Brooklyn, New York, a twenty-two-year-old private in the Third New York Cavalry. A sheet of Plexiglas covers the signature.

had 5,732 white residents, 5,481 slaves and 2,480 free blacks. It was a substantial black majority, and Nat Turner's rebellion, as well as the presence of escaped slaves in the Great Dismal Swamp, had made whites uneasy. Many slaves and free blacks joined the throng heading toward Fort Monroe where they would one day become Union soldiers.

On May 12, 1862, after the capture of Norfolk and Portsmouth, Union troops rode into Suffolk and Confederate forces withdrew to the Blackwater River. Riddick's lavish home, as well as the rebuilt Suffolk Courthouse, served as headquarters for the Union occupation. General John J. Peck commanded a garrison of twenty-five thousand men.

In early 1863, General Lee sent General James Longstreet and two divisions to southeastern Virginia to protect Richmond from an expected Union advance. When this failed to materialize, Longstreet launched a wide-ranging foraging expedition that filled wagons with foodstuffs for Lee's army. He also began building fortifications and laying Suffolk under siege. The Southerners reoccupied Fort Huger, an old earthwork fort on the Nansemond River. Attempting to cut off Union communications with Suffolk, they established other batteries along the Nansemond River, some of them positioned near the Norfleet house just upriver from Fort Huger. On one occasion, they succeeded in damaging and driving off Union vessels attempting to pass. The fort changed hands a couple of times, but then Lee, on April 29, summoned Longstreet to Fredericksburg and his troops soon found themselves marching to a place called Gettysburg. The siege of Suffolk was over.

Above: Black laborers at a wharf on the James River during the Civil War.
COURTESY OF THE NATIONAL ARCHIVES.

Below: General Wool's headquarters at Fort Monroe.
COURTESY OF THE HAMPTON HISTORY MUSEUM.

Princess Anne County, too, was under Union occupation. Troops were garrisoned at Kempsville, Chesapeake Beach, Princess Anne Courthouse and Pungo Ferry. While no battles were fought between armies around the sprawling rural landscape, roving guerilla bands constantly harassed the soldiers, destroyed bridges, and attacked the Cape Henry Lighthouse, smashing its lens.

The only instance of rebel troop movement in the county was a celebrated flight to safety. It involved ninety-seven Confederate prisoners who, on board the USS *Maple Leaf*, departed Norfolk on June 10, 1862, en route to Fort Delaware. Just off the Virginia Capes, the men overpowered the crew and took charge of the steamer. When they realized there was not enough fuel to make it to Nassau in the Bahamas, they beached the *Maple Leaf* south of Cape Henry and made their way overland to Knotts Island where they were given food and shelter. The next day they crossed Currituck Sound in stolen boats and tramped over back roads all the way to Richmond.

Even though most major battles occurred elsewhere, thousands of local men fought and

QUARTERS No. 1 IN 1862

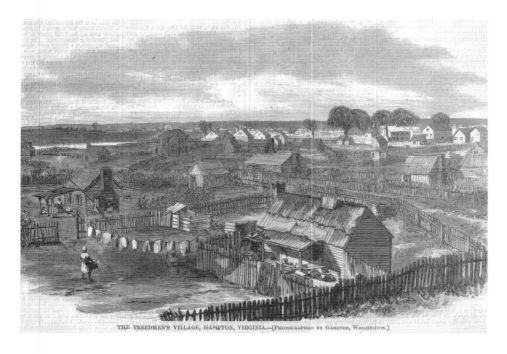

THE FREEDMEN'S VILLAGE, HAMPTON, VIRGINIA.—[Photographed by Gardner, Washington.]

bled for the Confederacy, and a dreadful weariness settled in for the duration. One Norfolk County schoolgirl, Katie Darling Wallace, 11, lamented in a letter to the editor in January 1864, "…all our dear boys…are gone to war. May they be spared to the end of this dreadful carnage."

AFTERMATH

During the period of Union occupation, former slaves were permitted to live on and farm abandoned land at such places as Sewell's Point in Norfolk, the Baxter Road area in Princess Anne County, Simonsdale in Portsmouth and Phoebus in Hampton. Many understood that they were given title to the land, and were greatly upset when President Andrew Johnson pardoned ex-Confederates and ordered their land restored to them. The now-landless African Americans had far less chance of making a go of it.

The odds against succeeding in this post-bellum world were immense. Some

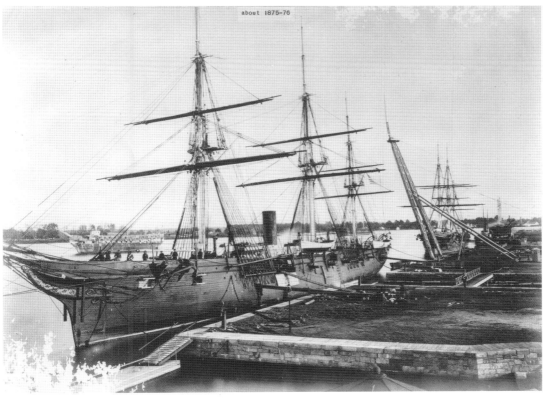

prospered. Samuel Harris of Williamsburg amassed a fortune selling dry goods on Duke of Gloucester Street. He owned a stable, barbershop, blacksmith shop, saloon and lumberyard, entered real estate ventures with prominent whites and was appointed to the school board and the board of the local bank. When tracks of land between Fort Monroe and Hampton Institute were subdivided into city lots, blacks purchased them and a new

⚓

Above: The USS Franklin *at anchor in the Southern Branch of the Elizabeth off Portsmouth, 1879.*

COURTESY OF THE WILSON MEMORIAL HISTORY ROOM, PORTSMOUTH PUBLIC LIBRARY.

Below: Former Confederate General William Mahone, a railroad magnate, helped lead Norfolk back to prosperity by merging rail lines that reached across the country.

COURTESY OF THE NATIONAL ARCHIVES.

residential subdivision called Phoebus came into being.

Hampton Roads was federally occupied territory until 1870. It was a bleak time for many who supported the Confederate cause. In Portsmouth, the burned-down shipyard was restored in 1866, with the promise of good-paying jobs. But former soldiers and sailors of the Confederacy, as well as those who did business with them, were barred from employment and stripped of their right to vote. Many had their property confiscated and sold or leased to former slaves.

Much of the rural land went uncultivated. If you had looked for news of Princess Anne County in Norfolk newspapers, you would have found mostly advertisements of farms for sale. Unable to keep up with debts and taxes, many families had to sell and move on. Princess Anne entered a long period of historical slumber from which it would not awake for several decades.

The region's economy, strangled by the war, was slow to recover. Cotton began to trickle into the ports in the 1870s, thanks to the establishment of better rail links. What had been 100,000 bales of cotton coming into Norfolk in 1869 grew to 400,000 by 1874, with peanuts and lumber not far behind. But the biggest boost was the arrival of coal on the tracks of Norfolk and Western Railroad. Mayor William Lamb, son of the Civil War-era

mayor, happened to be a coal merchant and predicted that the port would become "the most important coaling station on the Atlantic coast." In 1885, Pier I was opened at Lambert's Point just north of downtown, and the first of what would become thousands of colliers began loading coal for factories around the world.

The story throughout Hampton Roads after the Civil War was much the same: Federal occupation, followed by the Reconstruction Acts and a few decades of rapid advances for those who had been enslaved. For whites it may have been hard to swallow to see a new newspaper called *The True Southerner*,

published in 1866 by former slave Joseph T. Wilson. When a new state constitution was drawn up in Richmond in 1867-68, several black delegates took part, including former slave Sam Nixon, now Thomas Bayne of Norfolk, who emerged as a leading Republican. Among others were Willis A. Hodges of Princess Anne County, Daniel M. Norton of York County and George Teamah of Norfolk County. They supported a measure calling for public schools for all, regardless of race, but this was too radical, even for radical Republicans. By the mid-1880s, as whites began to regain power in Richmond and the courthouse, black gains were stripped away and a rigid system of segregation took hold. The Supreme Court's 1896 decision approving separate but equal facilities in railroad cars provided the justification for Jim Crow laws that ran the gamut of public facilities, from restaurants to schools, from busses to beaches, from voting booths to employment offices. The beginning of the end of the rigid system of public segregation would not arrive until 1954 when the Supreme Court reversed itself, declaring that separate was inherently unequal. A last-gasp struggle was soon to follow.

Above: Postcard showing how Granby Street looked in 1868 before the area that is now City Hall Avenue was filled in.
COURTESY OF THE SARGEANT MEMORIAL ROOM, NORFOLK PUBLIC LIBRARY.

Below: A six-masted schooner at the Norfolk and Western coal piers, 1905.
COURTESY OF THE SARGEANT MEMORIAL ROOM, NORFOLK PUBLIC LIBRARY.

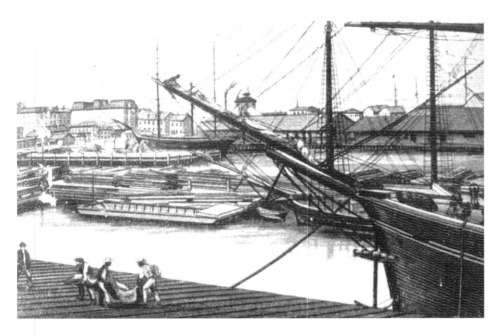

Above: Main Street docks, 1880.
COURTESY OF THE *VIRGINIAN-PILOT*.

Below: The huge and lavish Atlantic Hotel on Granby and Main, 1883.
COURTESY OF THE SARGEANT MEMORIAL ROOM, NORFOLK PUBLIC LIBRARY.

BOOM TIMES AGAIN

Meanwhile, the local economy was starting to chug along. For Norfolk, one of the star players was former Confederate General William "Billy" Mahone, an engineer who had built the Norfolk and Petersburg Railroad in 1853. It was a marvel of engineering, running straight through the Great Dismal Swamp and stretching out fifty-two miles to the west. After the war, with the help of political connections, Mahone ramrodded the first of dozens of mergers that would lead to a colossus, Norfolk and Western Railroad, with more than fifteen hundred miles of track. In 1882, Norfolk showed off its railroad might by building a downtown station topped by an eighty-foot clock tower. The next year, beginning almost as an afterthought to the city's spider web of rail lines, Norfolk Southern Railway began as a line linking the city with Edenton, North Carolina, connecting with steamers bringing produce to market. That venture would become part of Southern Railroad and, nearly a hundred years later, after merging with Norfolk and Western, lead to creation of Norfolk Southern Corporation, one of the nation's great railroad lines.

Norfolk's population was booming, with 46,624 at the turn of the century. As the city grew, so did its institutions. The Norfolk Public Library was begun in 1870, although it would not be until 1901, when steel tycoon Andrew Carnegie put up $50,000 for a library, that one was built in Freemason. Also in 1870, horse-drawn trolleys were introduced and then in 1894 electric-powered streetcars clanged through the city. In 1871 the Norfolk Fire Department was established, the third full-paid city department in the country. There was even room for wild animals. In 1892 the city purchased sixty-five acres along the Lafayette River that would eventually become home for the Virginia Zoo.

TURNING TO THE SEA

Through these years, the lifeblood of Princess Anne County was the Port of Norfolk. Steamships were leaving that city several times a week for points north, so farmers were eager for better transportation links. But shell roads like the one between Norfolk and Kempsville were about as good as they were going to get. What would one day truly drive the economy of this sprawling county was not so much its farms but its coastline. When one canal company president remarked in 1871 that the area that would one day become Virginia Beach was "one of the most lovely, healthy, and attractive places in the world for a summer resort," it was one of the first public signs that anyone knew this.

The fact that this was only six years after the end of the Civil War—and just a year after Virginia rejoined the Union—makes this observation remarkable. The region was still

Above: O'Keefe's Casino at Cape Henry, from the collection of Edgar Brown.
COURTESY OF THE *VIRGINIAN-PILOT.*

Bottom, left: Annie Elizabeth Herbert wrote many notes to friends who were enlisted in the Confederate Cavalry from Kempsville. In 1867 she married one of them, Charles Burroughs Foster.
COURTESY OF THE LOCAL HISTORY COLLECTION, VIRGINIA WESLEYAN COLLEGE.

Bottom, right: James Hill Bonney enlisted in the Confederate Army in May 1861. After the war, he was proprietor of the Inn at the Princess Anne Courthouse. He is seen here with his wife, Mary Elizabeth Atwood, and their children.
COURTESY OF THE LOCAL HISTORY COLLECTION, VIRGINIA WESLEYAN COLLEGE.

reeling from the effects of the war. Confederate money was next to worthless. Jobs were scarce and farms, now without slaves, were failing and residents were packing up and heading west, but some were imagining a very different world just within their grasp. And it wouldn't take long for the beginnings of a new dawn to glow on the horizon.

Before 1880 the Atlantic shoreline was mostly farmland that ended in pine forests and dunes. All up and down the coast there was barely a house or building, except for life-saving stations that were then being built six miles apart, beginning at Cape Henry. That year, however, the newly-formed Seaside Hotel and Land Company started buying what would amount to several thousand acres along five miles of oceanfront. The company had close ties to another enterprise, the Norfolk and Virginia Beach Railroad and Improvement Company—and the two ultimately merged. In January 1883, work was begun on a rail line that would run from Norfolk over a trestle bridge at Broad Creek and through farmlands and timber stands to

the beach. By July the first of several thousand visitors were dancing on the floor of a new pavilion, wading into the ocean and eating at picnic tables. The name "Virginia Beach," then only a footnote in the railroad company's charter, soon took hold.

The following year, 1884, saw the opening of the 60-room Virginia Beach Hotel. Complete with gas lighting and lavatories, it was considered one of the most luxurious hotels in America. It soon offered a host of outdoor activities, including golf and tennis, band concerts and operettas. It wasn't long before the rich, famous and powerful, including Alexander Graham Bell and President Benjamin Harrison, were disporting themselves at the seashore and wealthy Norfolk families were buying up lots and erecting summer retreats. One of them, with 22 rooms and 14-inch-thick walls, would eventually be known as the DeWitt Cottage, which stands today as the Atlantic Wildfowl Heritage Museum. By 1897 there were a few dozen year-round residents and they began lobbying for town status. Finally, in March 1906, a charter was granted. The town council met in what had been the Virginia Beach Hotel, refurbished and renamed the Princess Anne Hotel.

The region was gearing up for a new century.

Above: John Woodhouse Sparrow entered lifesaving service in 1883 at the Seatack Station and retired in 1916.
COURTESY OF THE OLD COAST GUARD STATION.

Left: Princess Anne Hotel forms the backdrop for visitors to the beach in 1887.
COURTESY OF THE VIRGINIAN-PILOT.

Below: Bathers at the beach, 1896.
COURTESY OF THE VIRGINIAN-PILOT.

JAMESTOWN TER-CENTENNIAL EXPOSITION

HISTORICAL - EDUCATIONAL - NAVAL - MILITARY - INDUSTRIAL

Commemorating the 300th Anniversary of the First Permanent English Settlement in America.
Located on Hampton Roads, close to Norfolk, Portsmouth, Newport News, Hampton, and Fortress Monroe.

OPENS APRIL 26. 1907.   GENERAL OFFICES: NORFOLK, VIRGINIA.   CLOSES NOV. 30. 1907.

Chapter IV

BIRTHPLACE OF A NATION

There is little evidence that Hampton Roads celebrated, or even observed, its first or second centuries, but by the third there was something to crow about. As 1907 approached, the region could look back on survival and recovery from a disastrous civil war and begin to feel the surge of economic might from its railroads and ports. Norfolk had grown north toward the shores of Hampton Roads and the expansionist dreams of a few would put the city on a new and, as it turns out, unexpected course.

Sewell's Point, an obvious strategic location, had served as fort and battery during two major wars, but had not witnessed any sort of sprawl, either urban or suburban. It had seen a temporary settlement of freed slaves after the Civil War, but those lands had been returned to whites. It was the perfect spot, leading lights realized, for a memorable party. Not just a local one, either. In 1903 a group of investors headed by Gen. Fitzhugh Lee, a hero of the Spanish-American War and nephew of General Robert E. Lee, bought a marshy open tract of 340 acres on the point for what was to be called the Jamestown Exposition. The grandiose project would represent America to the world. But first, water, electricity, telephones and everything else necessary for operating a small city, had to be brought in: miles of roadways, sidewalks, carriageways and a mile of piers along the Hampton Roads waterfront.

The ambitious scheme was slow getting off the ground, partly because the legislature balked at providing the $1 million expected from the state, and local investors literally delayed their commitment until the last minute. Nevertheless, twenty-two states erected grand exhibition halls, which would one day serve as "Admirals Row" officers' quarters. Pennsylvania came through with a three-quarter replica of Independence Hall. There was a miniature railway, a "Shoot the Chute" ride, restaurants and other attractions. There were gleaming automobiles—a phenomenon of only a dozen years—parading up and down the broad boulevards.

It was a kind of mega-world's fair, with Civil War cycloramas, including the battle of the *Virginia* and *Monitor*. There was a Wild West Show, with a huge cast of cowboys, cowgirls, Indians, and rancheros, and a Palace of Mirth, with a huge clown head atop the entrance. There were lions, polar bears, hyenas and ostriches. Mark Twain, Woodrow Wilson, Booker T. Washington, William Jennings Bryan, and many others made appearances.

To top it off, Hampton Roads hosted the largest gathering of warships in history, including sixteen battleships, six destroyers, three cruisers, and several smaller vessels, accompanied by more than a dozen foreign ships. The occasion was marked by all the pomp and ceremony that one might expect from such a gathering: bands and ceremonial salutes, rowing contests and regattas, feasts and dances. A "Grand Basin," complete with deep piers, was dug at the north end of the point. Railway spurs were run out to the grounds, as were trolley tracks and a new roadway, Jamestown Exposition Boulevard, later named Hampton Boulevard.

One notable exhibit hall was the Negro Building, with a vast collection of exhibits. Among them were 14 dioramas by Harlem Renaissance sculptor Meta Warrick, each of them depicting a stage in the African American journey. The first showed slaves arriving at Jamestown, shackled and traumatized by their journey. The series progressed through plantation life to freedom and then, contrary to the then-prevailing stereotype, showed former slaves leading normal, purposeful lives at home. The last portrayed a graduation ceremony at Howard University, with Frederick Douglass, the great emancipator, serving as commencement speaker.

The star attraction of the exposition was the Rough Rider himself, President Theodore Roosevelt, who opened the exposition on April 26. In a characteristically bully and expansive speech, Roosevelt welcomed visitors from around the world. "They have come to assist us in

⚓

Advertisement for what was to be a lavish celebration of the 300th anniversary of the first English settlement of America. At the center is Sewell's Point, with Willoughby Spit at left.

COURTESY OF THE MARINERS' MUSEUM.

Above: The Jamestown Exposition, a 300-year birthday party for the nation, brought exhibition buildings from 22 states, including a replica of Philadelphia's Independence Hall.
PHOTO BY WILLIAM O. FOSS. COURTESY OF THE *VIRGINIAN-PILOT*.

Below: President Teddy Roosevelt welcomed visitors from abroad who "have come to assist us in celebrating what was in very truth the birthday of this nation."
COURTESY OF THE SARGEANT MEMORIAL ROOM, NORFOLK PUBLIC LIBRARY.

celebrating what was in very truth the birthday of this nation," he declared, "for it was here that the colonists first settled, whose incoming, whose growth from their own loins and by the addition of newcomers from abroad, was to make the people which one hundred and sixty-nine years later assumed the solemn responsibilities and weighty duties of complete independence."

Roosevelt used the occasion to announce that the assembled battleships would set out from Hampton Roads on a flag-showing cruise around the world. "The Great White Fleet," as it was dubbed after the battlewagons received fresh coats of white paint from the Norfolk Naval Shipyard, would demonstrate to foreign governments, especially Japan, that the U.S. was now a major naval power. The sixteen battlewagons, belching black smoke from their coal-fired boilers, steamed out from the Roads on December 16 with 14,000 sailors aboard and TR watching from the rail of his yacht. The voyage would cover 43,000 miles and include 20 port calls on six continents. They returned in triumph in February 1909 and promptly sailed up the Elizabeth River to receive coats of the U.S. Navy's new official ship color, battleship gray.

As grand a spectacle as the Jamestown Exposition was, the crowd turnout was disappointing. Part of the blame went to the construction delays that resulted in a muddy mess on opening day and stinging criticism in the press. Then, too, it was one of the coldest, wettest springs in decades. In all, just three million visitors, not the expected 15 million—and many of these holding complimentary tickets—trooped out to Sewell's Point before the exposition closed seven months later. It was a financial failure that resulted in receivership for the investors.

THEODORE ROOSEVELT'S LETTERS TO
HIS SON KERMIT AFTER THE JAMESTOWN EXPOSITION

White House, April 29, 1907.

DEAREST KERMIT:

We really had an enjoyable trip to Jamestown. The guests were Mother's friend, Mrs. Johnson, a
Virginia lady who reminds me so much of Aunt Annie, my mother's sister, who throughout my
childhood was almost as much associated in our home life as my mother herself; Justice Moody, who
was as delightful as he always is, and with whom it was a real pleasure to again have a chance to talk;
Mr. and Mrs. Bob Bacon, who proved the very nicest guests of all and were companionable and
sympathetic at every point. Ethel was as good as gold and took much off of Mother's shoulders in the
way of taking care of Quentin. Archie and Quentin had, of course, a heavenly time; went everywhere,
below and aloft, and ate indifferently at all hours, both with the officers and enlisted men. We left here
Thursday afternoon, and on Friday morning passed in review through the foreign fleet and our own
fleet of sixteen great battleships in addition to cruisers. It was an inspiring sight and one I would not
have missed for a great deal. Then we went in a launch to the Exposition where I had the usual
experience in such cases, made the usual speech, held the usual reception, went to the usual lunch,
etc., etc.

In the evening Mother and I got on the *Sylph* and went to Norfolk to dine. When the *Sylph* landed
we were met by General Grant to convoy us to the house. I was finishing dressing, and Mother went
out into the cabin and sat down to receive him. In a minute or two I came out and began to hunt for
my hat. Mother sat very erect and pretty, looking at my efforts with a tolerance that gradually changed
to impatience. Finally she arose to get her own cloak, and then I found that she had been sitting
gracefully but firmly on the hat herself-it was a crush hat and it had been flattened until it looked like
a wrinkled pie. Mother did not see what she had done so I speechlessly thrust the hat toward her, but
she still did not understand and took it as an inexplicable jest of mine merely saying, "Yes, dear," and
with patient dignity, turned and went out of the door with General Grant.

The next morning we went on the *Sylph* up the James River, and on the return trip visited three of
the dearest places you can imagine, Shirley, Westover, and Brandon. I do not know whether I loved
most the places themselves or the quaint out-of-the-world Virginia gentlewomen in them. The houses,
the grounds, the owners, all were too dear for anything and we loved them. That night we went back
to the *Mayflower* and returned here yesterday, Sunday, afternoon. To-day spring weather seems really
to have begun, and after lunch Mother and I sat under the apple-tree by the fountain. A purple finch
was singing in the apple-tree overhead, and the white petals of the blossoms were silently falling. This
afternoon Mother and I are going out riding with Senator Lodge.

NORFOLK

The exposition may have flopped, but not Norfolk, which experienced one of the largest building booms in its history. By 1907 the city boasted forty hotels, including rather stately ones like the Lorraine, the Victoria and the Union Square. Two office buildings reached for the sky. A grand, million-dollar downtown Union Station for the Virginian and the Norfolk and Western railroads was due to open in 1909.

So much of Hampton Roads' future seems compressed within the first few decades of the twentieth century, including the dawn of naval aviation. That moment came on a stormy day, November 14, 1910, when Eugene B. Ely revved up the engine of his boxy, open-cockpit Curtiss-Hudson plane on a wooden platform hanging off the deck of the cruiser *Birmingham*. Ely, a racecar driver, chauffer and pilot, had waited all morning for the weather to clear. He and his backers were afraid that if he didn't make the attempt, the national press would head back to Washington and dismiss the whole idea.

When the storm paused, Ely didn't wait for the *Birmingham* to turn into the wind. Instead he gunned the fifty-horsepower engine and the plane lumbered down the platform. Ely couldn't swim and was afraid of water. He knew that he needed air speed,

and that's what he got as the plane nosed off the edge and plunged toward the water. It was almost not enough. The forward wheel touched the water momentarily, but a second later as pilot and aircraft achieved sufficient air speed, they climbed into the lowering sky. A few minutes later, he landed successfully near a row of cottages on Willoughby Spit. Ely went on to land successfully on one of the makeshift platforms on a ship in San Francisco Bay in 1911,before being killed in a crash later that year.

The Attucks Theater, named for Revolutionary War hero Crispus Attucks, opened in 1919 and played host to top performers of the day.
COURTESY OF THE CRISPUS ATTUCKS CULTURAL CENTER, INC.

REBIRTH OF A GEM

Post-World-War-I Norfolk was a place of separate, but in some ways thriving, cultures. Church Street was a focal point of black business and pride, and it was on this thoroughfare that a group of businessmen from Norfolk and Portsmouth decided to build a regional mecca for entertainment. They would call it the Attucks Theater, in honor of Crispus Attucks, an African American who was the first patriot to lose his life in the Boston Massacre of 1770. When it opened in 1919 the Attucks showcased plays, vaudeville shows and movies. During its heyday it hosted legendary performers like Cab Calloway, Duke Ellington, Mamie Smith, Nat "King" Cole, and Redd Foxx. The theater also served as a gathering place for civic meetings and an adjunct to local schools. There were poetry readings, music recitals, graduations, church services and concerts. It also provided office space for professionals like doctors, dentists, lawyers and realtors. The building was well-used and well-loved.

The theater closed in the mid-1950s and sat vacant for nearly half a century, but community leaders held onto a dream of one day restoring and reopening it. It took years for the Crispus Attucks Cultural Center to raise $8 million and years more for the meticulous restoration to take place. A half century later, in October 2004, an audience of black and white Norfolkians, many of them decked out in evening gowns and tuxedos, cheered as the curtain depicting the Boston Massacre rose again. The Preservation Hall Jazz Band, a seemingly timeless band from the New Orleans French Quarter, wailed into the night much as musicians had done there decades before.

Above: The "Great White Fleet" of sixteen battleships sailed out of Hampton Roads on Decemer 16 in a world-circling exhibit of the country's new naval might. Here they're seen returning in February 1909.
COURTESY OF THE MARINERS' MUSEUM.

Below: Ocean View train station, 1908. The line ran from downtown to the waterfront. After years of decline, Ocean View has emerged as a new gold coast at the sourth end of the Chesapeake Bay.
COURTESY OF THE VIRGINIAN-PILOT.

Congress was moved to vote the first funds for naval aviation, and in 1919, workers at Norfolk Naval Shipyard stripped down a coal ship, replaced the deck with a permanent landing platform and rechristened the ship the *Langley*. It was America's first aircraft carrier. The Navy was in the aviation business to stay.

NAVAL MIGHT

Then there was the matter of the investors who, it turns out, didn't do all that badly, thanks to the fact that they now owned one of the last open deepwater tracts of land in Hampton Roads. With the memory of the Great White Fleet still fresh, with the world's largest naval shipyard just a dozen miles away, with a burgeoning drydock and shipbuilding empire across Hampton Roads, a munitions arsenal at St. Juliens Creek south of Portsmouth and a refueling depot at Craney Island, it didn't take long for local and national leaders to realize where a new naval base ought to be built.

It is one thing to propose a giant new naval base and quite another to justify it and set plans in motion. But on April 5, 1917, caution went out the window as the U.S. declared war on Germany. Secretary of the Navy Josephus Daniels was persuaded to obtain the land and Congress promptly passed a bill providing for $1.2 million to buy 474 acres and $1.6 million for development of the base, including piers, aviation facilities, storehouses, storage for fuel and oil, a recruit training station, a submarine base, hospital and recreation grounds. It was the start of what was to become the greatest naval base in the world.

Ground was broken on Independence Day 1917, and within one month housing for 7,500 sailors had been competed. To make way for ships, eight million cubic yards of dredge spoil was removed and used to fill in the flats on the west and north. The Navy's air

capability was rapidly expanded and 30,693 enlisted men and 6,716 officers were welcomed. By then, the air detachment was recognized as one of the most important in the nation, and in August 1918 the station became Naval Air Station Hampton Roads, a separate entity under its own commanding officer. The first aircraft were, appropriately, seaplanes, flown across Hampton Roads and moored to stakes in the water until canvas hangars could be built. Their mission was to conduct anti-submarine patrols and train aviators and mechanics.

The end of World War I saw drastic cuts in naval appropriations, but air operations in Norfolk continued. The air station developed

Above: A year before the stock market crash of 1929, crowds assembled on the Lafayette River for a speedboat race.
COURTESY OF THE SARGEANT MEMORIAL ROOM, NORFOLK PUBLIC LIBRARY.

Below: The Chaumont *departs, June 10, 1933.*
COURTESY OF THE SARGEANT MEMORIAL ROOM, NORFOLK PUBLIC LIBRARY.

Right: The hurricane of August 23, 1933, generated 88 miles-per-hour winds at Norfolk Naval Air Station, dumping 10 inches of rain. It was the first time an eye of a hurricane had passed over Norfolk since 1821. In the aftermath, Norfolk citizens wade and paddle on Granby Street.

CHARLES BORJES PHOTO. COURTESY OF SARGEANT MEMORIAL ROOM OF THE NORFOLK PUBLIC LIBRARY.

Below: Baseball at City Park in Norfolk. The Spartans, at bat, playing the Cardinals.

COURTESY OF THE SARGEANT MEMORIAL ROOM, NORFOLK PUBLIC LIBRARY.

an arresting device to train pilots for deck landings and began work on a catapult to assist in launches. There would be no more nail-biting affairs like Ely's. After the stock market crash in 1929, the base survived but operated at a slower tempo.

As war clouds gathered again at the end of the 1930s, major construction resumed. By 1939, the Norfolk Naval Station was clearly the largest naval installation on the Atlantic coast and would grow even more after the bombs fell on Peal Harbor. By mid-1941, about 30,000 sailors were either living at the base or on ships stationed there, and by 1943, the height of the war, the number of military and civilian personnel leaped to more than 350,000.

Bawdy houses flourished in the city, along with gambling dens, tattoo parlors and cheap bars. National magazines sent reporters to the city to report on the raucous goings on. Finally, at the Navy's urging, the city cracked down, and the illegal activity moved just outside city limits. One calming influence was the service organizations that sprang up to meet the needs of lonely sailors. The USO built a formidable organization, opening up eight centers and sponsoring outdoor dances and, in 1943, took over the art deco Municipal Auditorium for major traveling USO shows. The auditorium would one day become part of the Harrison Opera House.

Meanwhile, the Navy base burst its bounds, expanding to the east to swallow up a former World War I army base. Runways, hangars, warehouses, barracks and ramps for seaplanes were built on hundreds of reclaimed acres. The base expanded to handle five aircraft carrier air groups and a training program for pilots. Again, the base grew, adding four hundred acres that included the old Norfolk airport. The base became the major training station for most Navy air squadrons, and several from allied nations, that fought in the war. Three 1,000-foot piers were built for convoy escort purposes.

Today, Naval Station Norfolk occupies about 4,300 acres, with 75 ships and 134 aircraft, 13 piers and 11 aircraft hangars for repair, refit and training. It is home to aircraft carriers, cruisers, destroyers, large amphibious ships, submarines and a variety of supply and logistic ships. Port Services controls more than thiry-one hundred ships' movements annually. The facilities extend more than four miles along the waterfront and include seven miles of pier and wharf space. Air Operations conducts over 100,000 takeoffs and landings each year, an average of 275 flights per day, or one every six minutes.

Right next to the naval base is a relatively new kid on the block. The land south of the base had been an Army quartermaster depot,

and the city of Norfolk realized that it would be a perfect site for one of the new container cranes that were just coming into widespread use. The city acquired the land in 1965 and installed a single crane. This was a new era for

Above: In May 1939, a crowd gathered on Granby Street to watch a flagpole sitter.
CHARLES BORJES PHOTO. COURTESY OF THE SARGEANT MEMORIAL ROOM, NORFOLK PUBLIC LIBRARY.

Below: Norfolk Naval Station sustained a horrific explosion on September 17, 1943, when depth charges ripped through the base, killing 40 sailors and destroying 16 buildings.
COURTESY OF THE SARGEANT MEMORIAL ROOM, NORFOLK PUBLIC LIBRARY.

Hampton Roads, which in the past had done most of its shipping by loading and unloading goods directly from pier to ship and ship to pier in "break-bulk" fashion. Now shipping would entail stacking and unstacking forty-foot containers brought in by truck and rail. At first, the cities of Norfolk, Portsmouth and Newport News competed for business, but that ended in 1981 when the Virginia Port Authority took over all three. In 2005, the ports handled sixteen million tons of freight, one of the largest such operations in the world.

The post-war years for Norfolk were both exciting and turbulent. First, the city had to recover from the explosive impact of the war, which left services and housing stretched to the limit and the city's reputation tarnished.

Left: Scope opens November 15, 1971, with Chrysler Hall next door.
MEDFORD TAYLOR PHOTO. COURTESY OF
THE VIRGINIAN-PILOT.

Right: Walter and Jean Chrysler.
COURTESY OF THE CHRYSLER MUSEUM.

A CULTURAL BONANZA

One of Norfolk's luckiest associations was forged by a sailor and a chance meeting.

Just after the outbreak of World War II, Walter P. Chrysler, Jr., son of the Chrysler Corporation founder, volunteered for service in the Navy. The thirty-two-year-old Chrysler was not your typical sailor, but world traveler, art collector, Broadway producer and film-maker. Like a lot of other sailors, though, he was stationed in Norfolk. And so it was that he met Jean Esther Outland from the Berkley section, and in 1945 married her.

Chrysler had already amassed one of America's most impressive art collections, thanks to a seemingly limitless appetite for everything from avant-guarde to Baroque, French impressionism to Italian Renaissance. He owned about 8,000 glass pieces, including many from one-time Long Island neighbor Louis Comfort Tiffany. Then, too, there was a growing portfolio of historic photographs. The collection of over 25,000 objects was then worth something like $60 million—and it was looking for a permanent home.

In 1968, Norfolk Mayor Roy Martin, a former classmate of Outland's at Maury High, got a call from the new Mrs. Chrysler, asking if the city would like to be considered. There are no records of Martin's reaction, but it must have been jubilant. The city was about to be handed a cultural bonanza. Chrysler was also prepared to give $1 million for adding a wing to what had been the Norfolk Museum of Arts and Sciences. The city agreed that the Italianate structure on the Hague would be renamed the Chrysler Museum, and, for good measure, soon named a new center for performing arts Chrysler Hall. Both Walter and Jean Chrysler were active in the city's cultural life until their deaths in the 1980s. In 1989, the city engaged a Washington architect and, with $13.5 million in public and private funds, renovated the museum. *The Torchbearers*, a dramatic cast aluminum sculpture in front of the museum, had been presented to the museum by sculptor Ann Hyatt Huntington, wife of another art benefactor, Archer Huntington, founder of the Mariners' Museum. Other impressive museums in Hampton Roads include the Contemporary Arts Center of Virginia in Virginia Beach and the Peninsula Fine Arts Center in Newport News.

There were vast areas of slum housing and an almost-deserted waterfront, with rotting piers and dilapidated warehouses. Just as vast were the inequalities that lingered from decades of rigid segregation, but that issue would remain on a neglected back burner for a while.

WRECKING BALL

The year 1946 was a watershed for Norfolk. A series of hard-charging mayors and city councils came into power, and the General Assembly approved a law allowing

cities to acquire and clear blighted land for private or public use. The new Norfolk Redevelopment and Housing Authority went to work almost immediately. The city became the first in the nation to receive loans and grants under the federal Housing Act of 1949. In December 1951, bulldozers knocked down the first of more than 10,000 units of substandard housing, and at the same time began building public housing projects. Gone were the honky-tonk bars and tattoo parlors of East Main Street, as well as run-down buildings everywhere.

But the city paused to endure a stinging lesson in old-style Virginia politics when the long pendulum of racial segregation finally swung the other way. At first the reaction to the U.S. Supreme Court's 1954 ruling that

separate schools were unconstitutional was as temperate as it could be. Norfolk School Board Chairman Paul Schweitzer declared, "We intend, without mental reservation, to uphold and abide by the laws of the land."

State educators were equally moderate, but the then-dominant Byrd Machine—the forces allied with Sen. Harry F. Byrd, Sr.—were having none of that. With the rallying cry of "massive resistance," they approved a briefcase full of laws requiring, among other things, that any school required by the courts to integrate must be closed. It wasn't long before these laws would be put to the test. In June 1958, U.S. District Court Judge Walter E. Hoffman ordered that Norfolk schools

Above: VE celebration on Granby, May 8, 1945.
COURTESY OF THE SARGEANT MEMORIAL ROOM, NORFOLK PUBLIC LIBRARY.

Below: Norfolk slums, 1940. Photo by the Norfolk Housing Authority.
COURTESY OF THE VIRGINIAN-PILOT.

assign 151 black students to all-white schools. Hoffman refused all attempts to delay or soften the order. Governor J. Lindsay Almond, Jr., a product of the Byrd organization, made it clear he would carry out the state law, and in fact did so in Charlottesville and Warren County. Norfolk would not be spared. On September 28, when Norfolk attempted to carry out the court order and integrate the schools, the governor had their doors chained and padlocked. So it was that ten thousand white students at Granby, Maury, and Norview High Schools and Blair, Northside, and Norview Junior Highs were barred from class. The seniors became the "lost class of 1959."

Norfolk, which by most measures was a progressive, even cosmopolitan city, suddenly found itself in the nation's eye as a throwback to the Old South. Furthermore, a majority on the City Council supported the closings, and threatened more. But several citizens groups, energized by the closings, launched an effective campaign to reopen the schools. Lenoir Chambers, editor of *The Virginian-Pilot*, added a clear, strong voice that eventually won him the Pulitzer Prize. Even the business community, fearful of what the closures meant for the city's business climate, took a stand. One hundred business leaders took out a full-page ad in the *Pilot* declaring that the "abandoning of our public schools is unthinkable." Finally, in January 1960, both the Virginia Supreme Court and a Federal Appeals Court panel struck down the massive resistance laws. The next month, 17 black students entered the six schools and put an end to segregation once and for all.

Meanwhile, urban renewal continued apace. New, wide boulevards now bisected downtown, and new public places like Scope, Chrysler Hall, City Hall and Kirn Memorial Library would soon be built. New bank buildings and a hotel changed the city's skyline. The old Atlantic City neighborhood would become

home to a medical complex that included Eastern Virginia Medical School and Norfolk General and Kings Daughters hospitals. Harbor Park, a triple-A minor league baseball park for the Norfolk Tides, a New York Mets franchise, opened on the Eastern Branch of the Elizabeth River. It would raise the bar for minor league franchises around the country.

Norfolk's education and cultural life kept pace with its growth. Even as the Great Depression settled on the region, the seeds for two universities were planted. Old Dominion University began in 1930 as a division of the College of William and Mary, and has since grown to a modern urban campus with over twenty thousand students. And Norfolk State University, founded in 1935 as a branch of Virginia Union University, gradually established itself as one of the largest and best predominantly black institutions in the country, with an enrollment of nearly eight thousand.

In 1961, Virginia Wesleyan College was founded on the Norfolk-Virginia Beach border. The four-year liberal arts college is technically in Norfolk even though most of its campus is in Virginia Beach.

The city became a cultural center for the southeast, with homes for the Virginia Symphony and Virginia Opera. But downtown needed a boost, and that seemed to arrive on December 1, 1981, when James Rouse, the man who developed Baltimore's Inner Harbor and Boston's Faneuil Hall, unveiled Norfolk's Waterside, a waterfront marketplace. Norfolk had recently discovered the magic of tall ships on its waterfront when John Sears and Captain Lane Briggs invited ship captains to bring their vessels to the harbor and thousands of the curious came to see them. Now, instead of turning its back to the water, the city was embracing it.

Nauticus, the National Maritime Center, took its bow on the water in 1992, joined by the battleship *Wisconsin*, which made its last journey from Norfolk Naval Shipyard to a permanent berth beside the gray waterfront structure on December 7, 2000, Pearl Harbor Day. Nauticus seemed to reinvent itself, developing battleship-related exhibits to go along with its new neighbor. This may have been the firepower a Navy town needed to

redefine itself, but the economic engine that drove the rebirth of the city was a new downtown mall, MacArthur Center. The $300 million center, with its Nordstrom and Dillards department stores and more than one hundred others, at last filled in the sprawling parking lots that had been created by urban renewal thirty-five years before. The center takes its name from General Douglas MacArthur who, with his wife, Jean, rests in a monumental rotunda at the former Norfolk City Hall, now the MacArthur Memorial.

The other changes came in a dizzying rush as suburbanites discovered the excitement of living in a vibrant downtown. Every vacant building, it

The USS Wisconsin *at its berth beside Nauticus.*
PHOTO BY PAUL CLANCY.

Below: Dawn on the Portsmouth waterfront, with the Navy Yard in the distance. The date of the photo is unknown.
COURTESY OF THE WILSON MEMORIAL HISTORY ROOM, PORTSMOUTH PUBLIC LIBRARY.

ambassador for the state at ports of call around the world. She was built by skilled boatwrights on Norfolk's historic waterfront and launched with great hopes and fanfare in December 2004. The *Virginia* took her place near the *American Rover*, the three-masted schooner that, with tanbark sails, has long served as icon for local waters.

PORTSMOUTH

Shrugging off the legacy of war, Portsmouth seemed to return to normalcy by the turn of the century. In January 1889, electric lights replaced gas lamps in homes and city streets. Horse-drawn carriages were replaced by electric streetcars by 1901. Steamboats began calling at the city docks and transporting produce to markets in the North. Its size doubled and its population soared to 17,427.

The Norfolk Navy Yard—there was already a Portsmouth Navy Yard in New Hampshire, so the old name survived—was the economic stimulus for the city's growth. During Theodore Roosevelt's presidency, the yard had about all the business it could handle. When Roosevelt visited Portsmouth in 1906, he received a hero's welcome. But what really sent the local economy into high gear was the nation's entry into World War I. The planned neighborhoods of Cradock and Truxton were built to house the growing

seemed, became a candidate for condominium units, and every vacant lot the site for new housing, from apartments to townhouses to condos. By the end of 2006, hundreds of units of new housing had either opened or were on the drawing boards. New restaurants seemed to open every week on the once-seedy Granby Street. They took their place beside the Norfolk branch of Tidewater Community College, a new presence that brought upwardly mobile students and faculty to downtown.

The region's maritime history has come alive with the addition of the tall ship schooner *Virginia* to Norfolk's skyline. The two-masted, black-hulled schooner, a replica of a 1917 pilot boat of the same name, is now a floating

population—which by 1918 stood at 57,000. The yard could even take responsibility for the nation's first aircraft carrier when it converted a collier, *Jupiter*, into the USS *Langley*.

The end of the war and the stock market crash of 1929 sent Portsmouth into a steep decline that would only end when the Japanese attacked the U.S. Naval Base at Pearl Harbor on December 7, 1941. Soon, shipyard workers were pouring into the city from across the state and nation. Shipyard employment rose as a steady stream of new ships was built. Employment peaked at an all-time high of 43,000. Before the war was over, the yard turned out 101 new ships and landing craft and worked on over 6,000 U.S. and allied warships.

By this time, the Norfolk-Portsmouth Ferry started running full tilt, with four ferry slips at the foot of High Street. These were substantial car ferries that disgorged scores of vehicles at each landing. There was so much demand for making the passage between the two cities that the need for a tunnel became clear. And so, on May 23, 1952, when the Downtown Tunnel opened, the ferries were doomed, and made their last run on August 25, 1955. Call it nostalgia or genuine need, a new passenger ferry would eventually return.

Portsmouth continued to grow, annexing neighborhoods like Cradock and Elizabeth Manor in 1960 and West Norfolk, Craney Island and much of Churchland in 1968. In the meantime, Norfolk County government, now isolated from much of its remaining population on the other side of the Elizabeth River, moved

Top: A downtown market, 1901.

COURTESY OF THE WILSON MEMORIAL HISTORY ROOM, PORTSMOUTH PUBLIC LIBRARY.

Above: Bilisoly's Drug on High Street, 1896.

Dr. A. L. Bilisoly is at left.

COURTESY OF THE WILSON MEMORIAL HISTORY ROOM, PORTSMOUTH PUBLIC LIBRARY.

AFRICAN-AMERICAN GAINS IN HAMPTON ROADS

Beginning in 1968, African Americans began to make rapid political gains. Raymond Turner and James Holley were elected to Portsmouth City Council and Joseph A. Jordan, Jr., to Norfolk's City Council. The following year, William P. Robinson, Sr., of Norfolk was elected to the House of Delegates. The year after that, Dr. Hugo A. Owens and W. P. Clarke took seats on the Chesapeake council and Jesse Rattley was elected in Newport News. Later, Rattley and Holley won election as mayor, and William A. Ward joined them as mayor of Chesapeake.

Nine members of the fourteen-member state legislative Black Caucus had been elected from the Hampton Roads area. Robert Scott of Newport News became the first African American to serve in Congress. Blacks have also been named superintendent of schools, chief of police, and city manager in several Hampton Roads cities.

Above: The USS Shangri-La *is launched February 24, 1944, at the Navy Yard. A crowd estimated at one hundred thousand was in attendance.*

COURTESY OF THE BORJES COLLECTION, SARGEANT MEMORIAL ROOM, NORFOLK PUBLIC LIBRARY.

Right: Olde Towne in Portsmouth, looking from the waterfront south on Church Street.

PHOTO BY PAUL CLANCY.

its seat to Great Bridge, setting the stage for the birth of a new city, Chesapeake. A new tunnel, the Midtown, was added in 1962, and in 1967, an impressive addition to the Portsmouth landscape, the Portsmouth Marine Terminal began operations at Pinners Point. Federal aid helped build a new seawall in 1968, with the added benefit of a breezy pedestrian walkway and an annual Seawall Art Show.

The Portsmouth waterfront seemed to

pause, almost to catch its breath. Then, as the century came to a close, the pace picked up again. In January 2001, the $48-million, 250-room Renaissance Portsmouth Hotel and Conference Center opened on the water. In July, the Ntelos Pavilion at Harbor Center, with its flowing white fabric roof, opened and the Irish Tenors filled the night with

Above: President Theodore Roosevelt visits Portsmouth, May 30, 1906.
COURTESY OF THE WILSON MEMORIAL HISTORY ROOM, PORTSMOUTH PUBLIC LIBRARY.

Left: Portsmouth High School girls' basketball team, 1918.
COURTESY OF THE WILSON MEMORIAL HISTORY ROOM, PORTSMOUTH PUBLIC LIBRARY.

crooning. Right beside the pavilion, opening the following spring, was the Ocean Marine Yacht Center, a repair facility for mega-yachts and marina. One could slip into a slip at the marina and listen to the next-door concerts.

And, fittingly, on July 31, 2003, the Elizabeth River Project, a grassroots environmental organization founded a dozen years before on a shoe-string budget and the desire to encourage people to work together, opened new headquarters on the ground floor of Admiral's Landing. The ERP had succeeded in its first major goal of getting major players on the river, including factories and the United States Navy, to work together as partners. By 2005, the river had seen the most significant water quality improvements of any tributary on the Chesapeake Bay.

All four cities in South Hampton Roads, Norfolk, Portsmouth, Chesapeake and Virginia Beach, agreed to support a $13 million program to clean up Scuffletown Creek and restore several wetlands. After

twelve years in a downtown Norfolk loft, the project had been able to buy space right on the river it so wanted to improve. For those who had founded the organization, it was thrilling to be at the center of the harbor and working river. All around them were their partners.

NEWPORT NEWS

At the end of the Civil War, the point of Warwick County land known as Newport News lay in ruins. A Yankee soldier described it as a "nothing more than a wild wilderness," with only a few houses and wild hogs roaming the woods. Chimneys were all that remained of some of the farms, which had been left uncultivated and covered with shrubbery. Everything, it seemed, had been wasted by the war. A prisoner of war camp designed to house up to 20,000 prisoners had been built on 25 acres. All of the prisoners would eventually have to be paroled and sent home. The five years immediately after the war were steeped in violence and lawlessness as freed African Americans and disenfranchised whites clashed. But a period of stability was ushered in after Virginia was readmitted to the Union in 1870. The period that soon followed brought Warwick County chugging and steaming into the twentieth century. A new railroad empire—and a new city to go with it—was about to be born.

⚓

Above: Main Street, Hilton Village, 1920. The village was built to house the burgeoning workforce at Newport News Shipbuilding.
PHOTO BY E.P. ELLIS. COURTESY OF THE LIBRARY OF VIRGINIA.

Below: Newport News Small Boat Harbor, 1917, with Curtiss Flying School at left. The school begun by famed aviator Glenn Curtiss in 1915, attracted many hopeful flyers from the U.S. and abroad.
COURTESY OF THE HAMPTON HISTORY MUSEUM.

The man who discovered the Peninsula's potential was Connecticut Yankee Collis P. Huntington. The driving force behind the nation's transcontinental railroad, Huntington was intrigued by the area's deepwater harbor and quickly raised the capital to run tracks for the once-bankrupt Chesapeake & Ohio Railroad right to the end of Newport News Point. In 1881, as rail service began, coal piers, grain elevators and cargo wharves were built to handle the freight between trains and ships calling at the point. A small city sprang up, with homes, churches, a library, and a newspaper. To be sure, there were rough spots, including a Hell's Half Acre of saloons in one part of town, with frequent blood-lettings.

But Huntington, who seemed to have things fall into his lap, found a ready-made work force among the vagrants and displaced persons who had discovered the point during the depressions that followed the Civil War. The ships bringing products for export on his rail cars needed repairing, so he founded the Chesapeake Dry Dock and Construction Company in 1896. That same year, the four square miles at the point officially became a city.

By 1898, when the U.S. declared war on Spain over Cuba, the company had already built three battleships and now had contracts for several more. Furthermore, the government made Newport News a military port of embarkation. National Guard troops were encamped in Casino Park while awaiting transport to Cuba. It was the beginning of the town's intimate association with wars. The same drama was played out in World War I. The government acquired Mulberry Island in 1918 to build Camp Abraham Eustis as a Coast Guard artillery training center. The camp would become Fort Eustis in 1923. The

once-quiet Peninsula fairly bristled with barracks, camps and ammunition piers. All this activity created a population surge and the need for housing.

A temporary Victory Arch, a memorial to American men and women returning from "over there" was dedicated in 1919. It would be replaced by a permanent stone arch in 1962. You can now walk down to the waterfront through the arch and imagine the scene: the shipyard working 24 hours a day, troops and supplies arriving and departing daily, streets crowded with jostling people and noisy automobiles, a swelling population searching for housing. In 1918, with the help of federal funds and the shipyard, a new town called Hilton Village was developed three miles north of city limits on two hundred acres. The village included five hundred English cottage-style homes and rows of stores, with small upstairs apartments. A streetcar line ran from the village to the city.

During the war, 583 convoy ships carried a quarter of a million troops from the city piers. The shipyard's labor force swelled to 14,000 and the city's population to 100,000. It was a giant bubble, and it burst in 1918 when peace was declared. There was a brief respite as the embarkation camps became receiving camps, but shipyard contracts were cancelled and the yard's workforce plummeted, finally reaching twenty-two hundred. When the Depression hit in 1929, the local economy plunged to depths it had not seen in half a century. It would not reemerge until war clouds again appeared on the horizon.

The Newport News Port of Embarkation was reactivated in 1942. Again, the Army leased the C & O piers and expanded them to get ready. In addition to thirteen million tons of military freight, Hampton Roads bid farewell to 730,000 soldiers and welcomed back nearly that many at war's end. Needless to say, the local USO was constantly jumping. The Peninsula swarmed with barracks and tent camps, and this time a new phenomenon, German and Italian prisoners of war. Some 134,000 disembarked and marched off to POW camps at Fort Eustis and several other places, including one near the James River Bridge.

Because of the lurking presence of German U-boats, Hampton Roads had the feel of an armed fortress. The Coast Guard placed submarine nets at the mouth of the bay and navy destroyers patrolled the coast. All of this played out as convoys of outward-bound ships, ever on guard against attack, stole away under cover of darkness. All the while, the shipyard was operating at full capacity. Between the main yard on the James River and its subsidiary in Wilmington, the shipyard turned out close to fifty vessels. When peace finally came this time, Newport News did not go into another financial swoon. The shipyard continued aircraft carrier projects, and Fort Eustis became the permanent home of the Army Transportation Corps. Camp Patrick Henry was converted to an airport and state hospital. And out on the James off Mulberry Island, the hulking carcasses of decommissioned merchant marine vessels, especially the Liberty and Victory ships that helped win the war, began to congregate. The reserve fleet, or "ghost fleet," as many called it, grew to more than 140 at its peak, then began to dwindle as the dangerously leaky ships were, one by one, towed to scrap yards.

The shipyard scrambled for work after the war, even taking on such distinctly non-

⚓

Soldiers about to sail on the SS Maripose, *for overseas duty, July 13, 1943. The soldier with the guitar is Hamilton Goodwin.*

After 140 years on the ocean floor, the turret of the USS Monitor returned to Hampton Roads and a permanent home at the Mariners' Museum. A ceremonial honor guard escorts the turret on its latest journey.

PHOTO BY GREGG VICIK. COURTESY OF THE MARINERS' MUSEUM.

maritime projects as wind tunnels and water turbines for places like Hoover Dam and Muscle Shoals. But the most exciting civilian project was the exquisitely beautiful super-passenger liner, the SS *United States.* The 990-foot luxury liner, christened on June 23, 1951, had her sea trials off the Virginia Capes and then, on her maiden voyage, set the transatlantic record of three days, 10 hours and 40 minutes—an average speed of 35.5 knots!

Now the city that the shipyard and railroad built was ready for the next leap, but the question was, in which direction—and how far? There was growing sentiment to merge, and not just with the rapidly growing Warwick County suburbs but with next-door Hampton as well. Could there be a super-city

called Hampton Roads? Norfolk, for one, which considered itself part of Hampton Roads, nixed the idea, and it seemed to collapse as Hampton merged with Elizabeth City County and Phoebus. And then Warwick went its own way. The county that had enjoyed the rapid suburbanization caused by the growth of Newport News, became the city of Warwick on July 15, 1952. But Warwick's independence was not to last. Its own growth pangs—as well as the loyalty that many residents felt toward the neighboring city where they worked—led to the mega-merger of Warwick and Newport News. Not only did Warwick lose its status as a city, but its proud name, as voters chose to call the new entity Newport News. And so it was that on July 1, 1958, the new city, with O. J. Brittingham, Jr., serving as mayor, was born. The former boundary at Sixty-fourth Street was extended all the way to the James City County line, encompassing six square miles and 113,000 residents. It would grow to 180,150 by century's end.

And the city, founded in the memory of Christopher Newport, would undergo changes that the old sea captain couldn't have imagined. In 1991, Christopher Newport University would take its bow and, at the end of 2005, so would the Ferguson Center for the Arts, designed by internationally acclaimed architect I. M. Pei. Newport News Shipbuilding and Dry Dock Company would be courted by giant defense contractors and become, in 2001, Northrup Grumman Newport News. Perhaps not least would be a cutting-edge high-tech installation, Jefferson Lab, with, among other distinctly non-seventeenth century concepts, a continuous electron beam accelerator.

Another cause for applause would be the opening, on the 145th anniversary of the Battle of Hampton Roads, of the *Monitor* Center at the Mariners' Museum. The museum, begun as a place to display the maritime art collection of Archer Huntington, the son of the city's founder, had become the custodian of artifacts recovered from the revolutionary ironclad. In a dramatic conclusion to a five-year effort, Navy divers, in collaboration with the National Oceanic and Atmospheric Administration, rescued the

The Camp Hill Quartet, January 13, 1945. Third from left is Corporal Lutrelle Palmer, Jr., son of the principal at Huntington High School who led the fight for equal pay for black teachers. "Lu" Palmer went on to become a famous Chicago columnist and civil rights advocate.

Monitor's turret from the depths of the sea off Cape Hatteras on August 5, 2002, and returned it to Hampton Roads. The center would also house many artifacts from the CSS *Virginia*, the Confederacy's ironclad champion.

HAMPTON

Following the Civil War, Hampton struggled to rise from the ashes. An Army artillery school was reestablished at Fort

EQUAL JUSTICE, EQUAL PAY

In 1920, Dr. Lutrelle F. Palmer was hired as principal of the new Huntington High School in Newport News. The school was cited for excellence, but it rankled Palmer that black teachers were, on average, paid two-thirds less than their white counterparts. Palmer's salary was supplemented by parents in the community. After his speech to the Virginia Teachers Association at Hampton Institute in 1937, the teachers voted unanimously to file equal pay lawsuits in partnership with the NAACP.

What the teachers needed was an individual to step forward. Aline Black, a science teacher at Booker T. Washington High School in Norfolk, held a masters degree from the University of Pennsylvania and was working toward a doctorate at New York University. At the risk of losing her job, she filed suit with the aid of Thurgood Marshall, then attorney for the NAACP. She lost the suit on a technicality, and the following year the Norfolk school board declined to renew her contract. At the same time in Newport News, Palmer was also dismissed.

But there was no stopping the movement toward equal pay. In June 1939, parents and teachers staged a parade in Norfolk protesting inequality between black and white schools. That fall, Melvin Alston, president of the Norfolk Teachers' Association, also went to court. This time, although the lower court ruled against him, a federal appeals court held the unequal pay scale to be unconstitutional, and the U.S. Supreme Court declined to review the case, a decision that had national implications. Newport News would later name an elementary school for Palmer.

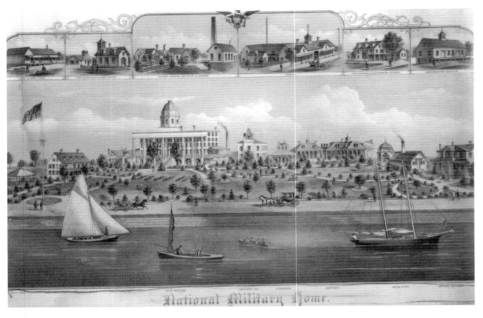

National Military Home.

Monroe in 1868. The former Chesapeake Female College on the waterfront, which had served as a Union hospital during the war, was joined by a new home for disabled soldiers. And on the east bank of Hampton Creek, in an area known as Little Scotland, a new symbol of freedom was born.

Union Army General Samuel C. Armstrong, now head of the Freedman's Bureau, received help from the American Missionary Society in 1867 to establish a school to train teachers for the small black schools that were springing up throughout

the South. In addition, it would teach agricultural and mechanical skills. When the Hampton Normal and Agricultural Institute opened the following year, there were two teachers and 15 students, mostly from black families in Hampton. It grew rapidly, thanks to Armstrong's inspired fundraising efforts. He organized the Hampton Singers, a group of students who in two and a half years gave over 500 concerts in northern cities. So impressed were wealthy northerners that they poured donations into the school's bank

July 12, 1895.

Sellie Bickford   John Ross   Susie Jones   Jennie Vaughan   Eliza Tabb   Howard S.
Fonnie Barnes   Mary Blackmore   Bessie Love   Annie Chisman   Mary Lee   Nanc.
Liv Whit...

account. Among its graduates was Booker T. Washington, who later taught there. The Institute, which added classes for American Indians in 1878 and a school for nurses in 1891, was to evolve into Hampton University, now one of the finest small institutions of higher learning in the country.

Hampton had begun its love affair with grand hotels shortly after construction was begun on Fortress Monroe in 1819. The Hygeia Hotel began as housing for construction workers and grew with several expansions until in 1841 it was described as "large and commodious." It was torn down during the Civil War, and then a second Hygeia, grander than the first, fell into disrepair toward the end of the century and was demolished to make way for a park. In the meantime, John Chamberlin, whose background included gambling clubs and race tracks, had formed a company in 1887 to build another luxury hotel near the fort. Lack of funds slowed it down, but then, with new investors, the Chamberlin Hotel opened its doors in 1896. It cost a staggering $5 million, had 554 rooms and was completely illuminated by electric lights. It served briefly as officers quarters in World War I, then in

March 1920 burned to the ground. On that same spot, a new Chamberlin-Vanderbilt Hotel, this one eight stories and containing an indoor pool supplied with sea water, opened in 1928. With the expected closing of Fort Monroe in the near future, the grand old hotel

Above: Buggy riders on Queen Street, July 12, 1895.

COURTESY OF THE HAMPTON HISTORY MUSEUM.

Below: A sketch of the Hygeia Hotel, 1895.

COURTESY OF THE HAMPTON HISTORY MUSEUM.

Above: The skipjack Pearl D. Evans *on Hampton Creek, 1900.*

Below: Queen Street at night, looking east, 1914.

was expected to become an independent living facility, with an emphasis on military retirees. Several other hostelries opened at Buckroe Beach in the early 1900s, bringing waves of beachgoers from across the state. The tourist boom lasted until 1957 when a new bridge-tunnel across Hampton Roads made it possible for beach enthusiasts to travel easily to the Atlantic seashore.

In 1916 the National Advisory Council for Aeronautics, predecessor to NASA, established the need for an airfield and proving ground for the Army and Navy and for its own aircraft. NACA determined that the site must be near

water and close to an Army post. Appointed by the Army, a group of officers went in search of a site, sometimes posing as hunters and fishermen to avoid potential land speculation. Fifteen locations were scouted before a site near Hampton was selected.

In 1917 the new proving ground was designated Langley Field for one of America's early air pioneers, Samuel Pierpont Langley. Langley had first made tests with his manned heavier-than-air craft, launched from a houseboat catapult, in 1903. Just before the Wright Brothers made their historic flight, Langley's Large Aerodrome "A" twice plunged

into the Potomac River. He died in 1906, shortly before a rebuilt version of his craft soared into the sky. Langley would become a prime training base for aircraft of all kinds. Brigadier General Billy Mitchell led bombing runs over captured German warships off the coast of Virginia, proving that the new aircraft could sink ships. The field also became the center of lighter-than-air activities, until a fatal accident doomed the program. In February 1922 the Italian-built *Roma* took off from Langley and lost its rudder over the Army base in Norfolk. The blimp plunged into electrical wires, igniting the hydrogen, and burst into flames, killing 34 men on board. That was the end of the program. In 1948, Langley Field officially became Langley Air Force Base. It is now home to more than 8,800 military and 2,800 civilian employees. At the same time that Langley was used as an airfield, it also became the nation's first civilian aeronautics laboratory. NASA Langley

Above: A streetcar connecting Hampton and Newport News, with Lewis Woodward Walter of Hampton in the foreground.
COURTESY OF WALTON FAMILY AND THE HAMPTON HISTORY MUSEUM.

Below: Lancers' Confectioners, Melon Street in Phoebus, 1930.
COURTESY OF THE CHENEY COLLECTION, HAMPTON HISTORY MUSEUM.

Research Center, with thirty-three hundred civil service and contract employees, focuses on improving today's military and civilian aircraft, while designing tomorrow's jets and spaceships. The soaring downtown Virginia Air and Space Center shows off a shuttle simulator, a command module and a three-billion-year-old moon rock.

Across the harbor, in what was once a visitor's center, the Cousteau Society—previously in Norfolk and Chesapeake—opened its American headquarters in 2003. Now, with exhibits that highlight the famed ocean explorer's adventures, visitors to Hampton could witness a bit of the sea as well as the stars.

Meanwhile, more down-to-earth enterprises helped rebuild Hampton. Its waterfront and accessibility to the open waters of the bay and ocean turned the city into a bustling seaport. The waterfront became crowded with packing plants and boats, and tall mounds of oyster shells rose near the docks. Hundreds of thousands of bushels, barrels and quarts of crabs and oysters were shipped from the city known locally as "crabtown." A neighborhood of stately Victorian homes, Little England, grew up just around the corner from downtown. Like Norfolk, however, the city became enamored with urban renewal in the 1970s and many of its turn-of-the-century stores, banks and movie theaters bit the dust. Fortunately, Queens Way survived and

now leads the city's recent efforts to revive its downtown.

VIRGINIA BEACH

Just as the Jamestown Exposition spurred development in Norfolk, it spread its influence to the fast-growing Virginia Beach. A new syndicate bought the Princess Anne Hotel and more than doubled its size with the addition of eighty rooms. Luxury appointments, like Irish linens embossed with the "Stuart" crest to honor Queen Anne, were waiting for exposition guests. But in June

Above: Frank W. Darling and family. He was the son of one of the biggest seafood company founders.

COURTESY OF THE CHENEY COLLECTION, HAMPTON HISTORY MUSEUM.

Below: B-17 Flying Fortresses at Langley Field, July 2, 1944.

COURTESY OF THE LIBRARY OF VIRGINIA.

HAMPTON ROADS' MILITARY MUSCLE

One hundred years after the Jamestown Exposition, Hampton Roads would play host to some 90 warships at Norfolk Naval Station and Little Creek Amphibious Base, straddling the Norfolk-Virginia Beach line. This is now the headquarters of the Atlantic Fleet, with responsibility for defending the entire Atlantic area. Combined with Oceana Naval Air Station in Virginia Beach, it is the largest naval complex in the world. In fact, Hampton Roads, with some 114,000 active duty and 30,000 civilian personnel, is now home to one of the largest concentrations of military bases and facilities of any metropolitan area in the world. More than forty thousand acres are devoted to the nation's defense.

With a population that exceeded 1.6 million, the area had begun to crowd its military installations. In 2005, the Defense Base Realignment and Closure Commission (BRAC) warned the city of Virginia Beach that Oceana would lose its jets unless severe steps were taken to curtail development. One definite casualty of the commission's work that year was Fort Monroe. The great old "fortress," as it was once known, the site of the first colonists' lonely outpost, would at last revert to the city of Hampton.

On the sprawling 4,300-acre naval base today, there is one neighborhood that doesn't conform to the expected look of military bases. "Admirals Row" is an avenue of former exhibition buildings that were built by 22 states a century ago. Now housing senior military officials from several service branches located at the base, the grand houses built by Connecticut, Delaware, Georgia, Illinois, Maryland, Michigan, Missouri, New Hampshire, North Dakota, Ohio, Vermont and Virginia look out over a small golf course toward Hampton Roads. Pennsylvania's entry, a replica of Independence Hall, is reserved for ceremonial purposes. The North Carolina and Rhode Island houses were combined after a fire and are now used for bachelor officer quarters. Around the corner from the front row, the "Chocolate House," an exhibit built by industry, is also an admiral's home. Off to the right, facing the water, masts fly from sailboats moored at a marina where the exposition's "Grand Basin" rested.

It is not difficult to imagine the great flotilla of ships standing out on the Roads, nodding toward an auspicious future.

1907, shortly after the grand reopening, a fire burned the hotel to the ground. It was a devastating setback that wouldn't be overcome for twenty years when another splendid oceanfront institution took its place.

Meanwhile, one of the most impressive pieces of real estate on the Atlantic coast, Cape Henry, was undergoing a dramatic change. There had been some vacation home development there, and a rail spur ran there from the resort area, but its location, overlooking the coastline and the entrance to the Chesapeake Bay, was too important for the nation's defense to remain a sun-drenched playground.

During the 1898 war with Spain, a company of naval reserves was stationed in temporary quarters at the cape. All the while, government officials were eyeing the spot for potential defense and even considered erecting an island fortification halfway between Cape Henry and Cape Charles. That would have been far too expensive, but the government decided in 1913 that a fort should be built. The next year, the Virginia General Assembly gave the land to the U.S. Government "to erect fortifications and for other military purposes." The War Department named the land Fort Story after General John Patton Story, one of the most noted coast artillerymen of his day. During World War I, which was soon to follow, two artillery companies guarded the bay's entrance there.

Children on the Buckroe Beach carousel.
COURTESY OF THE LIBRARY OF VIRGINIA.

Above: A horse and cart outside Virginia Beach's first public library, organized by a group of local women and given space in a store owned by Bernard P. Holland, the first mayor of the town.
COURTESY OF THE SARGEANT MEMORIAL ROOM, THE NORFOLK PUBLIC LIBRARY.

Below: Virginia Beach boardwalk, 1913.
COURTESY OF THE CARROLL WALKER COLLECTION, THE *VIRGINIAN-PILOT.*

The development of the resort area continued apace after the war. Water pipes and roadways and now the Cavalier Hotel, even grander that the lost Princess Anne, made it to the oceanfront, followed by a casino, streetlights and a boardwalk. Other hotels and apartment complexes quickly followed. It all came to a halt after Black

Monday in 1929, although the Cavalier managed to survive by attracting well-healed customers. It even kept lights burning at night to counter the stigma of depression. The hotel took on an entirely different character as World War II dawned. Thousands of artillery soldiers arrived at Fort Story to man a battery of guns. A training station for amphibious vessels opened at Little Creek and, in what would become the most far-reaching military move, the Navy bought a 328-acre farm near Oceana for use as an auxiliary landing field.

The war put many of Virginia Beach's hotels on hold. Even though the beach itself was open to the public during daylight hours, it had to be vacated at night and a blackout was observed. The Navy took over the Cavalier and used it as a radar school, commissary and dispensary, and several other hotels were commandeered for use as wartime facilities. So crowded with military personnel and families was the oceanfront that water restrictions were imposed. Meanwhile, Princess Anne County farmers worked overtime to meet the military's need for chickens. Farm workers were in short supply, but a new phenomenon of war, enemy prisoners, partly filled the bill. Camp Ashley in the Thalia section was used as a German POW camp, housing as many as 6,000

prisoners. Some who could demonstrate anti-Nazi sentiments were allowed to work on farms and in fertilizer plants.

By war's end, Fort Story, Oceana, Dam Neck and Little Creek remained military bases, and the population of Princess Anne continued to explode, more than doubling to 42,227 within the decade. Returning soldiers and sailors and their families bought homes in the suburbs, clogged the roads with new cars and the maternity rooms with babies. It didn't take long for the region to add a planning commission and adopt a master plan to control growth.

Left: Bathers and lifeguard, 1920s.

Right: Unidentified camper at Camp Awaisa, August 1932.

OLD COUNTY/NEW CITY

Because the mushrooming suburbs of Princess Anne County received their drinking water from Norfolk, it wasn't surprising that the growing city began eyeing its rural neighbor for expansion. First, in 1949, Norfolk moved to annex 40 square miles in Princess Anne, and the first signs of opposition surfaced. The idea was shelved, but in 1955, a new bid was launched, this time for 33 square miles. A judicial panel—the courts then had the say on annexation—reduced the area to 13.5 square miles, including the Poplar Hall section and the municipal airport. Even so, it was a densely populated chunk of land, with 38,000 people who, on January 1, 1959, suddenly became Norfolk residents.

At the same time, the town of Virginia Beach had been gobbling up unincorporated land to the north and west of her boundaries. To many in Princess Anne, it looked as though the most valuable land in the county would continue to be lost if they failed to put the brakes on. Sidney S. Kellam, onetime county treasurer, prominent Democrat and head of a powerful political machine, began lobbying the General Assembly in 1960 to change annexation laws to protect further encroachment attempts. Norfolk responded by imposing limits on water supply increases to Princess Anne, bringing development to a screeching halt. The battle lines were drawn.

Kellam bought some time by persuading Norfolk officials to postpone more annexation moves in exchange for putting further lobbying in Richmond on hold. At the same time, Kellam was named to head a committee that would study "metropolitan government" in the region. Any such effort was doomed to failure, but what the hiatus did was buy enough time for the Kellam forces to make their next move.

When Princess Anne County and Virginia Beach announced in October 1961 that they were studying a possible merger, Norfolk reacted with alarm. On December 5, Norfolk City Council voted to cut off water services to Princess Anne if voters ratified the merger. The threat backfired, generating almost as much support in the county for merger as the Boston Tea Party had for independence. When the votes were counted on January 4, 1962, the results were overwhelming: Virginia Beach, 1,539 for and 242 against; Princess Anne, 7,476 for and 1,759 against. It was all over but the hurrahing. On January 1, 1963, the city of Virginia Beach, 310 square miles of once-sparsely populated wilderness, became the state's fastest-growing city. The only surviving political remnant of Princess Anne was the seat of the new city government.

Above: Swimmers play in the surf before oceanfront cottages and guest houses, 1940s.

COURTESY OF *THE VIRGINIAN-PILOT.*

Below: Suffolk Seaboard Train Station, now owned by the Suffolk-Nansemond Historical Society, houses a railroad model and museum. The station, opened in 1885, was restored in 2000.

PHOTO BY PAUL CLANCY.

In 1964, one of the engineering marvels of the world, the Chesapeake Bay Bridge-Tunnel, was completed, stretching nearly twenty miles across the mouth of the bay. The spidery bridge fed into two mid-bay tunnels that made it possible for ocean-going ships to pass through deep channels. The city was now firmly connected to the once-lonely, remote Eastern Shore of Virginia. Thirty-five years later, a second parallel crossing was completed.

Decade after decade, Virginia Beach grew by about 100,000 residents until, by 2004 it reached 425,000. One of the exciting tourist attractions was the Virginia Marine Science Museum (now Virginia Aquarium & Marine Science Center), with its impressive tanks for sharks, sea turtles, and river otters. Without a

central commercial center, the sprawling city sprouted an estimated 125 shopping centers. Finally, in February 2000, work was begun on Virginia Beach Town Center across from Pembroke Mall on the city's main artery, Virginia Beach Boulevard. It would be a city within a city, a $300-million complex of office towers, hotels, condominiums, restaurants and shops. Soon there would be a performing arts center. Virginia Beach, the most populous city in Virginia, would finally have a skyline.

SUFFOLK

One of the things that helped Suffolk get back on its feet after the Civil War was the hard steel of railroad tracks. The first train out of Suffolk in 1834, the Portsmouth & Weldon, had actually been pulled by horses for the first two months. One morning in August 1837, a freight train loaded with lumber ran head-on into a passenger train from Portsmouth, killing three passengers and injuring 140 others. Nevertheless, Suffolk soon became a crossroads for trains; six different rail lines converged on the town: the Southern, the Norfolk & Western, the Atlantic Coast Line, the Seaboard Air Line, the Virginian and the Suffolk & Carolina. By the turn of the twentieth century, over thirty passenger trains and nearly hourly freight trains left Suffolk every day. In 1885 the elegant Seaboard Air Line Passenger Station, serving the Seaboard on one track and the

Virginian on the other, was opened. The station eventually became vacant for several years and was nearly destroyed by a fire. To the rescue came the Suffolk-Nansemond Historical Society. The station, just off Suffolk's Main Street, now welcomes visitors to exhibits that include an elaborate model railroad town.

Rail service began attracting companies looking for ways to get their products to market. Lumber mills, iron foundries, knitting mills and several peanut plants began

arriving. Suffolk was right at the center of what had become, since the oily, multi-purpose legumes were first imported from Brazil, a North Carolina-Virginia peanut belt. "Virginia" peanuts were considered the largest and tastiest of many varieties. And this was all that an entrepreneur named Amadeo Obici needed to know.

Obici, born in Oderzo, Italy, in 1877, had gone from Brooklyn to Wilkes-Barre, Pa., where he started a fruit and peanut stand. He migrated to Suffolk and in 1908 started Planters Nut and Chocolate Company. He also patented a sandpaper-cone shelling device that automated the production process. With a sure knack for marketing, he staged a contest for a logo and a school child came up with "Mr. Peanut," to which Obici added a cane, top hat and a monocle, and began a national advertising campaign. It was wildly successful and soon turned Suffolk into the world's largest peanut market.

Obici was as generous as he was inventive. During the Depression, he guaranteed his workers a minimum wage and started a hospital in his hometown in Italy. He and his wife, Louise, were childless, and decided to leave their estate to a future hospital for the city. In September 1951 the four-story Louise Obici Memorial Hospital, with 120 beds and space for 23 newborns, was opened on Main Street. It would serve the city for forty-one

⚓

Top, left: Amadeo Obici gravitated toward Suffolk because of its excellent peanut-growing conditions and access to railroads. Date unknown, probably early 1900s.
COURTESY OF THE HAMBLIN STUDIO COLLECTION, LIBRARY OF VIRGINIA.

Above: Planters salted peanuts rolling down conveyor belt and packed in cellophane bags.
COURTESY OF THE HAMBLIN STUDIO COLLECTION, LIBRARY OF VIRGINIA.

Below: Chuckatuck High School debating club, 1890.
COURTESY OF THE HAMBLIN STUDIO COLLECTION, LIBRARY OF VIRGINIA.

World War I parade in Suffolk.
COURTESY OF THE LIBRARY OF VIRGINIA.

years until, in April 2002, a new Obici Hospital was opened on Godwin Boulevard. The old hospital grounds would become the site for Obici Place, a condominium-office-retail development.

Following the trend of other Hampton Roads localities, Suffolk merged with Nansemond County in 1974, becoming, at 430 square miles, Virginia's largest city. It would become one of its fastest-growing, too, with a 2004 population of more than seventy-six thousand. Also like its sister cities, downtown Suffolk began seeing

condominiums. And hi-tech jobs, especially along the I-664 corridor, began spurring even more homes and raising real estate values.

CHESAPEAKE

The turn of the century saw the beginnings of what would become a muscular addition to the Hampton Roads scene. The city of South Norfolk sprang to life with the advent of electrified trolley service. One-time farms were converted to residential lots on which handsome homes were built, more than thirty

STANDING UP TO VOTE

Moses Riddick became a political activist in 1946, long before the civil rights movement was born. Although blacks outnumbered whites in Nansemond County, there were only 83 registered black voters in the county. It didn't discourage him, even when the Ku Klux Klan burned a cross on his lawn, even when someone put a bullet hole through his car door. He formed the Independent Voters League, urging blacks to pay the $1.50 poll tax and familiarize themselves with the blank ballot before they attempted to register. His efforts paid off quickly. In 1947, William A. Lawrence became the first African American on the Nansemond County Board of Supervisors. Riddick himself was elected to the board in 1963 and later served as vice mayor on the Suffolk City Council.

Riddick became friends with Dr. Martin Luther King Jr., who called him "Mose." He served as delegate to state and national Democratic Party conventions. He also helped create the Suffolk Redevelopment and Housing Authority and fought for improved housing for the underprivileged. He attended a civic league meeting the night before his death, at age 74, in March 1991.

stores opened and a new waterworks added. There were box factories, sawmills, churches, public schools and a post office. The town was incorporated in 1919 and not too many years later annexed its neighbors, Portlock, Money Point and Riverdale, becoming a first-class city in 1951.

As it grew and flexed its muscles, South Norfolk became home to some of the worst polluters on the South Branch of the Elizabeth River: an oil refinery and fertilizer, chemical,

guano and creosote plants. This section of the river, between Scuffletown and Jordan Bridge, would contribute to making the river one of the most toxic in the nation, causing cancerous sores on fish. It would become the focus of a long, difficult and costly clean-up campaign as the citizen-begun Elizabeth River Project joined with businesses and governments, declaring that "the goo must go."

The city in late 2004 came out with a "Forward Chesapeake" comprehensive plan in which it recognized that suburban sprawl has to be balanced with urban revitalization. Part of the plan includes saving and restoring

Above: Suffolk Fire Station, 1945.
COURTESY OF THE SARGEANT MEMORIAL ROOM, NORFOLK PUBLIC LIBRARY.

Bottom, left: Moses Riddick championed the cause of voter rights for African Americans in the 1940s and eventually succeeded in getting candidates, including himself, elected to the Nansemond Board of Supervisors.
COURTESY OF THE HAMBLIN STUDIO COLLECTION, LIBRARY OF VIRGINIA.

Below: Four children in a goat cart, 1942. Hamblin Studio.
COURTESY OF THE LIBRARY OF VIRGINIA.

many of the older homes and buildings in the historic city and turning what was becoming a blighted area into a mixed-use village, complete with luxury condominiums. Some of the city's planning documents refer to the area as "SoNo," a Chesapeake takeoff on New York's trendy SoHo section. Although some old-timers disliked the name, it seemed to catch on among those who wanted to preserve its interesting character, but at the same time spruce it up.

Just as South Norfolk grew beside a waterway, so too did Great Bridge and Deep Creek, prospering as they played host to the locks of two intracoastal waterways, the Chesapeake and Albemarle and Dismal Swamp canals. Deep Creek was a favorite stopping place for the James Adams Original Floating Theater, the waterborne stage on which Edna Ferber based her famous novel *Showboat*.

Deep Creek by 1850 consisted of about 50 houses, several taverns and two general stores. In its early days, the village was perhaps best known for Saturday night brawls between timber cutters and watermen. Another village, Gilmerton, grew up around the lock that once operated near an extension of the canal to the Southern Branch of the Elizabeth. The village was named after a former governor, Thomas W. Gilmer, whose name also lends itself to a lift bridge over the Southern Branch.

The vast area south of Norfolk known as Norfolk County was ripe for picking as cities like Norfolk and South Norfolk looked for elbowroom. In 1950 the county had a population of 99,000, but ten years later the number stood at 51,000 as municipalities gobbled up fast-growing suburbs. The biggest threat was an annexation suit that would

have left South Norfolk completely surrounded by Norfolk City. The only defense, many in the region felt, was to consolidate and form a separate city. They drew their inspiration from similar defensive moves then being made in Princess Anne County.

In the fall of 1961 the supervisors of Norfolk County and the city council members of South Norfolk began a series of meetings

Above: An old mill at Great Bridge, 1895.
COURTESY OF THE WILSON MEMORIAL HISTORY ROOM,
PORTSMOUTH PUBLIC LIBRARY.

*Below: An aerial photo of South Norfolk
in 1950.*

COURTESY OF THE *VIRGINIAN-PILOT.*

at the newly constructed county health center in Great Bridge. The pieces of the puzzle fell quickly into place as a law firm was engaged and a proposed consolidation agreement drafted. On December 22 the two governing bodies held simultaneous sessions, linked together by telephone. They agreed to petition the courts of their two jurisdictions to order that a referendum be held on whether a merger should take place.

There was a spirited debate on both sides of the issue, with signs and bumper stickers, posters and buttons sprouting everywhere, and on February 13, citizens were asked, "Shall the City of South Norfolk and Norfolk County consolidate?" The answer was a resounding yes: 1,809 to 1,376 in the city and 4,839 to 2,036 in the county. After a new charter was approved by the General Assembly, another referendum was held in June and Chesapeake, the name of a great Indian tribe that once dominated the region, was chosen. On Sunday, January 1, 1963—the same day that Virginia Beach came into existence—the city of Chesapeake was born.

Chesapeake, with a land area of 340.7 square miles, became one of Virginia's largest cities. And with an estimated 2004 population of 214,725, one of its fastest-growing, with a thriving economy but still a down-home atmosphere. The Greenbrier area, in fact, was declared the fastest-growing in South Hampton Roads, with an estimated 53,000 workers. A new 175,000-square-foot retail center, Town Place at Greenbrier, would soon makes its debut.

WILLIAMSBURG

During the siege of Yorktown, wounded American and French soldiers were treated at the Governor's Palace or the College of William and Mary. After the victory at Yorktown, French General Rochambeau set up his winter quarters in the city. On the night of December 22, 1781, the palace burned to the ground. The most destructive force, however, was neglect, as the largely abandoned former capital fell into disrepair. A visitor in 1793 found it "dull, forsaken and melancholy."

During the slow-moving peninsula campaign of the Civil War, Confederate General Magruder and his troops built a line of redoubts just east of Williamsburg. On May 5, 1862, an engagement took place and the Confederates fell back toward Richmond. Shortly afterwards, federal troops marched into the city. Williamsburg remained in Union hands for the remainder of the war, with the exception of one day in which control swung back and forth. During those encounters, the

Wren Building, suspected of housing Rebel sharpshooters, was put to the torch. There was more destruction during the occupation as forces dismantled some buildings for firewood. Following the war, Williamsburg went into a long slumber. And this is probably what saved it. Even though neglected, at least its structures weren't constantly being torn down and replaced.

The slumber went on well into the next century until the rector of Bruton Parish Church, W. A. R. Goodwin, embarked on a crusade. The strong-willed Goodwin succeeded in raising funds to restore the George Wythe House for the church rectory. He had almost given up on the rest of the town, but, in 1924, Goodwin spoke before the New York City chapter of the Phi Beta

A tugboat leaves the lock at Great Bridge, 2006.

PHOTO BY PAUL CLANCY.

Above: This scene on Duke of Gloucester Street in 1890 shows what a century of neglect could do.
COURTESY OF THE COLONIAL WILLIAMSBURG FOUNDATION.

Below: William Archer Rutherford Goodwin (left), former rector of Bruton Parish Church, persuaded John D. Rockefeller Jr. to restore the one-time colonial capital.
COURTESY OF THE COLONIAL WILLIAMSBURG FOUNDATION.

Kappa Society about the possibility of building a hall on the college campus where the society was founded. In the audience was John D. Rockefeller, Jr., and Goodman managed to position himself next to the billionaire philanthropist. Before the event was over, Goodwin persuaded Rockefeller to bring his wife and three of their sons to

Williamsburg, and then, at the dedication of the new Phi Beta Kappa Memorial Hall in 1926, gave him a tour of the one-time colonial capital.

Rockefeller thought it over on a long walk through the town, then at dinner that evening announced he would take on the restoration of not just a few structures but the entire

town. The opportunity to restore the beauty and charm of the old buildings, he would later write, was "irresistible." He immediately gave Goodwin the authority to hire an architect to prepare preliminary drawings of how the restored town might look. On December 7, when one of the old houses came on the market for $8,000, Rockefeller telegrammed Goodwin to make the purchase, signing it "David's Father," in hopes of remaining anonymous.

Almost immediately, architects and archaeologists began sifting through the evidence of the original town. They uncovered early maps, plats and deeds, poured over newspapers, wills and other documents. One of them, a drawing by of the palace by Thomas Jefferson, proved to be excitingly similar to foundations that were being unearthed. Early photographs of many of the buildings, before they were changed or collapsed, were invaluable. In 1929 an engraved copperplate dating from about 1740 was found in the Bodleian Library at Oxford University, with views of the Wren Building, the Governor's Palace and the Capitol. Without the plate, Rockefeller said, "we would have been acting in the dark; with it, we have gone forward with absolute certainty and conviction."

By 1934, after eight years, 400 modern structures had been torn down, and 150

⚓

The Prentis Store, the oldest commercial structure, was built in 1734. Before restoration, it served as an auto service company.
PHOTO BY PAUL CLANCY.

Right: Buildings and historical interpreters inside recreated James Fort at Williamsburg Settlement.

COURTESY OF THE JAMESTOWN SETTLEMENT.

Below: Crowds greet President Roosevelt as his motorcade glides through Williamsburg. 1934 photo.

COURTESY OF THE COLONIAL WILLIAMSBURG FOUNDATION.

restored or reconstructed, the first phase of Colonial Williamsburg was ready for its formal opening. President Franklin D. Roosevelt came for the dedication and, motoring down Duke of Gloucester Street, he called it "the most historic avenue in all America."

Today, Colonial Williamsburg, along with Jamestown and Yorktown, the "Historic Triangle," is one of the most popular tourist destinations in the nation. The city has a population of around twelve thousand, but the surrounding area has dozens of master-planned communities rambling along the James, with major theme parks like Busch Gardens and Water Country USA, golf courses and hotels for the ever-growing tourist hoards. Needless to say, the colonists would have been stunned.

JAMESTOWN

This is where it all began. Jamestown, the inviting but unforgiving island on the edge of the wide river. On the four hundredth anniversary of the colonists' landing, cities from around Commonwealth were planning eighteen months of celebrations. They were eager to acknowledge their debt to the original settlers and show their centuries-long-progress. All played major parts in the drama. The *Godspeed*, the replica of one of the three ships that arrived that day, was to visit several eastern seaboard ports, kicking off their celebrations.

Even as plans were being made for the quadricentennial observance, the story of the original settlement was changing, almost by the hour. In the dozen years since archaeological digs began on the island, hundreds of thousands of artifacts dating to the first half of the seventeenth century had been uncovered, including the nearly intact skeleton that could have been that of a prominent member of the original landing party. Archaeologists were finding, too, that the original settlers were not all the loafers that many historians judged them to be. Many were industrious, durable survivors.

Another major find was the footprint of the palisade that formed the triangle-shaped original fort. Many of the finds are

displayed in a new "Archaerium" on the island. At the state-run Jamestown Settlement next door, a new visitor center had been built, along with a full-size replica of the fort and a representation of a Powhatan Indian village. The center includes a museum that chronicles the history of Jamestown from its beginnings in the Old World through the first century of its existence.

This is where a nation began; not only the first region to be settled, but the first to form a representative government. The very idea that the average citizen has as much right to liberty, equality and all the other blessings of freedom as a king came from the flawed but enduring characters who made up the colony. From the gritty determination of the settlers, from the stirring ideals of those who followed in Williamsburg, from the planters and tradespeople who made the economy work, from the ship captains who sailed through rough seas to get here, from the mighty military forces that kept and secured the peace, from the courageous individuals, black and white, who fought for equal justice, from the dreamers and visionaries who made these cities and towns, this region draws its strength and character.

A historical interpreter shows a young visitor how to secure a line on board one of the replica ships at Jamestown Settlement.
COURTESY OF THE JAMESTOWN SETTLEMENT.

ACKNOWLEDGEMENTS

Writing about such a broad sweep of history requires standing on the shoulders of many others. This area is so rich in history, and the characters who made that history so incredibly interesting, that hundreds of volumes have been and are being written. I had some exceptional help from some of the best of these historians: Peggy Haile McPhillips, Norfolk City historian; J. Michael Cobb, curator of the Hampton History Museum, Peter C. Stewart, professor of history at Old Dominion University, Stephen S. Mansfield, director of the archives at Virginia Wesleyan College, and John Quarstein, director of the Virginia War Museum. They all kindly read the manuscript and offered valuable suggestions. I'm indebted to William L. Kelso, director of Archaeology for the Jamestown Rediscovery project, who took me on a tour of the digging site; Nancy Egloff and Deborah Pagett of the Jamestown Settlement; Jim Bradley and Marianne Martin of the Colonial Williamsburg Foundation; and numerous others, including many from the Association for the Preservation of Virginia Antiquities, the Colonial National Historical Park and the Old Coast Guard Station. I also want to thank Tommy L. Bogger of Norfolk State University, Joseph M. Judge and Michael V. Taylor of the Hampton Roads Naval Museum, as well as dozens of docents at Jamestown and Yorktown. As far as photo assistance goes, my hat is off to Claudia Jew at the Mariners' Museum, Robert B. Hitchings and W. Troy Valos at the Sargeant Memorial Room of the Norfolk Public Library; Edie Carmichael of the Wilson Memorial History Room at the Portsmouth Public Library and Ann Johnson of *The Virginian-Pilot*. Also, the librarians in the local history rooms of the Chesapeake, Hampton, Newport News, Suffolk and Virginia Beach public libraries. Lastly, I thank Barbara B. Clancy for sharing the adventure.

Replicas of the three small sailing vessels that brought English settlers to America four centuries ago.

COURTESY OF THE JAMESTOWN SETTLEMENT.

BIBLIOGRAPHY

Africans in America, "Virginia's Slave Codes," www.pbs.org

Albertson, Robert Brooke. *Images of America*. Portsmouth, Virginia: Acadia, 2002.

Bogger, Tommy, L. *Free Blacks in Norfolk, Virginia 1790-1860: The Darker Side of Freedom*. Charlottesville: University Press of Virginia, 1997.

Bogger, Tommy L. "A Historical Overview of African-Americans in Hampton Roads, 1619-1999."

Burke, Davis. *The Campaign that Won America, The Story of Yorktown*. Eastern National Parks, 1970.

Brundage, W. Fitzhugh. "Meta Warrick's 1907 Negro Tablaux." *Journal of American History*, March 2003.

Chesapeake Parks and Recreation Department. *The Battle of Great Bridge, December 9, 1776*.

Cross, Charles B. and Eleanor Phillips. *Chesapeake, A Pictorial History*. Norfolk: Donning Company, 1985.

Eighmey, Kathleen M. *The Beach: A History of Virginia Beach*. Virginia Beach: City of Virginia Beach Department of Public Libraries, 1976.

Evans-Hylton, Patrick. *Hampton Roads: The World War II Years*. Charlottesville: Acadia, 2005.

Harper, Raymond S. *South Norfolk*. Charleston: Arcadia, 2003.

Hobbs, Kermitt and William A. Paquette. *Suffolk: A Pictorial History*. Norfolk: Donning Company, 1987.

Hume, Ivor Noel. *The Virginia Adventure*. Charlottesville: University Press of Virginia, 1994.

Jones, Jennifer. *Middle Plantation in 1699*. Williamsburg: Colonial Williamsburg Foundation.

Kayaselcuk, Mary LaPrade. "Heroes Forever: The Story of the Newport News Victory Arch." Williamsburg: *The Virginia Gazette*, 1986.

Kelso, William M. and Beverly Straube. *Jamestown Rediscovery, 1994-2004*. Jamestown: Association for the Preservation of Virginia Antiquitries, 2004.

Mansfield, Stephen S. *Princess Anne County and Virginia Beach, A Pictorial History*. Norfolk: Donning Company, 1989.

Mapp, Alf and Ramona H. *Portsmouth, A Pictorial History*. Norfolk: Donning Company, 1989.

Mills, Eric. *Chesapeake Bay in the Civil War*. Centreville, Maryland: Tidewater Publishers, 1996.

Parramore, Thomas C., Peter C. Stewart, and Tommy L. Bogger. *Norfolk, The First Four Centuries*. Charlottesville: University Press of Virginia, 1994.

Quarstein, John V. and Parker S. Rouse, Jr. *Newport News, A Centennial History*. Newport News: City of Newport News, 1996.

Price, David A. *Love and Hate in Jamestown*. New York City: Vintage Books, 2003.

Roosevelt, Theodore's letter to his son Kermit, Bartleby.com

Rose, Ruth H. *Norfolk, Virginia, Black America Series*. Charleston: Acadia, 2000.

Rountree, Helen C. and E. Randolph Turner III. *Before and After Jamestown, Virginia's Powhatans and Their Predecessors*. Gainesville, Florida: University Press of Florida, 2003.

Stensvaag, James T., general editor. *Hampton, From the Sea to the Stars, 1610-1985*. Norfolk: Donning Company, 1985.

Tazewell, William L. and Guy Friddell. *Norfolk's Waters, An Illustrated History of Hampton Roads*. Sun Valley: American Historical Press, 2000.

Theobald, Mary Miley. *Colonial Williamsburg, The First 75 Years*. Williamsburg: Colonial Williamsburg Foundation, 2001.

Tucker, George Holbert. *Norfolk Highlights, 1584-1881*. Norfolk: Norfolk Historical Society, 1972.

Turner, Florence Kimberly. *Gateway to the New World, A History of Princess Anne County, Virginia 1607-1824*. Easley, South Carolina: Southern Historical Press, 1984.

Trudell, Clyde F. *Colonial Yorktown*. Gettysburg: Thomas Publications, 1938.

The *Virginian-Pilot*, available online at the Norfolk Public Library Website.

Wichord, Rogers Dey. *The History of Lower Tidewater Virginia*. New York City: Lewis Historical Publishing Company, 1959.

Wertenbaker, Thomas J. *Norfolk, Historic Southern Port*. Durham, North Carolina: Duke University Press, 1931.

Willyard, Kyle. *The Continental Line, Inc.*

Yetter, George Humphrey. *Williamsburg Before and After*. Williamsburg: Colonial Williamsburg Foundation, 1988.

An aerial view of the Governor's Palace.

SHARING THE HERITAGE

*Historic profiles of businesses,
organizations, and families that have
contributed to the development and
economic base of the Hampton Roads region*

Buildings and historical interpreters

inside recreated James Fort at

Williamsburg Settlement.

QUALITY OF LIFE

Healthcare providers, school

districts, and universities, and other

institutions that contribute to the quality

of life in Hampton Roads

BON SECOURS HAMPTON ROADS HEALTH SYSTEM

Above: Bon Secours Hampton Roads Health System is improving the patient experience by implementing quality best practices.

Top right: The Imaging Centers at Bon Secours DePaul and the Bon Secours Health Center at Harbour View now feature technology that can improve by twenty percent the likelihood of detecting breast cancer early. The R2 Image Checker is a computer-aided detection system that identifies masses or distorted areas that are nearly invisible to the naked eye.

Right: The employees of Bon Secours are focused on providing uncompromising customer service in comforting, healing environments.

Bon Secours hospitals in the Hampton Roads area are part of the Bon Secours Health System, a not-for-profit organization with twenty owned or joint-ventured acute-care hospitals and numerous other healthcare-related facilities in six states on the East Coast and in Michigan.

Bon Secours, which means "Good Help" in French, is focused on becoming a leader in Catholic health ministry through its commitment to bringing compassion to healthcare and to helping those in need. As a system of caregivers, Bon Secours is committed to bringing people and communities to health and wholeness as part of the healing ministry of Jesus Christ and the Catholic Church.

The health system is headquartered in Marriottsville, Maryland about fifteen miles west of Baltimore, as is the United States Provincial House of The Sisters of Bon Secours, an order of Catholic nuns that founded the ministry. The local system includes three hospitals serving the Hampton Roads area: Bon Secours DePaul Medical Center in Norfolk, Bon Secours Maryview Medical Center in Portsmouth, and Mary Immaculate Hospital in Newport News. The system also includes two assisted living facilities, two outpatient surgical facilities, two nursing care centers, and several physician practices, along with home care and hospice services.

Along with its twenty hospitals, the Bon Secours Health System owns and operates six long-term or nursing care facilities, four

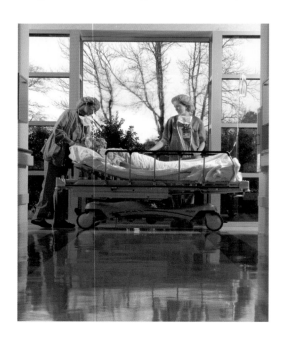

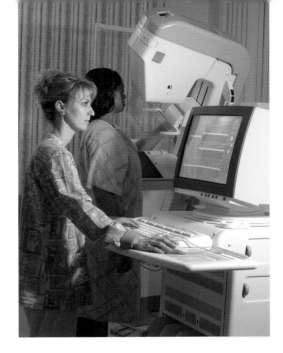

assisted- and independent-living facilities, and numerous primary care clinics, outpatient facilities, home healthcare services, and hospices. More than twenty thousand healthcare workers and thousands of physicians and volunteers carry out the healing ministry of the Sisters of Bon Secours.

The Sisters of Bon Secours began in 1824 in Paris when twelve young women committed themselves before God, as Sisters of Bon Secours, to minister to the sick, the suffering, and the dying. A rare form of ministry for religious women of the time, the Sisters stayed in the homes of the sick to nurse them, offer spiritual comfort, and help their families.

After extending the ministry to Ireland and England, the bishop of Baltimore in 1881 invited the Sisters to serve the sick and suffering in the United States. Three Sisters arrived in Baltimore in 1881 and began serving wherever they were needed. As their reputation grew, they were asked to care for people in other parts of the eastern United States.

Realizing they could better serve the sick, the poor, and the suffering in well-run facilities, the Sisters opened Bon Secours Hospital in Baltimore in 1919. Additional Bon Secours healthcare facilities followed in Michigan, Pennsylvania, Massachusetts, Florida, New Jersey, Virginia, and South Carolina. The ministry has grown to include the countries of France, Ireland, England, Scotland, the United States, and Peru. The Sisters formed Bon Secours Healthcare System in 1983, bringing several healthcare facilities under one organizational umbrella.

The oldest of the Hampton Roads hospitals is Bon Secours DePaul Medical Center, which joined the Bon Secours Health System in 1996. The hospital traces its roots to 1855, when the City of Norfolk was hit with a yellow fever epidemic.

Despite the dangers, eight Daughters of Charity, who had come to Norfolk in 1839 to operate the St. Mary's Orphan Asylum, offered to go from door to door to nurse the ill and dying in their homes and in makeshift hospitals. A wealthy patron of the orphanage, Ann Plume Behan Herron, opened her home to the sick and eventually donated her home to the Daughters of Charity to use as a hospital.

The Virginia Legislature incorporated the Hospital of St. Vincent DePaul, Norfolk's first public hospital, on March 3, 1856. The eight-room hospital served one hundred patients in its first year. As the Sisters' mission expanded, they added a clinic for the poor in 1892 and a training school for nurses a year later.

In 1939 the Sisters realized they needed a larger, more modern facility. They purchased land at the corner of Granby Street and Kingsley Lane and constructed a new building they named DePaul Hospital with a 259-bed capacity.

Throughout its long history, DePaul Medical Center maintained a strong commitment to meeting the needs of patients from throughout the region. The area's first intensive care and coronary care units opened in the early 1960s. The first island microvascular flap in the United States was performed at DePaul

Hospital and it was the setting for the Tidewater area's first ankle replacement.

By the 1970s, DePaul Medical Center had established itself as a state-of-the-art, 366-bed, full-service hospital, providing a comprehensive array of inpatient and ambulatory diagnostic and treatment services. In 1996 the hospital's leaders determined affiliation with Bon Secours Health System Inc. would allow for DePaul to best continue its ministry. The affiliation with Bon Secours became official on November 1, 1996.

Today, Bon Secours DePaul Medical Center is a 238-bed acute-care and teaching hospital. It combines the latest technological advancements and highly respected medical staff with dedicated and caring employees. Together, they provide a comprehensive range of inpatient, outpatient, diagnostic, and support services.

Centers of excellence include: Bon Secours Cancer Center at DePaul, DePaul Vascular Center, The Joint and Spine Center, Center for Birth, SeniorHealth Center, Transitional Care Center, Midwifery Center at DePaul, Comprehensive Wound Care Center, The Sleep Center, and The Women's Center for Healthy Changes.

Bon Secours DePaul also offers hyperbaric oxygen therapy, installed Virginia's first endovascular laboratory, and offers comprehensive imaging services.

Above: Bon Secours DePaul installed Virginia's first endovascular laboratory and continues to be a community leader by offering state-of-the-art 3-D imaging.

Below: Bon Secours DePaul uses the latest technological advances along with a highly respected medical staff and dedicated patient care team to provide high-quality, compassionate care to the community.

MARY IMMACULATE HOSPITAL

Mary Immaculate Hospital became a member of the Bon Secours Health System on November 1, 1996. This 110-bed hospital began around the turn of the twentieth century under the leadership of Dr. Joseph Buxton. The Elizabeth Buxton Hospital, as it was originally called, was located in the eastern part of Newport News on Chesapeake Avenue.

⚓

Above: Mary Immaculate Hospital is home to the Peninsula Center for Minimally Invasive Surgery. This innovative center is where skilled surgeons perform innovative procedures that result in less trauma to the body, therefore reducing pain and shortening recovery times.

Below: When it comes to matters of the heart, you want assurance that you can depend on the medical professionals who are caring for you. Using some of the most progressive technology available, the highly qualified and compassionate staff members of the Heart Center have your best interests at heart.

Dr. Buxton's son—Dr. Russel Buxton—did not share his father's fondness for running a hospital. He preferred to focus on his surgical practice. He eventually turned the administration of the hospital over to the Bernardine Franciscan Sisters, Third Order of St. Francis, who first came to the United States from Poland in 1894, establishing their mission in Pennsylvania.

In 1952, they assumed sponsorship of the hospital and renamed it Mary Immaculate Hospital. Two decades later, acknowledging the changing demographics on the Peninsula, the Sisters made plans to relocate the hospital to an area with limited healthcare services. In the 1980s the hospital relocated to its current campus in the Denbigh area of Newport News.

Throughout its long history, Mary Immaculate Hospital has maintained a strong commitment to meeting the needs of patients throughout the Peninsula. It does so by continuously expanding its breadth of services and its numerous community outreach programs.

The hospital is well known for its obstetrics and prenatal education programs, as well as other women's services. Emergency care is offered at all times and is staffed by board-certified physicians and a skilled nursing team.

Mary Immaculate provides cardiac catheterization and rehabilitation, extensive outpatient diagnostic services, outpatient and inpatient surgery, laser surgery, an intensive/coronary care unit, MRI and CT scans, women's services, renal dialysis, physical and occupational therapies, and speech pathology and audiology services.

The Heart Center houses the most technologically advanced cardiac catheterization lab on the Peninsula. The center also includes nuclear medicine, EKG, and more. Imaging services include the soft mammogram, bone density, MRI, and a state-of-the-art CT scanner.

Mary Immaculate is home to the Peninsula Center for Minimally Invasive Surgery that is comprised of the Surgical Pavilion and the Mary Immaculate Ambulatory Surgical Center. Together, there are ten operating rooms equipped with digital technology.

Mary Immaculate offers home health and hospital services, palliative care, physical and occupational therapies, Family Focus, and the most comprehensive health education offered on the Peninsula.

St. Francis Nursing Center, also a part of Bon Secours, is located on the Mary Immaculate campus. St. Francis is a 115-bed nursing center on the hospital campus offering 10 skilled and 105 intermediate care beds.

Mary Immaculate also provides extensive, no-cost or low-cost health and wellness classes and activities, including the Spirit of Women programs, Parcourse Exercise Trail, support groups, stress management workshops, and the Health Academy.

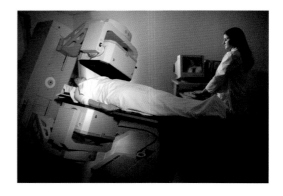

Bon Secours Maryview Medical Center, a 292-bed acute care hospital, became part of the Bon Secours Health System in 1984, when the Catholic Diocese of Richmond transferred sponsorship of the facility to the newly formed health system. The federal government founded Maryview Medical Center in 1945 to serve the healthcare needs of shipyard workers in the Portsmouth area and requested the Catholic Diocese of Richmond to run it.

It opened its doors on March 4, 1945, with 40 doctors, eight lay nurses, and 60 employees. The 150-bed hospital was named Glenshellah Hospital. It joined Portsmouth General Hospital as a healthcare provider to residents of the Portsmouth, Northern Chesapeake, Northern Suffolk, and Isle of Wight areas.

When the war ended later that year, Maryview dedicated its mission to caring for polio victims. The Catholic Diocese of Richmond called for organizations to manage the new healthcare facility, and the Daughters of Wisdom, an order of Catholic Nuns from Canada, answered the call.

They successfully operated the hospital until transferring sponsorship to the Bon Secours Health System in 1984. Bon Secours Maryview Medical Center continues to hold the best interests of the community at heart by caring for all those in need and expanding its breadth of services.

Through the years, Bon Secours Maryview has brought many "firsts" to the greater Portsmouth community. It brought the first cobalt treatment for cancer, the first cardiac catheterization lab, the first magnetic resonance imaging system (MRI), the first linear accelerator for radiation therapy in the treatment of cancer, and the first comprehensive pain management program. This tradition continued with the establishment of the hospital-based freestanding ambulatory surgery center and comprehensive diagnostic center, the Bon Secours Health Center at Harbour View, in the rapidly growing North Suffolk area. Bon Secours is dedicated to offering residents of

the area quality healthcare services as part of a comprehensive and coordinated delivery system.

Bon Secours Maryview offers surgical weight loss services, minimally invasive surgical procedures, emergency services, and orthopedic care. It is home to the Family Birth Center, the Spine Center, Maryview Center for Physical Rehabilitation, the Martha Davis Cancer Center, Maryview Joint Center, and—in affiliation with Columbia University College of Physicians and Surgeons—the Bon Secours Heart Institute. The Maryview Cancer Center offers specialty programs, which feature multispecialty physician teams for breast cancer, lung and chest, and colorectal cancer.

The hospital also offers diagnostic services which include EKG, echocardiography, holter monitoring, stress testing, vascular laboratory, cardiac catheterization and cardiac rehabilitation, sixteen-slice CT scans nuclear medicine, diagnostic X-rays, and MRI.

Bon Secours Maryview also offers behavioral medicine services (Behavioral Medical Center), assisted living residences (Providence Place of Maryview), an employee assistance program, physical therapy (Maryview Physical Therapy Center), urgent-care services (Maryview MedCare Centers), and several primary care physician practices.

Above: Bon Secours Heart Institute opened in November 2005 in affiliation with nationally ranked Columbia University College of Physicians and Surgeons.

Below: Bon Secours Maryview offers minimally invasive surgical services by some of the areas most skilled surgeons.

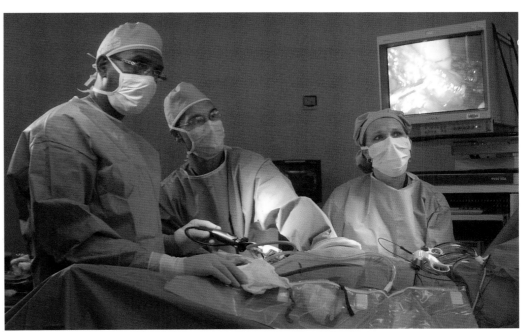

THOMAS NELSON COMMUNITY COLLEGE

Thomas Nelson Community College is an educational community unlike any other. The College offers high-quality educational programs and services at its two campuses, one in Hampton and one in Williamsburg. Thomas Nelson is the fourth largest community college within the Virginia Community College System (VCCS) which is comprised of twenty-three community colleges serving the Commonwealth of Virginia.

The College is named in honor of Thomas Nelson, Jr., who was among signers of the Declaration of Independence and an early colonial governor of the Commonwealth. Nelson spent his fortune to aid the revolutionary cause and died a pauper.

The College traces its development to a decision by the 1966 session of the Virginia General Assembly to establish a statewide system of comprehensive community colleges. A local committee investigated the feasibility of a community college to serve the residents of Hampton, Newport News, Poquoson, Williamsburg and the counties of James City and York and recommended that Thomas Nelson Community College be established.

A local board of advisors was appointed and a site was selected near the center of the Peninsula. The site was purchased by the City of Hampton and construction of the new community college began in the summer of 1967. The first classes were conducted for 1,232 students in September 1968 and the first class received associate degrees in 1970. Since

then, TNCC has graduated more than thirteen thousand individuals and provided credit and non-credit instruction to many more residents of the Peninsula and nearby communities.

Thomas Nelson Community College's mission is to prepare students for success in the global community and workforce of the future through the delivery of world-class comprehensive arts and sciences, transfer and occupational/technical programs and workforce development. Thomas Nelson enhances the quality of life for its citizens in its region by providing high-quality and accessible post-secondary education.

The diverse programs at Thomas Nelson are carefully tailored to support the economic development of the Commonwealth and meet the educational needs of citizens of all ages. Students at Thomas Nelson may choose from more than one hundred degrees and certificates in transfer or occupational programs in communications and humanities; business and public services; natural, health, and social sciences; mathematics, engineering, and technologies. Currently, the College offers associate degree programs, certificate programs and a diploma program. Thomas Nelson Community College is accredited by the Commission on Colleges of the Southern Association of Colleges and Schools to award associate degrees. The associate degree curricula have been approved by the State Council of Higher Education for Virginia. The College also offers many non-credit programs for professional certification or career upgrades.

Thomas Nelson has transfer agreements with many of Virginia's four-year institutions of higher education. These agreements allow

students to transfer to a four-year college after they complete their associate degrees. In addition, credits taken at Thomas Nelson are accepted by all 16 state colleges and universities and at least 22 of the private colleges in Virginia.

The College has direct involvement with the school systems in its service area through programs such as Tech Prep and Dual Enrollment. Thomas Nelson has dual enrollment agreements with the five school districts in its service area and two private schools, Hampton Christian and Denbigh Baptist Christian. The dual enrollment program allows students to earn college credit for courses they take while attending high school.

After providing a limited schedule of evening classes in the greater Williamsburg area for nearly three decades, the College opened its first facilities in the Busch Corporate Center in Williamsburg in 1998. In 2001, Thomas Nelson was designated as a multi-campus community college by the VCCS. This decision allowed the College to expand its offerings to citizens in Williamsburg, James City County and Upper York County. Four degree programs may now be completed by attending classes only in the Historic Triangle campus. These degree programs are: liberal arts, business administration, social science, and science.

Thomas Nelson is in the midst of planning for the construction of a permanent campus in the Historic Triangle on a seventy-three-acre site donated by James City County. The State Board for Community Colleges unanimously approved the land transfer agreement bringing to fruition a plan that began eleven years ago with the recognition of the significant population increases and growing educational needs of the residents of Williamsburg, James City County and Upper York County.

Strategically located with the Williamsburg-James City County (W-JCC) High School on the Warhill site, Thomas Nelson will work in collaboration with the W-JCC school system to develop programs and other educational opportunities that will facilitate the transition of high school students to college.

Based on a projected enrollment of 6,900 students at the College's Historic Triangle

campus, the master site plan includes five dedicated buildings for academic, administrative and faculty support, two 600-vehicle parking garages and a Physical Plant facility. The Historic Triangle campus is expected to be built in four to six major phases over several years, with a total of eight individual structures. The master site plan has also been approved by the State Board.

In Hampton, Thomas Nelson Community College has an 86-acre campus that includes eight academic buildings, a Wellness Center and support offices. Templin Hall, the newest academic building on the Hampton campus, opened in October 2002. It provides

the College with 49,143 square feet of instructional space including classrooms, faculty offices, computer and a graphics art lab and an outdoor amphitheater. The Mary T. Christian Auditorium, also located in Templin Hall, offers an array of cultural presentations for the community.

Thomas Nelsons' Workforce Development offers specialized education and training to meet local needs in a variety of fields. In 2005, Thomas Nelson Workforce Development became a partner in the four hundredth anniversary of the founding of Jamestown when the VCCS awarded a grant for its Institute of Excellence in Customer Service. A new guest service program was created with the Historic Triangle Jamestown 2007 Host Committee, the Greater Williamsburg Chamber and Tourism Alliance, and tourism industry representatives. Workforce Development has been able to secure over $50,000 through various grants to support the commemoration.

In a show of regional partnership, the school's Peninsula Workforce Development Center (PWDC) opened in October 2001. A two-story, 92,000-square-foot facility in Hampton on the College's main campus, the center serves everyone from existing businesses seeking to improve worker's skills to individual job seekers pursuing education or career opportunities, to high-tech companies moving to the Peninsula. The result of broad-based regional cooperation, the center is among the first of its kind.

The PWDC houses Thomas Nelson's workforce training programs, Old Dominion University's Peninsula Higher Education Center, the Virginia Employment Commission's Hampton and Eastern Regional Offices, and federally funded workforce development programs administered under the auspices of the Greater Peninsula Workforce Development Consortium and Workforce Investment Board.

The One-Stop Career Center is the focal point to assist job seekers and area employers. The center is equipped with computers, phones, fax machines and photo copiers. Career counselors are also available to assist with job searches, resume preparation, and provide training needs evaluations. The center also provides extensive support to employers in

their search and recruitment efforts. The Career Resource Center was jointly designed and funded by the Greater Peninsula Workforce Development Consortium, Thomas Nelson, and the Virginia Employment Commission.

Thomas Nelson's Workforce Development has been recognized statewide and nationally by the U.S. Department of Labor and the National Association of Workforce Boards. The College provided a broad range of services to more than 35,000 individuals and more than 630 businesses during 2005. Thomas Nelson was a leader in obtaining a federal grant of nearly $2 million for a regional consortium developing a workforce training pipeline.

In July 2004, Dr. Charles A. Taylor became Thomas Nelson Community College's sixth president. Dr. Taylor said, "Our commitment to excellence is present in all our programs at our two campuses in Hampton and Williamsburg. Our students are supported by a caring staff and a first-rate faculty who pursue innovative teaching techniques advancing the world of knowledge. We take great pride in the quality and dedication of our faculty and staff who are committed to student success. Our goal is to help build a better future for all."

For more information about Thomas Nelson Community College, please visit www.tncc.edu.

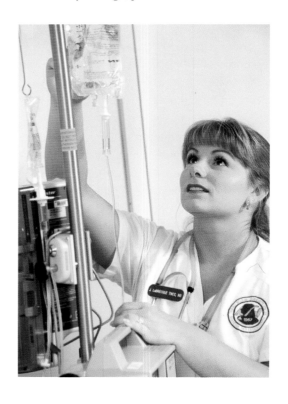

Walsingham Academy was founded through the vision of Father Thomas Walsh, who worked to establish a Catholic school in Williamsburg because he felt "that you reach parents most quickly through the children."

Father Walsh invited the Sisters of Mercy of Philadelphia to Williamsburg and offered the use of a World War II USO women's residence as a school. The Academy is still operated by the Sisters of Mercy as a co-ed, college preparatory school.

Walsingham Academy conducted its first class on September 16, 1947 at 601 College Terrace in Williamsburg. The school derives its name from Our Lady of Walsingham, a title of special devotion given to the Mother of God by medieval English Catholics.

Fifty-eight boarders and day students registered for Walsingham Academy's first year and the school's first graduate, Margaret Avery Leavitt, received her diploma in 1948.

Enrollment had jumped to 156 students in 1951 and the principal, Sister Mary Constance, arranged for the purchase of sixty-two acres on the historic road to Jamestown. The new school building was occupied in January 1952 and the old school continued to house boarders and the Sisters. Enrollment continued to grow and, in less than five years, a new wing was added to the building at 1100 Jamestown Road.

By 1963 enrollment at Walsingham Academy had reached 789, including 315 in the Upper School (grades 8-12). A new high school was dedicated in November 1964 and students in grades seven through twelve moved to the new building across the green.

The next addition came in 1997 when an athletic complex, including a large gym, administrative offices and classrooms, was built. Enrollment reached 700 in 1999 and over 760 for the 2005-2006 school year. Thirty percent of graduating seniors attended the school since first grade or kindergarten.

Although Walsingham Academy is a religious, Catholic school, the student body traditionally has been about fifty percent Catholic, with the remainder of the students from diverse religious backgrounds.

Walsingham Academy has received many honors for academic excellence, including the Blue Ribbon for the Lower School (Pre-K through grade seven) in 1998 and 2003. The Blue Ribbon Schools program honors public and private K-twelve schools that are either academically superior or demonstrate dramatic gains in student achievement.

The school's core values are proclaimed in this Mission Statement: "Walsingham Academy, a Catholic, Christ-centered learning environment, established by the Sisters of Mercy, commits itself to educational excellence and the development of the whole person through a spiritual and value-centered curriculum that emphasizes responsible leadership reflecting the Mercy heritage of compassion and service."

The first day of school at Walsingham Academy, September 16, 1947.

THE CHRISTIAN BROADCASTING NETWORK

⚓

Above: Pat Robertson praying.

Below: Pat Robertson running a camera at WYAH-TV.

Opposite, top: Pat Robertson at the CBN News Desk.

Opposite, bottom: The hosts of The 700 Club *(from left to right): Gordon Roberston, Terry Meeuwsen, and Pat Robertson.*

It was November 1959 when a young seminary graduate named Pat Robertson left New York City with his wife, Dede, and their three children and drove to the Tidewater region of Virginia where he hoped to purchase a bankrupt UHF television station in Portsmouth.

Robertson arrived in Portsmouth with only seventy dollars in his pockets but somehow managed to arrange the financing to buy the station. This led to the formation of The Christian Broadcasting Network in January 1960 and its very first broadcast on October 1, 1961. CBN was not only the first Christian television station in Virginia but also the first in the nation.

Today, CBN is one of the largest television ministries in the world and, with its many subsidiary and affiliate organizations, goes beyond the bounds of broadcasting in its mission to reach the world with a message of hope from the Bible.

The story of CBN's birth and early years is documented in Pat Robertson's autobiography, *Shout It From The Housetops*. CBN first went on the air with WYAH-TV (from Yahweh, the Hebrew name for God), a UHF television station with barely enough power to reach across the Portsmouth city limits. With a modest income from a few local supporters, CBN began broadcasting live half-hour programs from 7:00 p.m. to 10:00 p.m. each

night. Gradually, the broadcast day was expanded to 5:00 p.m. to midnight.

In the fall of 1963, CBN conducted its first telethon to raise the $7,000 per month needed for the following year's budget. Robertson told viewers that a "club" of 700 contributors, each giving $10 a month, would enable CBN to meet its expenses. As guests appeared to sing and share their religious experiences, Robertson invited the audience to pray for the seven hundred supporters who would help keep CBN going. Though its financial struggles continued, CBN had taken an important step in building community support for the ministry.

A year later, "The 700 Club" telethon was an important turning point for CBN. This telethon generated more contributions than the previous years, but not enough to meet CBN's growing budget. Then, in the final minutes of the broadcast, a remarkable outpouring of spiritual revival began to sweep through the viewing audience. Throughout the next several days, callers flooded CBN with prayer requests and pledges of financial support to CBN. A year later, Robertson added a program to the end of his station's broadcast day that followed the telethon format—prayer and ministry coupled with telephone response. He named it *The 700 Club*, hoping to build on the audience that had become familiar with CBN's telethons. The program's audience grew as other stations began carrying the show.

CBN, the second largest employer in the area, is one of the largest Christian television ministries in the world. A multifaceted nonprofit organization, CBN provides programming by cable, broadcast and satellite to 200 counties and is produced in 70 languages.

The CBN studios, located in Virginia Beach and Nashville, Tennessee, receive more than 2.5

million pieces of mail and welcome more than 10,000 visitors annually. A favorite event for CBN visitors is to attend a live taping of *The 700 Club*. The popular syndicated news magazine features co-hosts Pat Robertson, Terry Meeuwsen, Gordon Robertson, and Kristi Watts, with news anchor Lee Webb. Approximately one million viewers watch *The 700 Club* daily.

CBN also provides *The 700 Club* Prayer Counseling Centers (PCC) staffed with 350 trained prayer counselors who respond to nearly three million prayer requests in more than four million calls annually. The PCC provides live prayer, scriptural guidance and literature resources, at no charge, to people through the CBN toll-free prayer line. Increasingly, the prayer counselors are assisting callers with content from www.cbn.com. Prayer counselors support the daily *700 Club* broadcast as they provide spiritual ministry and encouragement from a biblical perspective, utilizing the CBN resources.

The 700 Club Prayer Counseling Center (PCC) processes approximately fourteen thousand calls daily. In 2005, 4,565,000 calls were handled. Since its inception, the PCC has received 71,225,000 calls.

One million viewers see CBN's national flagship program, *The 700 Club*, on ABC Family and syndicated stations daily. Seventeen million unique viewers watch the program each month and the program is seen in ninety-six percent of the U.S. markets.

The international edition of *The 700 Club—WorldReach*—has been viewed in more than 70 foreign languages, can be seen in over 200 countries, and is accessible throughout the year by more than 1.5 billion people around the world.

In 1977, CBN started the nation's first basic television cable network with satellite transmissions of religious and syndicated family TV shows. By 1981, CBN Cable reached nearly ten million homes. Renamed the CBN Family Channel in 1988, the commercial cable operation continues to prosper and was sold in 1990 to International Family Entertainment, Inc. (IFE), a publicly held company that trades on the New York Stock Exchange. IFE was sold in 1997 to Fox Kids Worldwide, Inc. Disney acquired the Fox

Family Channel and it was renamed ABC Family in 2001.

Operation Blessing International Relief and Development Corporation (OBI) is a nonprofit 501 (c) (3) humanitarian

Above: Pat Robertson with former President Ronald Reagan.

Top, right: Operation Blessing feeds the hungry.

Below: Pat Robertson with former Prime Minister of Israel Ariel Sharon.

organization, founded by Pat Robertson, which is dedicated to alleviating human need and suffering in the United States and around the world. Founded in 1978, OBI implements programs that provide hunger relief, medical aid, disaster relief and community development in order to make a significant, long-term impact and truly break the cycle of suffering.

In an unprecedented year of natural disasters, OBI was a first responder to the devastating Southeast Asia tsunami and Hurricane Katrina, providing emergency relief; and is still on the ground helping the survivors and communities rebuild. OBI has

touched the lives of more than 197.7 million people in 96 countries and all 50 states, providing goods and services valued at over $1.1 billion.

CBN News was founded as a news division of CBN in 1982. CBN News provides an alternative choice for those who are looking to understand the events and trends affecting their lives in a redemptive light. CBN News also produces *NewsWatch*, a half-hour nightly news program that is syndicated on cable systems, Christian networks and TV stations across the nation. Former CBN News guests include Ronald Reagan, Ariel Sharon, and Jimmy Carter.

M.G. "Pat" Robertson, the founder of CBN, is a native of Lexington, Virginia, and the son of A. Willis Robertson and Gladys Churchill Robertson. Robertson's father served thirty-four years in the U.S. House of Representatives and Senate.

Robertson received his B.A. degree from Washington & Lee University, a juris doctor degree from Yale University Law School and a master of divinity degree from New York Theological Seminary. He served as the assistant adjutant of the First Marine Division in combat in Korea.

All of CBN's efforts, including the daily flagship program *The 700 Club*, international programming projects and Operation Blessing, are focused toward the organization's primary mission: to prepare the United States and other nations of the world for the coming of Jesus Christ and the establishment of the Kingdom of God on earth.

Since its establishment in 1989, Chesapeake Bay Academy has served more than 625 families, graduated six classes from the twelfth grade, built and occupied a three-story, 50,000-square-foot, state-of-the-art building, achieved Virginia Association of Independent Schools (VAIS) accreditation, and launched The Dominion Education Center to provide supplemental services to additional families throughout Hampton Roads.

Chesapeake Bay Academy educates and empowers bright students with learning difficulties—including attention disorders (ADHD), dyslexia, and dysgraphia—to reach their full potential.

The Academy is the only kindergarten through twelfth grade school in Southeastern Virginia licensed by the Commonwealth of Virginia and accredited by VAIS to serve students with specific learning disabilities and other health impairments.

From the outset, family involvement has been critical to the success of Chesapeake Bay Academy. It is the Academy's belief that strong relations between children, parents and teachers are at the heart of teaching and learning.

The School's mission to educate and empower students, including those with learning and attention disorders, is reflected in its approach to academics.

Teachers and administrators create an individualized academic plan for each student that identifies specific weaknesses to be targeted, specific academic strengths that need to be accelerated, and accommodations needed for effective learning. Teachers then use individualized teaching methods to meet each student's needs. Teachers vary instructional strategies, provide direct instruction, implement creative techniques, and help students reach levels of achievement commensurate with their abilities. While each school division has specific, proven programs unique to their student body, the philosophy of individualization permeates the entire school.

In the Lower and Middle Schools, a combination of direct instruction in reading, writing, mathematics, social and learning skills and positive reinforcement in a safe environment sets the foundation for a student's success after transition to the Upper School.

In the Upper School, the accredited, SOL-based curriculum, paired with targeted reading and writing support classes, prepare students for successful transition to college, the workplace, or both. A school-to-work program

places all Upper School students in a work environment for three weeks and makes successful completion of the program a graduation requirement. This program has enjoyed tremendous success, securing excellent corporate and community partners who open their offices and work sites to our students and allow them to learn side-by-side with key personnel.

Athletics at Chesapeake Bay Academy are considered an essential part of a student-athlete's educational experience. The goals of the program are to help all students have access to age-appropriate opportunities to develop skills, compete, and increase their unique talents and skills. Programs are designed to provide maximum participation and help students develop a positive attitude about themselves, others and the school.

Chesapeake Bay Academy is located at 821 Baker Road in Virginia Beach. For additional information, please visit www.cba-va.org.

CHESAPEAKE BAY ACADEMY

NATIONAL COUNSELING GROUP, INC.

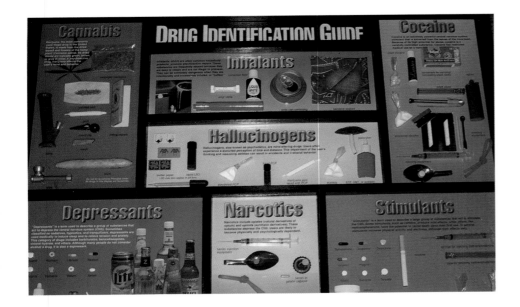

The National Counseling Group, Inc., (NCG) is a private, mental health and substance abuse counseling agency providing a large array of services to clients throughout the Commonwealth of Virginia. Thomas W. Minnick, LCSW, CSAC founded NCG in 1993 as the Northern Virginia Counseling Group, Inc (NVCG). Along with several key staff, including Sam Gray, Deborah Sikes, and George Young, who have been with the company over ten years, Minnick was able to realize his vision for developing a mental health agency that provides quality mental health client care and promotes the development of the community it serves. NCG currently has approximately 150 full time staff and will be adding another 50 by the end of 2006. During 2005, NCG provided approximately 120,000 counseling units of service throughout the state of Virginia.

Minnick's vision for NCG began after working in the field for several years and experiencing first hand the lack of coordination of services between various government and private entities. Clients frequently traveled between agencies to receive assistance, and professionals involved in their care were not cross-trained in treating multiple disabilities. As a result, there was neither a comprehensive nor a systematic approach to client care, and clients were underserved, inappropriately served, or ineffectually served. Given the challenges clients face in entering the mental health system and engaging in treatment, it seemed unfair to place them at further disadvantage by having to function in a faulty system. Thus, Minnick vowed to do something different and founded the National Counseling Group, Inc.

Coordinating services around a comprehensive and systemic view of client care became the cornerstone of NCG's philosophy and ultimate success. These services consisted of practices that were, at the time, considered unheard of or

beyond the scope of traditional outpatient treatment. However, NCG staff and clients experienced first hand the benefits of observed drug testing, in-home visits, collateral interviews with persons other than the identified client, and collaborative work with the courts, schools, and other mental health systems.

As NCG began its work in Northern Virginia, the court systems in this area were key early advocates. Probation officers Bob Bermingham, Scott Warner, Fran Deloatche, Jim Rankin, Ellen Patterson, and others helped refine our strategies for working with youth. NCG's first venture out of Northern Virginia was to the Richmond area. Supporters such as Debra Pierce of Goochland, Tony Collins of Powhatan, Wayne Frith, Greg Anderson, and Peggy Trickler of Hopewell, have assisted in making the Richmond NCG office a huge success. NCG personnel who were instrumental in the founding and success of this office are now important leaders in the agency; Chris Baham, Dennis Raabe, Sean Blair, and Holly Duggan.

NCG is dedicated to supporting its government and community partners and demonstrates that commitment in a variety of ways. NCG provides trainings and scholarship programs and sponsors many local school and community events. They also regularly participate in events throughout the state, such as the Virginia Juvenile Justice Association, Community Service Board Conferences, and Comprehensive Services Act Vendor Fairs. Furthermore, as evidence of NCG's commitment to the communities they serve, each year a significant portion of the revenue is donated to a variety of charities and causes.

Through the efforts and dedication of many, NCG was able to expand to the Tidewater region. Under the steadfast leadership of Terrie Pendleton and Clarence Payne, this office has

grown to over forty full-time staff and now has a permanent home in Virginia Beach. The success of this office in the community is owed to many individuals but particular notes of thanks go to Janice Douglas and Isiah Oliver of the Norfolk Department of Human Services, Judge Randy Carlson and Claudette Overton of the Norfolk Juvenile and Domestic Relations Court, Jeff Kail of the Chesapeake City Schools, and Mike Morton, formerly of Norfolk and currently of the Hampton Court Service Unit.

Although NCG got its start providing mostly outpatient services to dually diagnosed individuals, as the practice has expanded, so have the types and ranges of services offered. In fact, providing intensive, in-home services for children and mental health support services for adults utilizing the Medicaid funding program has become our largest source of activity. NCG invites you to call either of its two Tidewater offices—Virginia Beach at 757-467-8184 or Newport News at 757-240-5595. You can visit www.nationalcounselinggroup.com for more information on NGC's offices and services.

Opposite, top: NCG workers provide substance abuse education in all of its communities.

Opposite, bottom: CEO Thomas Minnick (center) and senior NCG staff. Seated (from left to right): Holly Duggan, Dimitri Haddad, Deborah Sikes, Thomas Minnick, George Young, Sam Gray, and Leslie Martin. Standing (from left to right): Latasha Blanding, Terrie Pendelton, Johnaton May, Gretchen Abell, Chris Baham, Oliver Agee, Christine Kelley, Michelle Schrotz, Frank Valentine, Clarence Payne, Patrick Slifka, Sean Blair, Jamie Slifka, Melissa McGinn, Dennis Raabe, and Julia Wilkins.

Above: NCG donated over $9,000 in support of Katrina families and relocating livestock.

Below: Team NCG participates in local fundraisers for its communities.

CITY OF NEWPORT NEWS

⚓

Above: A view of the Fountain Plaza I and Fountain Plaza II buildings in City Center at Oyster Point.

Below: The Herbert H. Bateman Virginia Advanced Shipbuilding and Carrier Integration Center (VASCIC).

Since it was founded in 1896, Newport News has grown from a small Chesapeake and Ohio Railway terminus at Hampton Roads to a metropolis of 185,000, surrounded on two sides by deep water and on the other two by the City of Hampton and York and James City Counties.

In little more than a hundred years, Newport News has become recognized for its advanced research and technology resources, state-of-the-art shipbuilding and naval engineering, cultural and recreational activities, historic preservation efforts, military facilities, and economic development opportunities.

Newport News is home to the Thomas Jefferson National Accelerator Facility (Jefferson Lab), a leader in particle physics research. The City's Economic Development Authority owns the 122,000-square-foot Applied Research Center next to the Jefferson Lab. Here, scientists from the Lab, the university community and private industry collaborate on a wide range of new technology.

NASA Langley Research Center, a world-class innovator of aeronautics and selected space science, is located less than ten miles from the Jefferson Lab. The 1,300 science and engineering professionals at NASA Langley Research Center are a major contributor to the intellectual infrastructure available on the Virginia Peninsula.

Located on the Newport News downtown waterfront is another world-class research and development facility, the Herbert H. Bateman Virginia Advanced Shipbuilding and Carrier Integration Center. Northrop Grumman Newport News, Virginia's largest manufacturer has teamed with other defense contractors and Virginia universities to design the next generation of nuclear aircraft carriers, integrating systems and the application of emerging technology.

Newport News is actively engaged in creating a highly livable community to attract the knowledgeable workers and creative individuals needed to support high-tech and corporate headquarters such as Ferguson Enterprises, Icelandic USA, and Specialty Foods Groups. City Center at Oyster Point, a high-density, high-quality, mixed-use development surrounding a magnificent five-acre fountain, includes Class-A office space, a Marriott Hotel and Conference Center, and a retail district that includes such stores as Ann Taylor Loft, Chico's, Coldwater Creek, Jos. A. Bank, Talbots, and Ten Thousand Villages. Port Warwick, the region's first new urbanism community, is a recognized model for developers of neo-traditional communities in other locations.

The award-winning Newport News Public School division educates nearly 33,000 children in 5 early childhood centers, 28 elementary schools, 9 middle schools, and 5 high schools. The school district offers twelve magnet or specialty programs in addition to its comprehensive education program. Newport News public schools have won 11 National Awards for Excellence and two Honorable Mention Awards— an unprecedented achievement. Rapidly expanding Christopher Newport University and other higher education centers support workforce development and lifelong learning.

The historic sites, museums and recreational facilities in Newport News foster a superb quality of life. The world-renowned Mariners' Museum, the newly expanded Virginia Living Museum and the Peninsula Fine Arts Center, an affiliate of the Virginia Museum of Fine Art, are just three of an array of cultural attractions to be found in Newport News.

Residents and visitors may step back in time with tours of four historic homes: Endview Plantation, the James A. Fields House, Lee Hall Museum, and the Newsome House Museum and Cultural Center. The region's important military ties are captured at the U.S. Army Transportation Museum at Fort Eustis and the Virginia War Museum.

In addition, Newport News is home to more than thirty city parks, including Newport News Park, the largest municipal park east of the Mississippi River. Newport News park features include boat ramps, championship golf courses, seasonal festivals, and an active recreation program that reaches out to all citizens.

The Mariners' Museum's new USS *Monitor* Center, scheduled to open in 2007, and the I. M. Pei-designed Ferguson Center for the Arts at Christopher Newport University are part of Newport News' urban revival.

Interstates 64 and 664 run the length of Newport News and the Virginia Peninsula, providing an efficient transportation corridor for moving people and goods. Six-laned arterial streets and well-planned traffic signal synchronization help move traffic smoothly, avoiding the unbearable congestion that plagues other cities. In addition, three airports within an hour's drive serve Newport News, including the Newport News/Williamsburg International Airport.

Newport News is transforming itself for the twenty-first century. Building on its shipbuilding heritage, Newport News looks to a future that includes high-energy physics and urban lifestyles that balance successful economic activity and livability.

For more information about the City of Newport News, please visit www.nngov.com.

Above: Styron Square in Port Warwick, the region's first new urbanism community.

Below: Icelandic USA corporate headquarters, located in Oakland Industrial Park.

TIDEWATER COMMUNITY COLLEGE

Enrolling more than 38,000 credit and noncredit students and serving more than 550 employers, Tidewater Community College (TCC) is the largest higher education institution and provider of workforce development services in the Hampton Roads region. From the number of students and employers it serves to its myriad connections and strategic partnerships throughout the region, TCC's influence across the region is often called its "best kept secret."

Founded in 1968 as a part of the Virginia Community College System, TCC serves the Hampton Roads cities of Chesapeake, Norfolk, Portsmouth, Suffolk, and Virginia Beach, with four fully comprehensive campuses and a regional Visual Arts Center in Olde Towne Portsmouth, the TCC Jeanne and George Roper Performing Arts Center in Norfolk's downtown theater district, and the Advanced Technology Center in Virginia Beach. A Regional Automotive Technology Center will be added in Chesapeake's Oakbrooke Business & Technology Center in 2007, and the new Fred W. Beazley Portsmouth Campus will open in 2008-09 as part of that city's live-work-play-learn redevelopment of its Victory area. That new campus will be home to a state-of-the-art school of nursing and the First College Program, an innovative initiative to provide up to 19 credits of college credit to 300 or more high school seniors each year.

Over the past decade, TCC has been pursuing the vision of being "a national model for community colleges in the twenty-first

century—the new millennium's strategic community college." The college's strategic plan explains the vision as framing "TCC as a vital academic resource, capable of directing its energies and shaping its programs to meet the changing needs of its many constituencies within the South Hampton Roads region, the Commonwealth of Virginia, the nation, and the international community of which it is a part."

TCC is committed to meeting the region's education and training needs as it advances the quality of life of the region through an educated, globally aware, and technologically engaged citizenry. Each year, more than forty-four percent of the South Hampton Roads residents who attend a college or university in Virginia enroll at TCC. And, when they transfer to four-year schools, TCC students perform as well as the native university students.

TCC has been nationally recognized for its work in incorporating the best of technological advances into the teaching and learning process, as well as for its work in international education. And area employers consistently register high levels of satisfaction with the performance of their employees who are TCC graduates. The college received the inaugural award of the Virginia Community College System for its work as a pacesetter in

responding proactively to the needs of business and industry in workforce development.

TCC offers over 150 programs that prepare students to pursue the baccalaureate degree or to enter or advance in the world of work, goals that are not mutually exclusive. Curricula that prepare students to transfer to four-year colleges or universities are offered in business administration, engineering, science, computer science, liberal arts, fine arts, theatre arts, social sciences, special education and developmental disabilities, and general studies. Career and technical programs that respond to the region's workforce needs by preparing students for employment or career advancement are offered in a wide variety of areas, including the health professions, culinary arts, truck driving, engineering and industrial technologies, horticulture, business, and information technology.

The college works closely with employers and economic development leaders to prepare and maintain a world-class, globally competitive workforce for the Hampton Roads region. For example, TCC's ability to respond quickly to develop training in the cutting-edge, technology-intensive modeling and simulation field is essential to the Commonwealth's initiative to make Hampton Roads the nation's premier center for military, government, and commercial modeling and simulation. Across the region, TCC provides responsive and affordable programs and services that ensure the kind of employee and organizational performance needed to compete in today's marketplace. Whether

through existing courses or special, customized training programs, workforce development services are provided to employers both on campus and at worksites.

TCC's commitment to the Hampton Roads region extends beyond access to educational opportunities and workforce development to include the sustained cultural vitality of the region. TCC's Jeanne and George Roper Performing Arts Center, restored to the original 1920s vintage grandeur of the historic Loew's Theater through a partnership with the City of Norfolk and private gifts, has served as the venue for a wide range of performances, from the premieres of locally produced films, to local theatrical productions, including the college's own, to artists of international stature, such as the Royal Shakespeare Company's only U.S. production of *The Tempest* and the Borromeo Quartet. And the Visual Arts Center in Olde Towne Portsmouth—the only facility of its kind at a community college in Virginia—features a full range of visual arts courses and programs, a public art gallery with six shows each year, and a forty-thousand-piece book and image library. The Center houses studios for three-dimensional design, sculpture, ceramics, hot glass blowing, photography, painting, printmaking, and computer and graphic design.

As the region and the nation at large face new challenges and opportunities, Tidewater Community College is moving strategically forward to enhance its ability to serve Hampton Roads. TCC will continue to anticipate and meet the increasingly diverse and sophisticated education and training needs of southeastern Virginia, while serving as a national example for a comprehensive community college in the twenty-first century,

LONDON BRIDGE BAPTIST CHURCH

Baptists were still a persecuted minority when London Bridge Baptist Church was established in 1784. Undaunted by the religious intolerance then common in Virginia, church founders William Morris and Elder Daniel Gould were determined to begin a Baptist church for the residents of London Bridge.

The first meetinghouse was a forty by sixty foot structure located on the road that ran from Norfolk to Virginia Beach. The frame building had four windows with clear glass along each side and an additional two windows behind the pulpit. The church had two entrances, one for men and one for women and, in the custom of the day, the sexes sat apart during services.

The walls were painted white and the ceiling was painted sky blue. The flooring was whipsawed oak.

The modern-day London Bridge Baptist Church, with more than two thousand members and a reputation as a growing, dynamic church, is located on the same property as the original church. Much has changed since 1784 but the

mission of London Bridge Church remains the same; sharing the good news of Jesus Christ.

The original congregation numbered fifty-five members and was ministered to by Reverend William Morris, a messenger of the Portsmouth Baptist Association. Described as a "preacher of much substance," Reverend Morris served the congregation for eighteen years until he and his family moved to Kentucky in 1802.

A number of circuit-riding ministers, who divided their time among several churches, served the London Bridge Church in its early days. The old-time circuit preachers received little pay for their services but church members provided them with food and lodging during their visits. It was considered an honor to take care of the minister's physical needs while he was looking after the congregation's spiritual needs.

Acceptance of Baptist doctrines increased in the early nineteenth century and the London Bridge Church grew along with the community. More than a hundred new members were baptized following a revival service in 1843.

Before baptisteries were constructed inside church buildings, baptizing was done mostly in the warm summer months. Early baptisms for London Bridge members were conducted in the nearby Lynnhaven River and later, on Chandler's farm on Linkhorn Bay. These services were always well attended and as the pastor and those to be baptized waded into the water, the congregation sang appropriate hymns

Above: An artist's rendering of the original church building.

Below: London Bridge Baptist Church is located at 2460 Potters Road in Virginia Beach.

from the shore, including Shall We Gather at the River.

The church building was enlarged and remodeled several times as the membership grew, but not all the changes were positive. Turning the church to face the road proved to be a mistake because the breezes that cooled the church during summer were no longer able to circulate.

The first remodeling, which included raising the ceiling to follow the line of the roof, cost $85 and increased the church seating capacity to 200. Unfortunately, many church artifacts were lost during the early remodelings because the thrifty church officers, who considered waste a sin, sold the old furnishings and lumber as the additions were made. The only tangible piece of church history still surviving is an old bell, which is now enclosed in a case in the mezzanine of today's building.

Tragedy struck the church family in 1889 when fire destroyed the home of the pastor, F. C. Clark, killing the pastor, his two daughters, a son, and a niece. Church members quickly came to the aid of the pastor's wife and two sons who managed to escape the fire but were left destitute.

Over time, kerosene lamps were used to light chandeliers, followed by Delco lights, powered by batteries. Coal and woodstoves gave way to a furnace, stained glass windows were added and brick veneer covered the exterior. Factory-made oak pews were installed and two side wings were added to house classrooms, a social hall and kitchen.

Church members helped the community cope with the shortages and heartaches of World War I and, by World War II; the church was a focal point of the war effort. Nearby Naval and Army installations turned the area into a growing metropolis and the church concentrated on ministering to the thousands of young men and women stationed far from home and facing an uncertain future.

Fire broke out in the 150-year old church building on November 16, 1946, and the building was destroyed, along with many of the church records. Services were conducted in the auditorium of Oceana School while members added their labor and materials to the $17,000 in insurance money and built a new church edifice. Dedication services for the new building were held October 10, 1948.

Church growth at London Bridge has been little short of miraculous in recent years. The church enjoyed a fruitful period under the seventeen-year ministry of Ed Hughes, a period that saw the McKenney Educational Wing dedicated.

Mark Stone was called as pastor in 1969 and his leadership and evangelistic zeal sparked rapid church growth. Reverend Mark Stone, who served for ten years, inspired a strong evangelistic outreach. Facilities were expanded to accommodate the growing membership, including a new sanctuary in 1971 and the Family Life Center in 1977.

London Bridge Baptist Church has continued to grow and serve the spiritual needs of its members under the leadership of Reverend Tommy Taylor, who has been pastor since 1979. A new worship center capable of seating twenty-four hundred was begun in 1999 and dedicated in 2001. Additional major renovations of the 1971 worship center into a new adult education wing; the former adult education wing into a new and exciting children's wing (The KOAST, for "Kids on Assignment Seeking Truth"); and Paradise Cove, a children's multimedia center, were completed in 2003 and 2004. The latest renovation has been to the middle and high school student areas, providing one of the most technologically equipped and exciting facilities available anywhere in the Tidewater Area. Stop by for a visit!

Pastor Tommy and Phillis Taylor.

NORFOLK STATE UNIVERSITY

The history of Norfolk State University is one filled with the joys, promises, and disappointments of building and working in a predominately black institution of higher education during the era of a segregated society. Norfolk State was established as one of the last historically black institutions in the state. According to Lyman Beecher Brooks in his book *Upward: the History of Norfolk State University 1935-1975*, the development of Norfolk State began as a result of a meeting of the city and University in which broad-based support grew out of the education of the public to the needs, purposes, and services of higher education.

The University opened its doors Wednesday, September 18, 1935, on the second floor of the Hunton Branch YMCA Building on Brambleton Avenue in Norfolk, Virginia with class registration and orientation. Classes began Monday, September 23, with a fall enrollment of 85 day students and 47 evening students. Today, Norfolk State University has an enrollment of more than six thousand students.

Over its seventy-year history, Norfolk State has passed through five distinctive periods of growth, namely the Norfolk Unit of Virginia Union University, the Norfolk Polytechnic College, the Norfolk Division of Virginia State College, Norfolk State College, and Norfolk State University. The mission of the University is "to provide an affordable, high-quality education for an ethnically diverse student population, equipping them with the capability to become productive citizens who continuously contribute to a global and rapidly

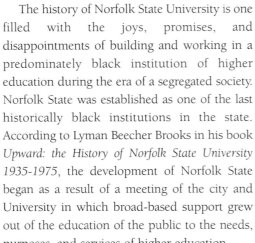

Samuel F. Scott
(1935—1938)

Lyman B. Brooks
(1938—1975)

Harrison B. Wilson
(1975—1997)

Marie V. McDemmond
(1997—2005)

changing society." From the years of the Great Depression to today's Digital Age, Norfolk State has been under the leadership of four visionary leaders who have guided the University to a new level of "Achieving With Excellence."

- Samuel Fischer Scott, a native of Portsmouth, Virginia, was the first leader who served as director of the Norfolk Unit, a two-year (junior college) division of Virginia Union University in Richmond, Virginia. For this first period of growth, Virginia Union assumed responsibility for the academic credit of the Norfolk Unit. The Norfolk Unit had its own budget and a local advisory board.

- Lyman Beecher Brooks, a native of Mathews County, Virginia, who received his doctorate from the University of Michigan, took over the junior college's helm in 1938 and relocated it to two successively larger facilities before it was permanently located on Corprew Avenue in 1955. He also led the junior college through several reorganizations until it became the independent Norfolk State College in 1969, and the title of president was bestowed upon him. The growth of Norfolk State was guided by

Above: The presidents of NSU.

Below: Summer Science Training Program, 1960.

Brooks' strong belief in community relationships and service. Under his leadership, students from diverse and sometimes poor socioeconomic backgrounds moved upward to academic and life achievements beyond their greatest dreams. Brooks remained at Norfolk State for thirty-seven years, from June 1938 to July 1, 1975.

- On July 1, 1975, Harrison B. Wilson, a former administrator at Fisk University, became the second president of Norfolk State. A native of Amsterdam, New York, Wilson received his doctorate from Indiana University. He firmly believed that the mission of Norfolk State was to serve everyone who was qualified. To that end, he added challenging programs, recruited outstanding faculty and administrators, acquired additional land for campus expansion, and diversified the student population by increasing national recruitment. During his tenure, he led the college to University status in 1979. Wilson successfully negotiated with the Office of Civil Rights during the higher education desegregation crises, obtained funding for a new administration building, the L. Douglas Wilder Performing Arts Center, five dormitories, and the William "Dick" Price Stadium, which holds thirty thousand spectators. Wilson served Norfolk State University from 1975-1997, twenty-two years.

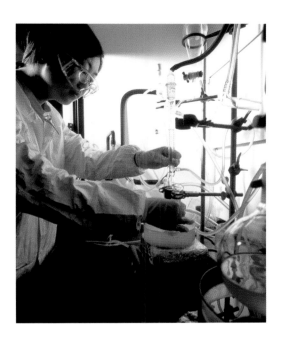

- Marie V. McDemmond became the third president at Norfolk State University on July 1, 1997. She received her doctorate in higher education administration and finance from the University of Massachusetts at Amherst. McDemmond eliminated a $6.5-million budget deficit, restored the fiscal integrity of the University, gained an increased level of funding from the General Assembly, increased fundraising in the community, and introduced a marketing campaign to improve the University's image. In a major agreement with Tidewater Community College, she developed a PASSPort program for students not meeting admission's standards at NSU. Through her conceptualization and implementation of a bold new initiative, Research and Innovations to Support Empowerment (RISE), Norfolk State is on the verge of introducing a new telecommunications infrastructure, which will stimulate economic development throughout the Hampton Roads area. McDemmond served the University for eight years, 1997-2005.
- Alvin J. Schexnider, who held the position of executive vice president, served as interim president of Norfolk State University from July 2005 through June 2006 after McDemmond resigned from the University for health reasons in March 2005.
- After an intensive and nationwide search, the NSU Board of Visitors held a special meeting on February 2, 2006, and selected Carolyn Winstead Myers, provost and vice chancellor for academic affairs at North Carolina A & T State University, as NSU's next president, effective July 1, 2006.

From 1935 to the present, Norfolk State University remains committed to providing a quality education to students from the Hampton Roads community, the Commonwealth, the nation, and around the world.

⚓

Above: The West Campus marquee.

Below: A NSU student conducting a scientific experiment.

CITY OF VIRGINIA BEACH

Above: Town Center at night.
COURTESY OF VIRGINIA BEACH CITY PHOTOGRAPHER,
CAROLE OSTE.

Below: Strawberry fields.
COURTESY OF VIRGINIA BEACH CITY PHOTOGRAPHER,
CAROLE OSTE.

There is archaeological evidence that European explorers and English Colonists were not the first people to set foot on Virginia soil. The evidence indicates that small bands of nomadic hunters roamed the area for thousands of years prior to the European encounters with Native Americans.

The first European landing occurred on April 26, 1607, when the vessels *Sarah Constant*, *Godspeed* and *Discovery* arrived in Virginia with 104 Englishmen aboard. The first landing consisted of twenty-eight men who disembarked near what is now Cape Henry. On the second day, another party went ashore, penetrating about eight miles inland. On the third day, the Englishmen sent a party northwest on a body of water that would become known in 1610 as Hampton Roads. On April 29, 1607, the settlers erected a cross at Chesapeake Bay and named the place Cape Henry in honor of King James' son, Henry, Prince of Wales.

The English settlers brought few personal possessions with them; however, they did bring the English systems of religion, law and local administration to Colonial Virginia.

Once the colony was established, adventurers were granted land to be settled and civilized. Plantations began to be established about 1634 and corporations were grouped into larger administrative units called shires (counties). The area, which would become Princess Anne County was initially part of Elizabeth City County and extended on both sides of Hampton Roads with a population of 1,670 persons. Princess Anne County was formed in 1691 from the eastern section of Lower Norfolk.

The modern history of the city may be traced from the 1880s when Colonel Marshall Parks, a prominent developer and entrepreneur, focused his attention on an area he named Virginia Beach.

Colonel Parks erected a wooden clubhouse at Seventeenth Street, the first structure in the area known then and now as "The Resort Strip." Railroad service from Norfolk to the new city began in 1883 and the first hotel opened in the early 1880s with accommodations for seventy-five guests. The Princess' Anne, a larger, more luxurious hotel with rooms for four hundred guests, opened around the turn-of-the-century and soon became a popular resort destination. The Princess Anne was destroyed by fire in 1907, one day before the city's first fire fighting equipment was placed into service.

Except for a treacherous dirt road, the railroad provided the only transportation between Virginia Beach and Norfolk until 1907. The first concrete roads were built in 1913 and, in 1921, Virginia Beach Boulevard, the first hard-surfaced road from Virginia Beach to Norfolk, was opened. More recently, Interstate 264 connected to the Virginia Beach

Expressway, which was built as a toll road. The Chesapeake Bay Bridge Tunnel, a major engineering feat, which crosses seventeen and one-half miles over the Bay to the Eastern Shore, opened in 1964.

The small resort community was incorporated in March 1906 as the Town of Virginia Beach. The first Mayor was B.P. Holland, who also served as postmaster and telegrapher. Holland built the town's first year-round brick home for his bride in 1895 and the structure, known as the DeWitt Cottage, is still in existence today.

Affluent society was attracted to Virginia Beach with the opening of the luxurious and exclusive Cavalier Hotel in 1927. The $2-million project featured a 75-by-25-foot heated pool and soon earned the reputation as the "Queen of the Beach." The famous wooden boardwalk, built in 1888, was replaced by a concrete walk in 1926 and replaced again in the early 1990s with a sea wall built by the Army Corps of Engineers. The first Boardwalk Art Show, which later became the Neptune Festival, was held in 1956 and is now considered one of the top twenty tourist attractions in the southeastern United States.

Virginia Beach's reputation as a "first class beach resort" continued to grow during the decades and, by the early 1950s, land in Princess Anne County adjacent to the City of Norfolk has become suburbanized. In 1959, Norfolk became the Commonwealth's largest city by annexing thirteen and one-half square miles of Princess Anne County with a population of thirty-eight thousand.

Fearful of losing their identity, as well as additional population and land, Virginia Beach residents began a long battle that ended in the merger of Virginia Beach and Princess Anne County in 1963.

Visitors are attracted to Virginia Beach for its beautiful beaches as well as the many historic treasures in the area.

Several of the homes built in the early years of Princess Anne County, including the 1732 Francis Land House, are open to the public and some are listed on the *National Historic Register*. The first Coast Guard Station has been relocated several times and currently serves as the Lifesaving Station Museum.

Several churches lend their historic significance, including Old Donation Episcopal Church, formed from the original Lynnhaven Parish in 1736. Several other churches date from the 1700s and early 1800s.

Virginia Beach continues to thrive as the largest city in the Commonwealth of Virginia with a population of approximately 450,000. "Pembroke Downtown," an unsuccessful development twenty-five-years ago, was revitalized and has blossomed into the "Town Center," a mixed-use neighborhood of offices, industry, multi-choice lodging, shopping and dining. The Resort Area now boasts the new multi-faceted Convention Center, the new Neptune Park and a hurricane-protection seawall.

Some of the background data for this profile was gleaned with permission from *The Beach Book*, a history compiled by the Virginia Beach Public Library.

Above: The original Cape Henry Lighthouse.
COURTESY OF VIRGINIA BEACH CITY PHOTOGRAPHER, CAROLE OSTE.

Below: Strawberries.
COURTESY OF VIRGINIA BEACH CITY PHOTOGRAPHER, CAROLE OSTE.

NEWPORT NEWS PUBLIC SCHOOLS

The purpose of public education has historically been to prepare children for citizenship, cultivate a skilled workforce, and create a culturally literate society. Newport News Public Schools has embraced these timeless values while effectively responding to major transformations in American society. The school district has created a community of learning that links all citizens in a shared mission for academic excellence.

During its early history, from the Revolutionary War through the Civil War, this area of the Virginia Peninsula, known then as Warwick County, has always strived to provide its children with a good education. Those efforts became more vigorous in 1870, when George Peek was appointed as Warwick County's first Superintendent of Public Schools. At the time the county was divided into three school districts—Newport, Denbigh, and Stanley. The City of Newport News and its schools experienced new growth with the arrival of railroad and shipyard tycoon, Collis Huntington. Newport News incorporated in 1896 and three years later opened three new schools. Warwick County was also growing, especially in the northern area called Denbigh. With the consolidation of Warwick County and Newport News in 1958, new schools and

Above: The area's rich history influences many aspects of school division life, such as the Colonial outfit worn by this student musician.

Below: Students gain a global perspective as part of their experience in Newport News Public Schools.

facilities were built at a furious pace. The administration building and Todd Stadium, along with fourteen new schools, opened during the 1960s.

Today, the Newport News School Division is the largest on the Virginia Peninsula, and among the largest in the Commonwealth, with 45 schools, pre-kindergarten through twelfth grade, and approximately 5,000 employees. Additionally, more than 3,000 volunteers contribute over 80,000 hours of their time annually to help improve the schools, and approximately 400 business partners work with schools and students to provide career guidance and workplace field trips, build outdoor classrooms and other services.

The Newport News School Board has adopted a dynamic six-year strategic plan called a "Blueprint for Excellence" that guides the division's efforts to improve academic achievement for all students. The five priority goals of the blueprint are:

- Improving academic achievement for all students while closing achievement gaps;
- Ensuring safe, orderly, nurturing schools and facilities that support quality teaching and learning;
- Maintaining efficient, effective, and accountable management of the school division;

- Supporting the recruitment, professional development, and retention of a quality workforce; and
- Promoting strong home, school, business and community relationships.

This dedication to excellence, led by the School Board and Superintendent Dr. Marcus J. Newsome, resulted in the selection of the Newport News School Board as the 2005 School Board of the Year by the Virginia School Boards Association. The award recognized the School Board for governance, promoting quality education, and Board development. The honored School Board members are Debbie H. "Dee" Johnston, chairman; Richard B. "Rick" Donaldson, Jr., vice chairman; Effie C. Ashe; Dr. William J. "Bill" Collins, III; Everette A. "Teddy" Hicks, Sr.; Michael W. "Mike" Wagner; and Dr. Patricia P. "Pat" Woodbury.

The implementation of the "Blueprint for Excellence" has resulted in a number of outstanding achievements for Newport News, including meeting one hundred percent of the adequate yearly progress standards mandated by the Federal No Child Left Behind Act and nearly all schools "fully accredited" under the Virginia Standards of Learning (SOLs) Program. The school division has raised achievement level in all areas while narrowing achievement gaps.

A significant number of students continue to receive recognition by the College Board as Advanced Placement (AP) Scholars, Scholars with Honor, or Scholars with Distinction. The number of students awarded National Merit and National Achievement Scholars continues to increase as well.

In recent years Newport News Public Schools has earned a number of national and state awards for excellence. All five high schools—Denbigh, Heritage, Menchville, Warwick, and Woodside—were recognized by *Newsweek* magazine as being among "the best high schools in America." Newport News Public Schools has received more National Blue Ribbon School awards from the U.S. Department of Education than any other school division in Virginia. These Blue Ribbon schools winners are Dunbar-Erwin Middle School, Huntington Middle School, Dutrow Elementary School, Denbigh High School,

Hines Middle School (winning twice), Gildersleeve Middle School, McIntosh Elementary School, Greenwood Elementary School, and Menchville High School (winning twice). Additionally, McIntosh Elementary School was named a 2005 "Distinguished Title I School" for Virginia, and Newport News Public Schools was named one of twenty "Tech Savvy" school divisions by *Scholastic Administrator* magazine.

Educators and staff members have earned numerous awards for excellence, including national board certification, awards for alternative certification, and state and regional awards for excellence in library media, defensive driving, and athletics. Of the 2,500 teachers on staff, more than 1,000 hold at least two college degrees.

"It is a fact of life in the twenty-first century that change is not an option" says school superintendent Dr. Marcus Newsome. "Students are different, families are different, society is different, and because this is so, public education faces unprecedented challenges. I am encouraged that Newport News Public Schools and its staff are responding to these challenges with creativity, innovation, and hard work."

For a more comprehensive look at Newport News Public Schools, please visit www.nnschools.org.

⚓

Above: Preparing students for success in the high-tech world is a key goal of the school division.

Below: Ensuring that every child has a safe and nurturing learning environment is a priority in Newport News Public Schools.

SENTARA HEALTHCARE

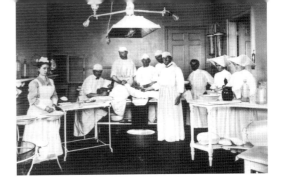

Sentara Healthcare, a not-for-profit health provider, got its start on June 1, 1888, as the twenty-five-bed Retreat for the Sick. The twenty-five bed hospital opened in Norfolk, with a simple mission: to give Hampton Roads the best medical care possible. While much has changed since those early days, Sentara remains committed to providing the best medical care. Today, Sentara is a nationally recognized leader in healthcare, offering services to more than two million residents in southeastern Virginia and northeastern North Carolina.

Sentara Healthcare operates more than 87 care giving sites, including 7 acute care hospitals with a total of 1,722 beds, 3 outpatient care campuses, 7 nursing centers, 3 assisted living centers, and over 265 primary care and multispecialty physicians. Sentara also offers award-winning health coverage plans, home health and hospice services, a school of health professions, physical therapy and rehabilitation services, and Nightingale—the region's first air ambulance service.

Here is a look at how far Sentara has come in 118 years:

- The Retreat for the Sick opened on June 1, 1888. In 1903 the facility relocated with a new name: Norfolk Protestant Hospital. Meanwhile, two other hospitals that would one day become Sentara facilities were also established. In 1891, Hampton General Hospital (Dixie Hospital) opened as a two-room facility and relocated in 1892 to expand. And in 1903,

Sarah Leigh Hospital, a twenty-eight-bed private facility, opened in Norfolk's Ghent.
- By 1936, Norfolk Protestant Hospital was renamed Norfolk General Hospital and Sarah Leigh Hospital was renamed Leigh Memorial Hospital.
- In 1951 the original Louise Obici Memorial Hospital in Suffolk was dedicated.
- The 1960s marked a number of firsts. In 1961, General Hospital of Virginia Beach, a twenty-five-bed hospital, began serving patients at the Virginia Beach Oceanfront. Across the water, construction began on Williamsburg Community Hospital. The new Williamsburg hospital opened in 1961 and replaced the antiquated Bell Hospital that had served the area since 1925. In 1965, Virginia Beach General Hospital relocated to its present site in Virginia Beach. Then in 1967, Norfolk General Hospital became the site of the first open heart surgery in the region.
- In 1972, Norfolk General and Leigh Memorial merged to form Medical Center Hospitals. In 1975, Bayside Hospital opened in Virginia Beach and in 1977, Leigh Memorial moved to its present site in Norfolk. In 1979, Norfolk General developed as a tertiary center.
- The decade of the 1980s brought more firsts to the organization. In 1981, Elizabeth Carr, America's first in-vitro baby, was delivered at Norfolk General. In 1982, Nightingale air ambulance service, home healthcare agency, nursing homes and urgent care centers all became part of Medical Center Hospitals. In 1983, Life Care was created. In 1984, Optima Health Plan HMO was introduced and in 1985, Norfolk General became a Level 1 Shock Trauma Center. In 1986 the system adopted the name Sentara. In 1988, Sentara merged with Hampton General Hospital. In 1989, Sentara performed Hampton Roads' first heart transplant surgery.
- During the 1990s, Sentara continued to grow and change. In 1991, Bayside Hospital in

Above: Sentara Healthcare, a not-for-profit health provider, got its start on June 1, 1888, as the twenty-five bed Retreat for the Sick. While much has changed since those early days, Sentara remains committed to providing the best medical care. Today, Sentara is a nationally recognized leader in healthcare, offering services to more than two million residents in southeastern Virginia and northeastern North Carolina.

Below: Sentara Heart Hospital, located on the campus of Norfolk General Hospital, is the region's only dedicated heart facility. It is unique to Southeastern Virginia and Northeastern North Carolina in that it provides comprehensive cardiac services— from diagnostics and interventional cardiology to open heart surgery and transplantation—all under one roof.

Virginia Beach was acquired. In 1994 Optima Family Care Medicaid HMO was introduced. In 1995, Sentara CarePlex Outpatient Center opened on the Peninsula. In 1996, Sentara established a formal affiliation with Williamsburg Community Hospital. In 1997 Optima Health received its first National Committee for Quality Assurance (NCQA) accreditation. And in 1998, Sentara merged with Tidewater Health Care.

- The Sentara Health Foundation was established in 1998 to improve health and quality of life and to further Sentara's not-for-profit mission of serving the community.
- In 2000, Sentara became the first in the nation to pioneer and develop eICU®, a remote monitoring system for intensive care.
- In 2001 Sentara was recognized nationally as the top integrated healthcare network in the country as published in *Modern Healthcare's* annual survey of the "Top 100 Integrated Healthcare Networks" in the nation.
- In 2002, Sentara CarePlex Hospital opened in Hampton and Sentara merged with Williamsburg Community Hospital.
- In 2002 the new Obici Hospital, located on Godwin Boulevard in Suffolk opened.
- In 2004, Sentara's Culture of Safety initiative was recognized by the American Hospital Association, which awarded Sentara Norfolk General the Quest for Quality award.
- In 2005, Sentara was awarded the 2005 John M. Eisenberg Patient Safety and Quality award from the Joint Commission on Accreditation of Healthcare Organizations (JCAHO) and the National Quality Forum.
- Also in 2005, for the eighth straight year, all commercial HMO products administered by Optima Health earned the highest NCQA accreditation.
- Sentara Heart Center and West Wing at Sentara Virginia Beach General Hospital opened in 2005.
- In 2006, Sentara Heart Hospital, the region's only dedicated heart hospital opened. And in April 2006, Obici Health System officially joined Sentara.
- Sentara continues to receive national recognition by consistently ranking among the nation's top one hundred integrated healthcare networks as published in *Modern*

Healthcare. Sentara is the only healthcare system to be ranked in the nation's top ten all nine years the survey has been conducted. Also, for the seventh year, the heart and heart surgery program at Sentara Norfolk General Hospital ranked in the top fifty of the nation's best hospitals in *U.S. News & World Report's* annual survey of America's best hospitals. And, for the third year, the urology program at Norfolk General ranked in the top fifty of the nation's best hospitals in the *U.S. News & World Report* annual survey.

The next decade will be characterized by growth and change—all dedicated to improving the health of the community. Examples of how Sentara is building for the future include:
- Sentara Port Warwick II, an ambulatory surgery center, opened in summer 2006;
- Sentara Williamsburg Regional Medical Center, a hospital and medical campus, opened in August 2006; and
- Sentara Princess Anne, a comprehensive health campus, opened in late summer 2006.

Sentara will continue to grow as one of the nation's leading healthcare organizations by creating innovative systems of care that help people achieve and maintain their best possible state of health.

For more information such as finding a physician, location of facilities, job opportunities or even to make a donation, please visit Sentara on the Internet at www.sentara.com.

⚓

Above: In 2000, Sentara launched the nation's first eICU. This groundbreaking telemedicine system is designed to reduce mortality and shorten ICU stays. The eICU uses two-way communication to connect critical care specialists in an off-site control center with staff and patients at numerous hospitals throughout Sentara's system. Combined with coverage by on-site intensivists, Sentara hospitals can meet The Leapfrog Group's ICU physician staffing standards. This innovative system of care continues to improve the outcomes of these most acutely ill patients.

Below: Sentara operates Southeastern Virginia's first hospital-based air ambulance service, Nightingale, which began in 1982 as the nation's thirty-eighth air medical program. Based at Sentara Norfolk General Hospital, Nightingale serves a 125-mile radius, flying as far north as Washington, D.C., as far south as Ocracoke Island, east to the Eastern Shore and west to Charlottesville, Virginia.

HAMPTON UNIVERSITY

One day in 1863, members of the Virginia Peninsula's black community gathered to hear a prayer answered. On that day, under the peaceful shade of a tree that became known as the Emancipation Oak, they heard the first reading in the South of President Lincoln's Emancipation Proclamation. The act accelerated demand for African-American education and the Emancipation Oak served as the first classroom for newly freed men and women eager for an education.

That passion for education led to the establishment, in 1868, of Hampton Normal and Agricultural Institute, known today as Hampton University. Brigadier General Samuel Chapman Armstrong, the twenty-nine-year-old son of missionary parents, founded the school during the reconstruction era. With the aid of the American Missionary Association, the school was established to train young African-American men and women to "go out to teach and lead their people" and to build a viable industrial system on the strength of self-sufficiency, intelligent labor and solid moral character. With this mandate, Hampton became an oasis of opportunity for the thousands of newly freed people.

Hampton Institute's most illustrious alumnus, Booker T. Washington (Class of 1875), founded Tuskegee Institute and

became a national leader. Washington also became a great orator and national figure who fought for the elimination of racism.

In 1878, Hampton established a formal education program for Native Americans, by beginning the institution's lasting commitment to serving a multicultural population. Hampton's historic Native American education program spanned more than forty years, with the last student graduating in 1923. Recent initiatives have attracted Native American students to renew their ties with Hampton.

In the early days, support for Hampton came from the Freedman's Bureau, Northern philanthropists and religious groups, with the first classroom building erected in 1870. The first baccalaureate degrees were awarded in 1922. Two years later, the school's name was changed to Hampton Institute, reflecting college-level accreditation. In 1984, Hampton's Board of Trustees formally adopted a university structure and changed the name to Hampton University, which today represents the unparalleled standard of excellence in American higher education.

With its deep commitment to multiculturalism, Hampton University serves students from diverse national, cultural and economic backgrounds. From its beginnings to the present, the school has enrolled students

⚓

Above: Brigadier General Samuel Chapman Armstrong, founder of Hampton University.

Below: Hampton Institute alumnus and founder of the Tuskegee Institute, Booker T. Washington.

from the continents of North and South America, Africa, Asia and Europe, including the countries of Gabon, Kenya, Ghana, Japan, China, Armenia, Great Britain, and Russia, as well as the Hawaiian and Caribbean Islands and numerous American Indian nations.

Placing its students in the center of its planning, Hampton University provides a holistic educational environment. Learning is facilitated by a range of educational offerings, a rigorous curriculum, excellent teaching, professional experiences, multiple leadership opportunities and an emphasis on the development of character.

In addition to the main campus in Hampton, the University operates the College of Virginia Beach in Virginia Beach and a branch of the Hampton University College of Continuing Education in Roanoke, Virginia.

The school currently enrolls more than 6,300 undergraduate and graduate students and employs a faculty and staff of more than 1,100. Student enrollment has grown by nearly ten percent since 2000.

The Southern Association of Colleges and Schools and the Department of Education of the Commonwealth of Virginia accredit the University. Various schools and departments within the University also maintain specialized accreditations of their own. The University holds membership in the Council of Graduate Schools, the Council of Independent Colleges in Virginia, and the American Council on Education.

Hampton University is comprised of seven schools—business, engineering and technology, liberal arts and education, nursing,

pharmacy, science, and journalism and communications—as well as a graduate college and a college of continuing education. The University offers thirty-eight bachelor's degree programs, fourteen master's degree programs, and doctoral degrees in nursing and physics, the doctor of physical therapy and the Pharm.D. in pharmacy.

In recent years, Hampton has added dozens of programs to offer students more choices among academic majors and professional careers, including music engineering technology, marine and environmental science, entrepreneurial studies, and sports management.

Research and public service are integral parts of Hampton's mission. In order to enhance scholarship and discovery, faculty members are engaged in writing, research and gamesmanship. Faculty, staff and students provide leadership and services to the University as well as to the global community.

The University's $200-million campaign for Hampton, "Dreaming No Small Dreams" was the most aggressive and ambitious fundraising campaign of any historically black college or university. After reaching the goal three years early, Hampton's Board of Trustee's increased the goal to $250 million. The campaign helped maintain the academic, cultural and historical prominence Hampton has enjoyed for more than a century.

Hampton University has been blessed through the years with many able, visionary leaders, including the founder, General Samuel Chapman Armstrong (1968-1893). Presidents who have provided exemplary direction since then include Drs. Hollis B. Frissell (1893-1917), James Grigg (1918-1929), Arthur Howe (1930-1940), George Phenix (1939), Malcolm MacLean (1940-1943), Ralph Bridgeman (1944-1948), Alonzo Moron (1949-1959), Jerome Holland (1960-1970), Roy D. Hudson (1970-1976), Carl M. Hill (1977-1978), and William R. Harvey (1978-present).

As it continues to achieve its mission, Hampton University offers exemplary programs and opportunities, which enable students, faculty and staff to grow, develop and contribute to society in a productive, useful manner.

Above: The Memorial Church, built in 1886, serves as a sanctuary for nondenominational religious services.

Below: The Emancipation Oak was the site of the first Southern reading of the Emancipation Proclamation.

VIRGINIA ASSOCIATION OF INDEPENDENT SCHOOLS OF HAMPTON ROADS

⚓

Above: Small class sizes allow faculty to focus on individual students.

Below: Students from various backgrounds enrich VAIS learning communities.

If you've ever considered independent private education for your child, read on…

Learning is very personal in independent, private schools. Challenging studies, balanced by individual attention and encouragement, help the young people in our care master core knowledge at an early age and acquire advanced skills that pave the way for success in college.

Small classes and dedicated teachers help students develop self-esteem, responsibility, and strong moral values. Diverse learning environments prepare students for careers in the global workplace of the twenty-first century. Independent private schools offer a strong sense of community beyond the classroom. Parental involvement, personal pride, and respect for others are cornerstones of an independent education.

Visit these Independent Schools and find the best education for your child. All of the following schools are accredited by the Virginia Association of Independent Schools and recognized by the Commonwealth of Virginia.

- Broadwater Academy
  P.O. Box 546, 3500 Broadwater Road
  Exmore, VA 23350
  (757) 442-9041
  www.broadwateracademy.org
  Broadwater Academy, founded in 1966, is a college-preparatory, co-educational day school that combines challenging academics with athletics, the arts and community service. Broadwater is committed to developing respectful, intellectual leaders. Prekindergarten through twelfth grade.

- Cape Henry Collegiate School
  1320 Mill Dam Road
  Virginia Beach, VA 23454
  (757) 481-2446 • www.capehenry.org

Cape Henry Collegiate School has over 1,000 students on a 30-acre campus. With a ten-to-one student/teacher ratio, emphasis is placed on the core values of community, opportunity, integrity, and scholarship. The school has a competitive athletic program, extensive summer offerings, financial aid, transportation, and a nationally recognized study abroad program. Prekindergarten through twelfth grade.

- Chesapeake Bay Academy
  821 Baker Road, Virginia Beach, VA 23462
  (757) 497-6200
  www.chesapeakebayacademy.org
  Chesapeake Bay Academy is the only licensed and accredited prekindergarten through twelfth grade independent school in Southeastern Virginia specifically dedicated to providing a strong academic program and individualized instruction for bright students with Learning Differences (LD) and Attention Disorders (ADHD).

- Christopher Academy
  3300 Cedar Lane, Portsmouth, VA 23703
  (757) 484-6776
  www.christopher-academy.org
  Christopher Academy, founded in 1970, is a nonsectarian school that provides a learning environment in which students are challenged to achieve their full potential. Our students develop a love of learning that lasts a lifetime. Prekindergarten through fifth grade.

- Hampton Roads Academy
  739 Academy Lane
  Newport News, VA 23602
  (757) 884-9148 • www.hra.org
  The purpose of Hampton Roads Academy is to culvitate a community of compassion and excellence that nurtures the whole student while preparing them for college and life. Sixth through twelfth grades.

- Hebrew Academy of Tidewater
  5000 Corporate Woods Drive, Suite 180
  Virginia Beach, VA 23462
  (757) 424-4327 • www.hebrewacademy.net

Hebrew Academy of Tidewater students graduate with a foundation in history, math, English and science, and Jewish history, language and values. HAT fosters intellectual curiosity and scholarship, and provides for successful higher education and lifelong Jewish learning. Preschool through eighth grade.

- Nansemond-Suffolk Academy
3373 Pruden Boulevard, Suffolk, VA 23434
(757) 539-8789 • www.nsacademy.org
Established in 1966, Nansemond-Suffolk Academy is a coeducational, college-preparatory day school serving prekindergarten through twelfth grade. NSA offers a dedicated faculty, extensive Advanced Placement (AP) courses, comprehensive extra-curricular offerings, an Honor System, and one hundred percent college placement.

- Norfolk Academy
1585 Wesleyan Drive, Norfolk, VA 23502
(757) 455-5582 • www.norfolkacademy.org
Chartered in 1728, Norfolk Academy enrolls 1,200 boys and girls in first through twelfth grades. The college preparatory program emphasizes character development, rigorous academics, athletics, fine arts, and community service. Academy graduates consistently attend the country's most selective colleges and universities.

- Norfolk Collegiate School
7336 Granby Street, Norfolk, VA 23505
(757) 480-1495
www.norfolkcollegiate.org
Founded in 1948, Norfolk Collegiate School provides a challenging college preparatory and AP curriculum that nurtures intellectual curiosity, stimulates personal growth, and encourages critical thinking. Athletics, service learning, character development and the arts enhance the supportive learning environment. Kindergarten through twelfth grade.

- Southampton Academy
26495 Old Plank Road
Courtland, VA 23837
(757) 653-2512
www.southamptonacademy.org
Southampton Academy, challenging academics—for college and career; team sports and the arts—for leadership, character,

integrity; the prospects and promise of a diverse community; the joy of learning; and the support of family and friends. Prekindergarten through twelfth grade.

- St. Andrew's Episcopal School
45 Main Street, Newport News, VA 23601
(757) 596-6261
www.standrewsschool.com
St. Andrew's Episcopal School is a Prekindergarten through fifth elementary school located in historic Hilton Village. Founded in 1946, SAES offers a challenging academic program, a Christian atmosphere, and resource classes in art, music, French, computers, physical education, and library.

- Tidewater Academy
217 Church Street, Wakefield, VA 23888
(757) 899-5401
www.tidewateracademy-pvt-va.us
Tidewater Academy provides its students a college-preparatory educational foundation that fosters a lifelong love of learning, while instilling the core values of family, community, and good citizenship, best preparing them for the challenges of an ever-changing world. Prekindergarten through twelfth grade.

- Virginia Beach Friends School
1537 Laskin Road
Virginia Beach, VA 23451
(757) 428-7534 • www.friends-school.org
Established in 1955, Virginia Beach Friends School emphasizes critical thinking, problem solving and creativity. Through a college-preparatory curriculum, VBFS helps students of all ages develop a love of learning and the skills needed for success. Prekindergarten through twelfth grade.

- The Williams School
419 Colonial Avenue, Norfolk, VA 23507
(757) 627-1383
www.thewilliamsschool.org
Since 1927, The Williams School has provided a learning environment offering academic rigor, building self-esteem and confidence, and instilling integrity and honor for students in Kindergarten through eighth grade. We offer extensive resources and expansive opportunities in technology, the arts, and athletics.

⚓

Above: Saxophone serenade, just one of the many performing arts opportunities.

Below: Sports participation teaches valuable lessons on and off the field.

AMERIGROUP
CORPORATION

⚓

AMERIGROUP Chairman and Chief Executive Officer Jeffrey L. McWaters.

When AMERIGROUP Corporation was founded in 1994, a deliberate decision was made to base the new managed healthcare company—with its envisioned national potential—in Virginia Beach, a vibrant part of historic Hampton Roads.

The belief was that the company would thrive in the region's dynamic business environment. Future employees would find the area's educational and recreational opportunities great for raising families. And the new venture would have room to prosper in the popular coastal location.

That decision fit well with the vision Jeffrey L. McWaters set forth in his business plan. A vision for a new kind of healthcare company, one that addressed critical needs which were not being met for a growing segment of the nation's population.

AMERIGROUP's chairman and CEO, McWaters had lived in Virginia Beach for several years. He knew that leading ideas thrived in Hampton Roads. After all, the region was host to the American experiment's first business incubator. And while America was an experiment with a vision, so was the establishment of AMERIGROUP.

Not all of McWaters' contemporaries in the mid-nineties agreed with the vision. But with tenacity and focus, he and his early associates won their point. They raised startup capital, developed networks and opened their first health plans in 1996.

Up until then, the disadvantaged were served primarily by inefficient and costly healthcare systems that saddled state governments with ballooning costs and spotty health outcomes.

And as McWaters foresaw, it was to get worse. His vast amount of experience in managed care—he had served as CEO of a managed behavioral health company before starting AMERIGROUP—lead to the idea that coordinating all aspects of individuals' healthcare would work for the population then served mainly by

Medicaid in an inefficient and costly open-ended system.

Riding the wave of that vision, by the end of its first decade AMERIGROUP had become the largest publicly traded company in the nation with a sole focus on coordinating the healthcare of people in programs like Medicaid and the Children's Health Insurance Program.

Its success sent a message; and if imitation is the sincerest form of flattery, then AMERIGROUP was complimented. Its early detractors learned that a new way of getting good healthcare to people was not only necessary but also a concept whose time had come.

Through preventive care for the well and efficient disease management for those who need it, members are given primary care physicians. From this medical home care, the possibilities were endless and able to go in any necessary direction under an informed, professional guidance of care managers.

Pregnancy shows how the system works. Actively reaching out to members, AMERIGROUP guides expectant moms into a prenatal care program that effectively reduces the rate of pre-term births, an expensive proposition that can lead to disastrous health consequences for many children born too soon.

Asthma and diabetes are also prevalent problems that need to be addressed early. In so doing, the company not only helps youngsters grow up healthier but also helps society avoid the burden of the alternative—higher adult healthcare costs. After all, diabetes alone is a growing problem among youngsters. Left untreated, it can lead to increased risk of heart disease, stroke, and other health risks later in life.

Having a doctor in an organized system of care for people who otherwise might have gone without—or used expensive alternatives like emergency rooms—has led to success for AMERIGROUP. It has been contagious, drawing national attention. At any given time, for example, the company is working with as many as twenty state governments, showing them how the AMERIGROUP brand of care can benefit members while saving scarce taxpayer healthcare dollars.

The company's message has resonated not only in state capitols but on Wall Street as well. AMERIGROUP went public in November 2001 and in 2003 began trading on the New York Stock Exchange. By early 2005, membership had grown beyond the one million mark, and AMERIGROUP was recognized by *Forbes* magazine as one of the "best managed companies in America." A few months later, it was listed by *Fortune* magazine among the top ten health insurance and managed care companies in the magazine's list of the country's one thousand largest companies.

AMERIGROUP forged success amidst a chorus of early naysayers who said it could not be done. It improved the techniques of the once-maligned managed care industry. And it has realized the early vision of its Mission Statement "…offering a continuum of education, access, care and outcome, resulting in lower costs, improved quality and better health status for Americans."

When the early English settlers sailed inland from Hampton Roads in 1607, their prospects were unknown. They would face extreme privation, yet they survived; and some of the same spirit that went with them survives today. AMERIGROUP is proud to share that spirit and their legacy.

The national headquarters for AMERIGROUP is located at 4425 Corporation Lane in Virginia Beach, Virginia. For more information, please visit www.amerigroupcorp.com.

AMERIGROUP's 'round-the-clock National Support Center adjacent to the busy Interstate 64 corridor in Virginia Beach, Virginia.

CITY OF HAMPTON

With its rich history, vibrant high-tech economy and growing reputation as a popular choice for conventions and tourism, the City of Hampton is fast becoming the most livable city in Virginia.

Hampton, established in 1610, is America's oldest continuous English-speaking settlement. Those roots, however, go even deeper. Captain John Smith's company landed at Point Comfort in 1607 and later established Jamestown upriver. In 1610 the English colonists settled on the site of the Kecoughtan Indian Village, and this date marks the first English-speaking settlement on land that would eventually become the City of Hampton.

That same year, the settlers founded Elizabeth City parish, which remains North America's oldest continuous Anglican parish. The parish's present site, St. John's Episcopal Church, was constructed in 1728 and was one of the few buildings left standing following the burning of Hampton by Confederate troops in 1861.

Landmarks of the past mingle with exciting innovations of the future throughout Hampton. The city is home to the NASA Langley Research Center, Langley Air Force Base, Fort Monroe, the Hampton Coliseum and Hampton University, one of the top hundred universities in the nation. Hampton focuses on projects to revitalize the entire city, including redevelopment plans for Buckroe, Kecoughtan, downtown Hampton, Coliseum Central and Phoebus.

NASA first took flight in Hampton and the city is home to the new National Institute of Aerospace, which will be a leader in research for the aerospace industry. Hampton is second only to Silicon Valley, California in having the highest per capita concentration of scientists, engineers and technicians. From NASA's Technology Commercialization Program to Old Dominion University's Langley Full-Scale Wind Tunnel, companies have discovered that Hampton has vast resources for private use. Companies such as AMSEC, Sverdrup, Computer Science Corporation, Howmet Casting, Lockheed Martin and Nextel have selected Hampton as an ideal place to do business.

In addition, Hampton boasts a strong military and technology presence. Fort Monroe, on whose moat-encircled stone wall construction began in 1819, is home to the Army Training & Doctrine Command. Langley Air Force Base, first established as Langley Field in 1917, is home of the First Fighter Wing. NASA Langley Research Center, where America's first astronauts were trained, continues to be a major center for aviation research.

As an education center, the city is home to Hampton University, dating to 1868, offering numerous bachelor, master and Ph.D. programs. The university has played a vital role in Hampton's economic and cultural development. The city also hosts Thomas Nelson Community College, a two-year institution offering associate's degree curricula.

Above: The downtown Hampton waterfront.

Below: The Hampton Roads Convention Center.

In May 2005, Hampton opened the Hampton Roads Convention Center, which firmly established Hampton and its surrounding offerings as a national meeting destination. A dramatic, sail-like tensile structure at the center's entrance salutes Hampton's maritime heritage.

Visitors and residents alike enjoy the Virginia Air & Space Center and the Riverside 3D IMAX® Theater. The visitor center for NASA Langley and Langley Air Force Base, the center features a full-size DC-9 aircraft, air and space artifacts, and more than one hundred hands-on, entertaining exhibits. Next door along the waterfront, the Hampton Carousel, having entertained riders for nearly a century, is housed in a weather-protected pavilion.

The Cousteau Society's U.S. headquarters, harbor tours, an arts center and historic landmarks lure visitors with entertaining offerings complimented by eclectic restaurants and small town charm. The city's districts present a delightful variety of antique and specialty shops unique to Hampton. Major retail favorites may also be found in Hampton at Coliseum Mall, soon to become the Peninsula Town Center, and the Power Plant of Hampton Roads, which is anchored by Bass Pro Shops Outdoor World.

Major annual entertainment events include the Hampton Blackbeard Festival and Hampton Jazz Festival, both in June, and Hampton Bay

Days in September. Sports fans are drawn to the NASCAR races at Langley Speedway and the Hampton Cup Regatta, which celebrated its eightieth anniversary in 2006.

Other Hampton attractions include the beautiful, relatively uncrowded Chesapeake Bay beaches and the novel historic area of Phoebus. Buckroe Beach is a favorite spot for sunbathing, swimming, paddle boating and fishing. The nearby Grandview Nature Preserve has over two miles of beaches in a 578-acre preserve and estuary. Phoebus is the location of the four-hundred-seat American Theatre. Built in 1912 the theater was

renovated and reopened in 2000 to feature year-round performances. Eclectic shopping and dining are also found here.

The livability of Hampton's communities received national attention due to the city's efforts to ensure that children are born healthy and enter school ready to learn. The Hampton Family Resource Project received favorable reviews in *Newsweek* and other national publications, including *Sesame Street Parents* magazine, which named Hampton "the most family-friendly city in America."

Hampton was named an All-America City by the National Civic League in 2002 and in 2005 received a nod as one of the "Best 100 Communities for Young People."

With nearly 150,000 residents, 650,000 yearly visitors, and 14,000 college and university students, Hampton is truly a city on the move.

⚓

Top: Hampton presents unique boutique shopping.

Middle: Memorial Church on the Hampton University Campus.

Bottom: Quarters of Lieutenant Robert E. Lee at historic Fort Monroe.

EASTERN VIRGINIA MEDICAL SCHOOL

Eastern Virginia Medical School is the only school of medicine in America founded as the result of a grassroots effort by the local community.

Planning for the medical school started in the early 1960s as the region turned its attention to improving the quality of medical in the region. The idea of a medical school in Hampton Roads gained momentum in 1964 when local citizens persuaded the Virginia General Assembly to create a medical authority charged with starting a school.

Fundraising for the proposed school began in 1970 when a group of community leaders launched a $15 million campaign. By the time Eastern Virginia Medical School matriculated its first class in 1973, the EVMS Foundation had attracted $17 million in gifts and pledges.

The school had also attracted much-needed medical specialists to a region where many basic services were lacking.

Today, 2,300 physicians hold degrees from EVMS, including 500 who practice in Hampton Roads and 300 who practice in other areas of Virginia. In addition, the school has a growing health professions program, with programs in biomedical sciences, public health, and other specialties.

Approximately 180,000 people have received medical care from physicians and health professionals at EVMS.

Located in Norfolk, EVMS is part of the Eastern Virginia Medical Center campus, which contains two hospitals, Sentara Norfolk General Hospital and Children's Hospital of The King's Daughters and a number of EVMS-related institutes and centers.

Sentara Norfolk General Hospital is the region's primary tertiary care center and Children's Hospital is a full-service, acute care facility, which serves as the regional referral center for pediatrics.

Campus facilities include Lewis Hall, EVMS's primary education and research facility, named for Richmond philanthropists and early EVMS supporters Frances and Sydney Lewis.

The Edward E. Brickell Medical Sciences Library is a state-of-the-art facility with an advanced information infrastructure allowing access to a host of digital resources. The library houses the school's original Moorman Library collection, a computer lab, computer classroom, historical collections, archives, and group and individual study seating.

Hofheimer Hall, named in honor of Elise and Henry Clay Hofheimer, II, houses the Office of the President, and various clinical offices for members of EVMS Health Services.

Fairfax Hall houses a variety of clinical, educational and administrative offices; the Jones Institute for Reproductive Medicine is home to EVMS's renowned division of reproductive medicine; and South Campus Building houses the Center for Pediatric Research and the Leonard R. Strelitz Diabetes Institutes.

Smith-Rogers Hall was originally part of Leigh Memorial Hospital and served as EVMS's temporary home in the early '70s while Lewis Hall was being constructed.

Today, it houses EVMS administrative offices.

EVMS works in partnership with hospitals, physicians, and clinics throughout the region, providing students and residents with a broad base of clinical experience. These educational partnerships spread the benefits of an academic medical center throughout the region, improving the quality of life and the quality of healthcare for the entire community.

Students at EVMS are immersed in their disciplines while attending a manageably sized school with a wide range of programs, approachable teachers, and a homey atmosphere that encourages interaction with students from other disciplines. The school offers a wide variety of educational programs including medical doctor, Ph.D. in biomedical sciences, master of physician assistant, master of public health, and others.

The Commission on Colleges of the Southern Association of Colleges and Schools to award the doctor of medicine degree, master's degrees, doctoral degrees, and certificates accredits EVMS.

Research activities at EVMS include an Epidemiology-Biostatistics Core, which fosters excellence in research through faculty with epidemiologic and biostatistical expertise who provide consultation and education to the academic health center and develop independently funded research projects.

The National Center for Collaboration in Medical Modeling and Simulation is a joint project of EVMS, Old Dominion University and a variety of academic, governmental and commercial partners. The center works to improve the quality and quantity of medical care available to U.S. military forces.

In addition, EVMS offers special programs in such areas as cardiovascular and renal research, pediatric research, contraception research and development, and geriatrics and gerontology. The Clinical Research Center conducts clinical investigations of new medications and therapies, particularly in the field of women's health.

The school's Leonard R. Strelitz Diabetes Institutes provides education, in-patient and outpatient care and research focused on minimizing complications of diabetes and finding a cure based on stimulating the growth of new islet cells.

A seventeen member Board of Visitors governs EVMS. The Cities of Chesapeake, Hampton, Newport News, Norfolk, Portsmouth, Suffolk, and Virginia Beach appoint eleven of the members. The EVMS Foundation Board of Directors appoints the remaining six members. The president of HVMS is Harry T. Lester.

Besides boosting the Hampton Roads economy by more than a half billion dollars annually and creating more than 10,500 jobs, EVMS has put the Hampton Roads region on the map internationally for biomedical research. Reproductive medicine and research in pediatrics, geriatrics, diabetes and cancer are among the areas where EVMS excels.

For more information about Eastern Virginia Medical School, check the school's website at www.evms.edu.

THE VIRGINIAN-PILOT

Above: The Virginian-Pilot scooped the entire country with its coverage of the Wright Brothers' first flight at Kitty Hawk, North Carolina.

Top, right: Samuel L. Slover.

In 1900, a man from Tennessee had a dream that is embodied today in *The Virginian-Pilot*, a daily newspaper that is the source for news and information in South Hampton Roads, Virginia, and Northeast North Carolina.

But Samuel L. Slover's path wasn't easy.

Slover came to Virginia as an advertising salesman for a New York trade journal and quickly realized there were few newspapers of consequence in the state. Sensing an opportunity, Slover began selling advertising for the Richmond paper. He was so effective he was offered half interest in a Peninsula paper—if he would pull it out of debt within a year.

Despite his success there, his ultimate goal was to own and operate a newspaper in South Hampton Roads. Through a series of purchases and mergers, he built a daily paper that would become *The Virginian-Pilot*. At the same time, he established a standard of journalistic excellence which continues to this day.

In fact, *The Virginian-Pilot* scooped the entire country with an account of the Wright Brothers' first flight at Kitty Hawk, North Carolina. *The Pilot* offered the story to twenty-one newspapers throughout the United States, but it seemed so far-fetched that only five asked to review it. Of those five, only two actually printed the story.

By 1954, Slover had laid the foundation on which his nephew, Frank Batten, would build Landmark Communications. Educated at The

University of Virginia and the Harvard Graduate School of Business, Batten earned his newspaper stripes in *The Pilot*'s news, advertising and circulation departments.

Soon after he succeeded his uncle as publisher, Batten faced an enormous challenge. It was a time when the area was wracked with "massive resistance" against school desegregation. Calm, persistent editorials championing the Supreme Court's ruling in favor of integration won *The Pilot* a Pulitzer Prize in 1960.

In 1963, Batten began implementing his long-term expansion plan, acquiring other newspapers, as well as cable, television and radio stations.

Reflecting its growth and diversification, the company changed its name to Landmark Communications in 1967.

But through the years, the commitment to journalistic excellence never wavered. In 1985, *The Pilot* was awarded a second Pulitzer Prize for its investigation of a Chesapeake city official's personal use of public funds.

Today, *The Virginian-Pilot* is the state's largest newspaper, with more than 758,000 adult readers every week. It is the flagship of Landmark Communications, a diversified media company with interests in newspapers, specialty publications, broadcasting and cable, including The Weather Channel.

The Virginian-Pilot may be viewed on the Internet at www.pilotonline.com.

CITY OF NORFOLK

When John Smith traveled down the Bay in 1608 to check out the colonists' rumored neighbors, the Chesapeakes and the Nansemonds, he sailed up a "narrow river" (today's Elizabeth) to the place where Norfolk now stands. There he saw two or three little garden plots, with houses and shores overgrown with the largest pines he had ever seen in the country. After exploring and visiting tribes, he returned to Jamestown.

Four hundred years later, Norfolk still sports gardens, including the beautiful Norfolk Botanical Garden. No longer a side trip for explorers, Norfolk is Virginia's water gateway to the world, home to the Atlantic Fleet, the North American Headquarters of NATO, one of the East Coast's busiest container ports, which spans the waterfronts of Norfolk, Portsmouth and Newport News, and a growing cruise port. Today the tallest objects on Norfolk's shoreline are high-rise condos and office towers providing a dramatic backdrop to the working harbor into which schooners still sail.

Norfolk owes her existence to the water. Along its sixty-six square miles, Norfolk sports 140 miles of shoreline. In 1680, England's King Charles II ordered the purchase of fifty acres of land along the waterfront in each of Virginia's then twenty counties to establish a port system. Before the act was rescinded in 1681, several counties took advantage of the opportunity to establish towns. Norfolk Towne was established by a deed recorded on August 16, 1682.

Events occurring in Norfolk waters have had worldwide impact. It was here that the first battle between ironclad warships the USS *Monitor* and the CSS *Virginia* (formerly *Merrimac*)—was fought in 1862. Naval aviation was born at Willoughby Beach in 1910. The nation's first ferry service ran on the Elizabeth River in 1636; and Operation Torch, the World War II Allied invasion of North Africa, was planned and practiced at Ocean View.

If the early settlers bypassed Norfolk on the way to Jamestown, Norfolk was very much at the center of the 1907 Jamestown Exposition celebrating the dawn of a new age of manufacture and technology, as well as curiosities from around the world. Many of the original Exposition buildings still stand in what is now Naval Station Norfolk.

A hundred years later, Norfolk is the cultural, financial, educational and artistic center of southeastern Virginia, home to four institutions of higher learning, the Virginia Opera, Virginia Stage Company, Chrysler Museum of Art and the International Arts Festival. Once a footnote in Smith's journals, this sparkling city on the harbor annually draws millions to learn, to live, and to celebrate life.

⚓

Above: Once a footnote, now a sparkling destination on the river—Norfolk today.

Below: The Jamestown Exposition, c. 1907.

HAMPTON HISTORY MUSEUM

The façade of the Hampton History Museum proudly bears the words of Captain John Smith that describe his welcome by the Kecoughtan Indians in 1608. Quotations about Hampton from other prominent persons, including Thomas Jefferson and Booker T. Washington, are displayed in the rotunda that introduces Hampton's four hundred year history.

Above: The Hampton History Museum and Visitor Center.

Below: McMenamin & Co. logo, 1878. It was once one of the largest crab factories in the United States.

A rich display of artifacts and images combine to tell how Kecoughtan, once a part of Chief Powhatan's empire, became a fortified English village and then a busy seaport. Visitors enter a ship's hold loaded with imports and exports. On leaving the ship they are confronted with the head of Blackbeard, the pirate who harassed Virginia shipping.

Entering the ruins of Civil War Hampton, the visitor grasps the enormity of the destruction as voices from the past compare the pretty pre-war village to the burnt-out shell. How Hampton then became "crabtown" is shown, along with the beginnings of Hampton University and the air base and research facilities at Langley.

The Museum traces its beginnings to 1952 and was housed in a succession of buildings until an enthusiastic group of leading citizens emerged to form the Hampton History Museum Association. They sought support for a more comprehensive history facility. With encouragement from a positive feasibility study funded by City Council, the Association, composed entirely of volunteers, undertook the tasks of producing a building design and raising the funds to construct it. The first director was hired in 2002 and an impressive two-story structure was constructed in downtown Hampton on Old Hampton Lane.

The $5-million, 18,000-square-foot facility, designed by Glave and Holmes Associates of Richmond, opened on May 3, 2003. The facility includes meeting rooms, a fully equipped kitchen for catered events, and a gift shop.

With more than seven thousand square feet allotted for exhibits, nine permanent and one changing gallery tell the exciting history of Hampton, which so closely parallels that of the nation. The building also houses the Hampton Visitor Center. In addition to tours of the facility, the Museum offers educational programs, workshops, lectures and exhibits for both children and adults. A strong corps of volunteers supports the Museum staff in all aspects of the Museum's operation and mission.

The Museum continues to grow and improve as a vibrant part of the community. An additional two thousand square feet of space will store the bulk of the city's extensive artifact and archival collection and, for the first time, the Museum and collections will be brought together.

Today, more than ever, the Hampton History Museum is accomplishing its mission of maintaining an educational and research center for "collection, exhibition, interpretation, preservation, and promotion of the vast historic resources of the city."

Peninsula Catholic High School is a regional high school of the Catholic Diocese of Richmond. Its mission is to develop young men and women who are spiritually, intellectually, socially and morally mature.

The school achieves its mission by providing a disciplined and nurturing college preparatory environment rooted in the Catholic tradition. Peninsula Catholic, open to students in grades eight through twelve, strives to meet the needs of students of all levels. Emphasis is placed on teaching skills for lifelong learning to help students become critical thinkers and problem-solvers. The goal of every academic area is to prepare students to be successful in the workplace and life.

Peninsula Catholic began in 1903 as St. Vincent de Paul School, the first Catholic girls' school in Newport News. It belonged to St. Vincent de Paul Catholic Church and operated in a two-story brick building on Thirty-third Street. Four Sisters of Charity of Nazareth, Kentucky, arrived to staff the school three days before it opened.

During the first year the school enrolled 104 girls and held its first graduation in 1910 with three graduates. A private Catholic boys academy closed its doors in 1929 and St. Vincent became a co-educational school.

In 1931, supporters dedicated a new school on Thirty-fourth Street. The grade school occupied the lower floors and the high school occupied the second floor. In 1945, Monsignor Gill announced that the school would be tuition-free for parish children. Enrollment soared to its highest level ever—704 students by 1953.

In 1960, grades eight to twelve were named St. Vincent's Central High School to recognize the fact that students came from the entire Peninsula. At that time, school ownership transferred from St. Vincent Church to the Diocese. In 1966 the school's name was changed to Peninsula Catholic High School. Three years later, the Diocesan School Board ordered the elementary school closed.

The school introduced a community service program in 1975 and received accreditation from the Southern States Association of Colleges and Schools in 1986.

Bishop Sullivan purchased property on Harpersville Road in 1989 for construction of a new school, which opened in 1995.

Peninsula Catholic, which celebrated its centennial in 2003, participates in the Tidewater Conference of Independent Schools. In 2005, a second gym, weight center, additional science lab, an additional computer lab and four new classrooms were dedicated. Future plans call for a fine arts center, additional classrooms, more administrative space and expanded outdoor athletic facilities.

The Catholic identity of Peninsula Catholic is apparent in the religious studies classes, daily prayer, liturgical worship, retreats and service program. Faith and values are integrated throughout the curriculum and school life, while service to the community exposes students to the needs of others and instills in them a spirit of openness and giving to others.

Peninsula Catholic High School is located at 600 Harpersville Road in Newport News. Additional information on Peninsula Catholic High School—"Home of the Knights"—may be found on the Internet at www.peninsulacatholic.com.

PENINSULA CATHOLIC HIGH SCHOOL

Left: Peninsula Catholic High School on Harpersville Road in Newport News from 1995 to present.

Below: Peninsula Catholic High School (formerly known as St. Vincent de Paul School and St. Vincent Central High School) on Thirty-fourth Street in Newport News from 1931 to 1995.

ARMED SERVICES YMCA IN HAMPTON ROADS

Above: Civil War reenactors with a U.S. Christian Commission coffee wagon. The wagon is owned by the Armed Services YMCA.

Below: A dedicated staff and volunteers help the Armed Services YMCA of Hampton Roads serve more nearly 4,000 military families each year.

The world has changed dramatically since YMCA volunteers first went onto the battlefields of the Civil War at the encouragement of President Abraham Lincoln to provide physical and spiritual comfort to the troops.

With the outbreak of the Civil War in 1861, the normal activities of the Association were interrupted and its energies and resources largely devoted to the support of the Army through creation of the United States Christian Commission. Every YMCA member who worked for the Commission during the Civil War was a volunteer. Commission volunteers provided support to soldiers in the field many ways, from coffee and tea to spiritual help to medical assistance.

Since then, through the Spanish-American War, two World Wars, Korea, Vietnam, and more recently in the Middle East, Somalia, Haiti and the Balkans, the Armed Services YMCA has continued to serve military men and women and their families.

The oldest ASYMCA branch with a continuous existence began as an Army YMCA at Fort Monroe, Virginia. Today, the Fort Monroe Army YMCA has evolved into a branch of the Armed Services YMCA of the USA, serving all services well beyond the physical confines of Fort Monroe.

The ASYMCA of the USA operates thirty-four branches or affiliates for young men and women serving far from their hometown friends and families. These branches and affiliates are located in major concentrations of military throughout the United States. Among these centers is the ASYMCA of Hampton Roads, with six locations in Virginia Beach and Norfolk.

The mission of the ASYMCA of Hampton Roads is to improve the quality of life for junior enlisted military personnel, and their families, through values oriented social, recreational, personal development, crisis prevention, and deployment separation and child development programs.

The childcare program includes preschool for children two through five years of age, kindergarten before- and after-school care, and before- and after-school care for children through the fifth grade. Operation Hero provides after-school mentoring and tutoring for children ages six through twelve who are experiencing the temporary school related difficulties sometimes faced by children of military families.

Other services provided by the ASYMCA of Hampton Roads include a food pantry with commissary gift certificates to assist military families experiencing financial difficulties, and an airport lounge at Norfolk International Airport where military personnel may relax, obtain information, even enjoy a movie.

The ASYMCA also provides family support group meetings to keep spouses informed of events during ship deployments.

A dedicated staff and volunteers help the Armed Services YMCA of Hampton Roads serve more nearly 4,000 military families each year.

Local and corporate support is crucial to the mission of the ASYMCA. Nearly forty percent of the organization's operating budget comes from local United Way and corporate support.

The remaining sixty percent of the budget comes from a variety of sources including programs that require modest fees—childcare, for example—and public contracts.

With your support, we are able to build programs and services that help our young men and women in the military remain strong and healthy. Military leaders often tell us how much they need and appreciate this vital support.

The ASYMCA is a bridge between military and civilian communities, building strong kids, strong families, and strong communities in support of the Armed Forces and the ongoing sacrifices required of military men and women and their families.

In 1978, Dr. Pat Robertson established Regent University as a place where Christian men and women could be trained to the highest academic standards and become Christian leaders who would engage key cultural sectors including business, communication and the arts, divinity, education, government, law, leadership, and psychology and counseling. Regent University has since emerged as a world-class institution—a leading center of Christian thought and action that attracts some of the highest-caliber students from around the world.

Nearly four hundred years ago Robertson's ancestor, Reverend Robert Hunt, landed in Virginia and planted a cross on the historic landing place in Virginia Beach, just a few miles from the present campus of Regent University. When Robertson and his family moved to Virginia Beach more than thirty years ago, his historical family tie to the Hampton Roads area came full circle.

With a father who served thirty-four years in the U.S. House of Representatives and Senate, Robertson saw the need for a Christian graduate school that would blend Christian values with solid academic and professional training. In 1977 land was cleared for Regent University's seven hundred-acre campus and the following year seventy-seven communication and arts students began classes in modest, rented facilities nearby.

Word spread quickly that Regent had captured the spirit of America's first universities—schools that were dedicated to applying biblical principles to all of academic and professional life. In less than a decade, enrollment grew to eight hundred students and six additional disciplines were added. Today, Regent University has more than nine thousand alumni and more than four thousand students currently earning their bachelor's, master's and doctoral degrees.

Regent University is surrounded by beauty and steeped in history. The stately campus is located between the pristine beaches of the Atlantic Ocean and the Virginia countryside once traveled by the great thinkers and committed believers who established this

nation. These early Americans deeply believed that their contributions would help establish an important legacy. Following the example of our forefathers, Regent University is establishing a powerful national and international legacy of principled leadership and courageous faith.

Regent has attracted such distinguished faculty as former U.S. Attorney General John Ashcroft, who serves as distinguished professor of law and government; former Regent University President David Gyertson, who now serves as distinguished professor of leadership formation and renewal; and Charles W. Dunn, dean of the Robertson School of Government, whose former posts include serving as special assistant to the minority whip in the U.S. House of Representatives and deputy director of the Republican Conference in the House.

Degree programs at Regent University blend solid professional training with sound biblical principles. From defending the Pledge of Allegiance to being the first Virginia Beach native elected as state attorney general, Regent alumni are truly involved in world-changing endeavors. Regent graduates are CEOs and teachers, state senators and media professionals, judges and pastors, entrepreneurs and counselors—all fulfilling significant roles that extend the mission that brought them to Regent University.

VIRGINIA ARTS FESTIVAL

British colonists found a new world in Jamestown. And each spring, the historical area and all of Hampton Roads welcome a world of performers to the Virginia Arts Festival.

Since 1997, the Festival has treated Virginians and visitors to a stellar array of musicians, actors, dancers and visual artists. From the Royal Shakespeare Company to Yo-Yo Ma, from the Chamber Music Series to the grandeur of the Virginia International Tattoo, there's something for every taste, every year. Itzhak Perlman, the Martha Graham Dance Company, Van Cliburn and Joshua Bell are just a few of the Festival's high-profile guests.

In just a decade, the Festival has established itself as one of the premier cultural events on the East Coast. It has nearly as many venues as the Olympic Games, with performances spread out over a seventy-mile region extending from Cape Charles on the Eastern Shore to Norfolk to Williamsburg. Artists also participate in extensive educational activities including master classes, workshops and symposia throughout Hampton Roads. More than 75,000 people attended the Festival's 130 public performances in 2005 and 28,000 students experienced its 79 outreach programs.

The profile of Hampton Roads is raised every year as national media cover the Festival and its artists. *A Prairie Home Companion* with Garrison Keillor has broadcast live from the festival three times. Concerts from the Chamber Music Series led by André-Michel Schub are broadcast nationally on NPR's flagship program *Performance Today*. And the Festival's CD recordings include Mozart flute quartets with the Miami String Quartet and flutist Debra Wendells Cross, and *Peter and the Wolf: A Special Report* with the Virginia Symphony Orchestra, music director JoAnn Falletta and the staff of NPR's *All Things Considered*.

A signature Festival event is the Virginia International Tattoo. CBS *Sunday Morning* called it, "a spectacle of music and might" and fans of all ages thrill to the pageantry of marching bands, massed pipes and drums, Scottish dancers, vocalists and more. More than 22,000 people attend the Virginia International Tattoo every year, with 6,000 young people at the annual student matinee.

A major initiative of the Festival is boosting Hampton Roads tourism during the spring "shoulder season." The Festival works collaboratively with municipalities, convention and visitor bureaus and corporate partners, particularly local hotel and restaurant partners, in attracting visitors to the region. A recent survey revealed that about twenty-two percent of Festival attendees come from outside Hampton Roads; in its first decade, the Festival has had a $50-million economic impact on the region.

For more information about the Virginia Arts Festival, please visit www.vafest.com, call 877-741-ARTS, or visit the Festival box office at MacArthur Center, downtown Norfolk.

Above: André-Michel Schub.

Below: Virginia International Tattoo.

Old Dominion University promotes the advancement of knowledge and the pursuit of truth on a local, national and international basis. The university takes its unique character from the Hampton Roads area, a complex of seven major cities that together serve as a microcosm of the opportunities and challenges of contemporary America.

Hampton Roads is a major center for research and development and a home for extensive scientific and technological activities in marine science, aerospace, ship design and construction, advanced electronics and nuclear physics. Old Dominion University has played an important role in the development of these fields and, in turn, businesses and individuals in these areas have contributed to Old Dominion's success and growth.

Old Dominion University's Virginia Modeling, Analysis and Simulation Center (VMASC) meets the growing demand for simulation experts in government, industry and academia by offering master's and doctoral programs. The programs, combined with the highly successful research activities in the field, continue to be an essential component of the region, accounting for more than 4,000 local jobs and contributing nearly $500 million to the Hampton Roads economy each year.

The area provides special opportunities for science and engineering faculty to emphasize research and graduate programs in marine science, aerospace and advanced electronics. Global ocean studies and cooperative research at NASA receive particular attention, as university researchers collaborate with U.S. and foreign engineers and scientists. Programs in public administration, education, the social sciences and health professions address urban issues in these areas.

The newly constructed Innovation Research Park @ ODU, an $80 million economic development project, will bring together university intellectual capital, faculty and students with private-sector companies to pursue research, technology development and business-creation opportunities. Located in the seventy-five-acre, mixed-use University Village, the research park will serve as the ideal location for high tech companies.

OLD DOMINION UNIVERSITY

Old Dominion offers 67 bachelor's, 65 master',s and 26 doctoral degrees in a wide array of fields, all of which meet national standards of excellence. Every undergraduate student follows a general education program designed to develop the intellectual skills of critical thinking and problem solving and to encompass the breadth of understanding needed for personal growth and achievement and for responsible citizenship.

The university enrolls a student body with a diversity of age, gender, ethnic, religious, social and national backgrounds, including some 1,200 students from 108 countries. In recent years, Old Dominion has produced a Rhodes Scholar, a Truman Scholar, and three *USA Today* All-Academics.

In celebrating its seventy-fifth year, Old Dominion University is old enough to value tradition yet young enough to facilitate change. The university is ready to meet the challenges of the twenty-first century through a spirit of creative experimentation, innovation, research and technology.

HAMPTON ARTS COMMISSION/ THE AMERICAN THEATRE

⚓

Above: The American Theatre in 1930.

Below: The interior of The American Theatre as it appears today.

The Hampton Arts Foundation was established in 1994 by then Vice Mayor T. Melvin Butler to facilitate private, corporate and foundation giving to the arts. Hampton Arts, the trade name for the Hampton Arts Commission and the Hampton Arts Foundation, is now one of the leading arts institutions in Southeastern Virginia. Consistently drawing the highest praise for the quality, diversity and reach of its programs and exhibitions, Hampton Arts is a model among public/private arts councils.

The Hampton Arts Foundation owns The American Theatre and the Charles H. Taylor Arts Center, two of Hampton's most historic buildings. Both have been painstakingly renovated and are now vibrant centers for the performing and visual arts as well as for numerous educational programs.

The American Theatre, built in 1908, has taken its place as a leading presenter of the very best in the performing arts from throughout the world. Prior to its purchase and a $2.9-million renovation, Hampton Arts offered a world-class series of 6 to 8 performances in rented facilities throughout the City of Hampton. Now that the theatre has been successfully and artistically renovated, those numbers have increased dramatically.

During the 2006-07 year, Hampton Arts presented more than fifty different events and attractions in the theatre. Attendance is growing with each successive season and the goal is to reach seventy percent of capacity as an average audience.

In 2006, the Hampton Arts Foundation purchased the building and parking lot adjacent to The American Theatre on Mellen Street. The five-thousand-square-foot building, constructed in 1939, will become the center of the Foundation's burgeoning educational program. The addition will also provide much needed additional lobby space as well as additional wing space on the theatre stage.

The Charles H. Taylor Arts Center, one of the most familiar and well loved buildings in downtown Hampton, was built in 1925 and given to the City of Hampton as a free public library by Grace Taylor Armstrong. When the city built a new library in 1987, the Charles H. Taylor Building was renovated and became the Charles H. Taylor Arts Center.

Hampton Arts works closely with many of the leading visual arts organizations in the presentation of annual exhibitions at the Arts Center. These include the Peninsula Glass Guild, the Tidewater Artists Association, the Hampton City Schools System, the Hampton Arts League, Hampton Bay Days and the Hampton University Museum.

A year-round program of educational programs and classes especially for children and young adults is also offered at the Arts Center and there are monthly lectures, demonstrations, workshops, and a weekly painters group.

During 2006, more than 100,000 people enjoyed the many offerings and programs of Hampton Arts and more than 30,000 Hampton school children were exposed to various artistic disciplines with programs funded by the Hampton Arts Commission.

The vision of Hampton Arts is to ensure that world-class performing and visual arts are accessible to and appeal to the diverse citizenry of the Hampton Roads region.

Suffolk High School football team, 1929.
COURTESY OF THE HAMBLIN STUDIO COLLECTION,
LIBRARY OF VIRGINIA.

Tourists watch as "patriots" open fire with
loud, smoky cannon.

PHOTO BY PAUL CLANCY.

THE MARKETPLACE

Hampton Roads' financial institutions, service industries, and retail and commercial establishments provide the economic foundation of the region

SPECIAL THANKS TO

Hampton Roads Vending & Food Service

Hawthorne Suites

HARBOR TOWER APARTMENTS

Harbor Tower, a high-rise apartment building that opened in 1983, served as the spark for what turned out to be an explosion of revitalization in downtown Portsmouth that began in the 1980s and flourishes to this day. Harbor Tower was built the same year as Waterside Festival Market Place on the other side of the Elizabeth River in Norfolk, a development that helped spur growth in that city as well.

That same year, the Elizabeth River Ferry began shuttling pedestrians between Portsmouth and Norfolk seven days a week, resuming service that had been offered for 319 years until the Portsmouth Tunnel led to its demise in 1955. The ferry transports pedestrians and bicyclists between High Street Landing and North Landing on the Portsmouth side to Waterside Festival Market Place in Norfolk.

These developments and more have led to a rebirth of the Portsmouth and Norfolk areas. Portsmouth is a charming port city with a historic seawall and three centuries of history. Harbor Tower is a five-minute ferryboat ride from downtown Norfolk, a twenty-minute drive from Virginia Beach and less than an hour from Colonial Williamsburg. Six museums, numerous historic landmarks, unique shopping and fabulous dining are all within walking distance.

Harbor Tower's reputation has grown as residents and visitors marvel at the buildings' dominating position on the waterfront and the spectacular views its location affords. This high-rise apartment building features 189 luxury one- and two-bedroom apartments with dramatic views, spacious floor plans and amenities that make the term "first-class" seem lacking. The nation's oldest naval shipyard—Norfolk Naval Shipyard—is situated close to Harbor Tower. It was established in 1767 under the British flag, thirty-one years before the United States Navy was born. Still in use today, it is the largest shipyard on the east coast and serves as a frequent destination for Navy ships.

Imagine watching a nuclear-powered aircraft carrier or an enormous Navy hospital ship move past your window. Watch the beautiful, black Disney cruise ship dock at

one of the private shipyards across from Harbor Tower, where Navy ships, gigantic cruise ships and other sea-going vessels dock. A menagerie of private yachts sails past on their way to the recently constructed Ocean Marina. Others head south on the Intracoastal Waterway from the zero mile marker where Harbor Tower is located, marking the halfway point between New York and Florida. Other views include the City of Norfolk skyline, Historic Olde Towne (including several historic churches and their steeples) and, at night, harbor lights that sparkle like diamonds on black felt.

Harbor Tower offers unfurnished apartments for long-term residents, as well as furnished and accessorized apartments for short-term visitors. Both types of apartments offer breathtaking views by day and mesmerizing sparkles from the harbor lights at night. Each apartment is equipped with a Whirlpool range, refrigerator, walk-in kitchen pantry, dishwasher, and individually

Harbor Tower sits majestically on the Elizabeth River. The Elizabeth River Ferry docks next to Harbor Tower and runs between Portsmouth and Norfolk every thirty minutes.

controlled thermostat. Other amenities include a garbage disposal, intercom system, access system, and, of course, world-class views. Choose from five distinctive apartment styles in one- or two-bedroom floorplans. You will enjoy open space illuminated with natural light from either a balcony or full-length picture window.

The short-term furnished apartments don't skimp on amenities, either. Each comes with a fully equipped kitchen that includes utensils, dinnerware, linens, major appliances, and small appliances. Furniture, twenty-five inch televisions with basic cable and HBO, phone service, bedroom and bathroom linens, and a free reserved parking space in a covered parking garage are also provided for the short-term guest. Furnished apartments are ideal for the extended stay, business travelers, corporate relocation, or anyone in need of temporary housing. Utilities are included in the price and short-term guests enjoy all of the amenities on which long-term guests have come to rely. A community room is available for private meetings and complimentary coffee is offered each weekday morning. Rates are all-inclusive and are flexible according to season and length of stay (rates are subject to change). Harbor Tower honors most major credit cards.

Harbor Tower amenities don't stop there. The apartments also offer concierge service for messages, packages and local information, valet service, controlled access, free reserved garage parking, dry cleaning delivery and pick-up service, evening and weekend valet service and the aforementioned community room where you can enjoy

social activities. Other amenities include a fitness center, showers and saunas, outdoor riverside pool and deck, billiards room, tennis courts, barbecue grilling and picnic area, and movie rentals at the concierge desk. There are smoke detectors and sprinkler systems in all common areas and in all apartments. Each apartment has individually controlled heating and air conditioning as well as energy efficient heat pumps. They also come with ceiling fans, oversized walk-in closets, balconies or large picture windows.

Like the Portsmouth area itself, you will find a wide variety of lifestyles represented in its attractive and comfortable confines. All enjoy the relaxed, no-maintenance lifestyle offered by Harbor Tower as well as its

⚓

Above: From your Harbor Tower apartment, enjoy panoramic views of the harbor and city. The scenic vista changes daily on the Elizabeth River.

Below: The Portsmouth waterfront district is a scenic, vibrant waterside environment and Harbor Tower is at the very center of it all!
PHOTOGRAPH COURTESY OF TRI-CITY PHOTOGRAPHY.

proximity to corporate, cultural and social influences in the nearby downtown area, commonly referred to as Olde Towne.

Olde Towne is the central portion of Portsmouth and home to two thousand people. Listed on the *National Register of Historic Places*, it is bounded by the Elizabeth River on the east, Effingham Street on the west, Interstate 264 to the south and Crawford Bay to the north. A walking tour of Olde Towne with a costumed guide at twilight (Olde Towne Lantern Tour) is a popular attraction for those interested in combining a history lesson with a pleasant stroll. This hour-long tour gives visitors a taste of the legends and folklore of Olde Towne and the district's unique architectural styles, including Colonial, Federal, Greek Revival, Georgian, and Victorian.

A one-mile, self-guided walking tour of Olde Towne will take you past forty-five sites in the city's historic district, where you can see hand-hewn pews made by slaves. Portsmouth's center is home to the largest collection of historic homes between Alexandria, Virginia, and Charleston, South Carolina. It also houses numerous early twentieth century buildings that have been restored or are in the process. The town's oldest building, the House & Commercial Building, dates to the mid-1700s. Benedict Arnold, the Revolutionary general who betrayed his fellow patriots, used the building as his headquarters during the Revolutionary War.

Portsmouth has been welcoming visitors for 250 years. William Crawford, a wealthy merchant and ship owner, founded the city in 1752 on sixty-five acres of land on the shores of the Elizabeth River. In addition to his business holdings, Crawford served at various times as the Norfolk County presiding court judge, high sheriff, militia lieutenant colonel and representative to the House of Burgesses.

He is frequently referred to as Colonel Crawford because of his militia service. The sixty-five acres on which Portsmouth was founded were part of Colonel Crawford's extensive plantation and became a town by an enabling act of the General Assembly of Virginia. Portsmouth was named after the English naval port of that name and many streets reflected the English heritage.

Portsmouth is home to the world's largest natural harbor, the nation's first shipyard and the site of the Civil War battle between the *Monitor* and the *Merrimac*, a site that can be viewed aboard a replica of a nineteenth century Mississippi riverboat. Visitors can also explore the Chesapeake Bay on a scenic four-hour cruise between Portsmouth and Crisfield, Maryland. Tangier Island Cruises offer cruises in and out of Portsmouth on the luxurious, climate-controlled ship known as the *Captain Rudy Thomas*.

Portsmouth separated from the county government and became an independent city

in 1858. Its location as an East Coast deepwater port has contributed greatly to the city's development throughout its two-and-a-half centuries of growth. The two World Wars brought economic growth to Portsmouth via thousands of jobs in the city's shipbuilding industry. Suburban migration deflated Portsmouth's economy and culture, and in the 1960s the Olde Towne area began to decline.

Revitalization began in 1980 with new streets, lighting and landscaping. Today, the area is teeming with restaurants, specialty shops, antique shops and art galleries. Festivals, musicians, and fireworks displays provide visitors with an array of entertainment, and both the Portsmouth and Norfolk waterfronts provide year-round opportunities for fun.

The Waterside Festival Marketplace offers food, family entertainment and nightlife along with shops, restaurants and nightclubs lining the banks of the Elizabeth River. MacArthur Center offers great shopping in a state-of-the-art, three-level urban marketplace that brings new levels of shopping, dining and entertainment to Southeasten Virginia. The Olde Town area is a natural setting for museums dedicated to preserving and chronicling the area's history. The Children's

Museum of Virginia, the state's largest children's museum, offers children more than eighty hands-on exhibits, temporary rotating exhibits, a sixty-four-seat planetarium and a one million dollar antique toy and model train collection. Virginia Sports Hall of Fame and Museum is located in downtown Portsmouth across from the Children's Museum of Virginia. This popular attraction honors Virginia sports heroes ranging from golfer Sam Snead to tennis star Arthur Ashe.

The Portsmouth Naval Shipyard Museum & Lightship Museum pays tribute to the Norfolk Naval Shipyard. Uniforms, cannon balls, models of ships and a piece of the CSS *Virginia,* also known as the *Merrimac,* are included among the memorabilia. The Lightship Museum includes a restored lightship, listed on the *National Register of Historic Places,* commissioned in 1915 to guide ships through dangerous waters.

Harbor Tower is a short walk or ferry ride from all these attractions and more. It's easy to see why Harbor Tower is considered a prime spot for both permanent and short-term residents. Visit us in person or online at www.harbortowerapartments.com and see why we've earned a reputation as both a great place to visit and to live.

Above: From your Harbor Tower Apartment you can see the picturesque Norfolk Skyline.

Below: In June 2005 the Pride of America *along with the "Live with Regis and Kelly" cruised into Hampton Roads and attracted thousands to the Portsmouth and Norfolk waterfront.*

CREWESTONE TECHNOLOGIES, INC.

Crewestone Technologies, Inc., was founded on the belief that creative genius and technical expertise can coexist in the same environment. Guided by this vision, the founders proved that creative and technical talents are a good match and can work in harmony to produce astonishing results.

Larry D. Crewe and corporate partners Wesley K. Jones and Robert A. Taborn founded Crewestone in 1999. These founders provided Crewestone with a well-grounded foundation in the science of film, television and video engineering. Crewe, who serves as president of Crewestone, was part of a research team at NASA that worked with Disney on the design of 3D software and hardware systems to produce the then cutting-edge animation for the highly acclaimed film, *Who Framed Roger Rabbit*.

A native of Newport News, Crewe started Lectronic Services as a sole proprietorship in Hampton. As he developed the business, he simultaneously launched a career at NASA Langley Research Center that spanned nearly thirty years.

Prior to co-founding Crewestone, Taborn, a native of Roanoke, Virginia, and veteran of Desert Storm, began his twenty-year technical career in the United States Air Force as a broadcast maintenance engineer for Combat Camera and, later, moved to Armed Forces Network (AFN). Following military service, Taborn worked at local ABC affiliate WVEC-TV and, soon after, NASA Langley Research Center.

Above: Larry Crewe, CEO and president of Crewestone Technologies.

Below: The corporate officers of Crewestone Technologies.

Prior to co-founding Crewestone, Jones, a native of Queens, New York, worked for Cable Vision Systems, CNN, WVEC-TV 13 and NASA Langley Research Center. He has more than twenty years experience in promotions, live events and broadcast television. Jones, who serves as chief operations officer for Crewestone, has coordinated events to include a visit from former President Clinton to the Norfolk Naval Base, to a multi-camera video recording of a live concert in St. Marteen for FUBU Clothing.

The principals of Crewestone have more than sixty years combined experience in the broadcast, video production, and technology systems integration fields.

Larry D. Crewe
President & CEO

Wesley K. Jones
Vice President & COO

Robert A. Taborn
Vice President & CTIO

Crewestone Technologies is a certified Small Business 8(a) firm employing a staff of television professionals, video producers and engineers, each of whom possess an average of eighteen years experience in their respective fields.

Crewestone provides award-winning professional audio and video services and products to government and commercial industry. Services include design and installation of audio, sound and video systems in businesses and churches, as well as video production services to include live, live-to-tape and field production projects. Crewestone provides staffing for audio/video contract-supported services.

Crewestone has provided state-of-the-art visual communications solutions to government and commercial clients for more than five years. Offering turnkey, totally managed communications solutions, they are a recognized leader in the areas of video production, postproduction, video system design, analysis, integration, operation, and support.

Crewestone provides high-quality, script-to-screen productions; graphic and animation presentations; audio and visual systems design; engineering, installation and support; duplications; and outstanding customer service. Crewestone is a specialist in all aspects of media production and design.

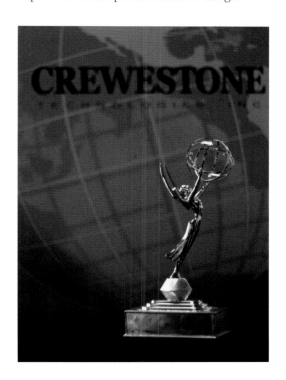

In just a few years, Crewe and his co-founders, Jones and Taborn, have assembled a creative and technical staff that has received more industry awards than most companies realize in a lifetime. Crewestone has grown from revenues of $1,400 its first year of operation to more than $2 million per year today. Employment has grown from four employees to more than 20.

Crewestone Technologies, Inc. provides marketing media, film and video production, and media systems integration for commercial and government clients. Collectively, Crewestone's three divisions—Visual Media Group, Strategic Marketing Group, and Systems Engineering Group—form a global solution for business presentation and media communication requirements.

Specifically, Crewestone develops business and educational television programming, creates marketing and public awareness media campaigns, and designs and installs an array of media communications systems from television broadcast studios to conference room presentation systems.

The bread and butter of the business is video production. Crewestone's pride and many awards come from their production of *NASA Connect* and *The NASA Sci Files*, which air nationally on PBS stations once a month. Local residents may remember when actor

Above: Crewestone Technologies is the recipient of more than fifty national awards.

Below: Crewestone Technologies is a producer of Emmy Award-winning productions.

Jackie Chan came to Hampton in 2000 to guest-star in the shows.

NASA Connect is aimed at grades eight through ten and has a viewing audience of about nine million.

The show, also shown to military children at overseas grade schools, has been shot in locations such as Norway, where the program explained the northern lights.

"It encourages that age group to like math, science and technology," said Lauren Yee, executive producer and program director at Crewestone.

⚓

The Crewestone staff frequently travels to promote the company's services and meet with its customers.

The NASA Sci Files has a similar aim, except that it's geared to grades three through five. The show features six young "treehouse detectives" who solve problems using math, science and technology skills.

Crewestone also does a lot more than film and edit. The company has been awarded contracts to do technical audio/video work at local universities and with the cities of Hampton, Newport News and Suffolk. The work ranges from video surveillance and conferencing to maintaining VCRs and cable systems.

The company has also done projects such as setting up the audio system when the Virginia Symphony played at local schools.

Crewestone set up the microphones, speakers and a video conferencing system on

the stage for a teachers' conference in Washington, D.C. And it helped a Virginia Beach judge set up a system so he could turn courtroom microphones on and off from the bench. "It was a simple process, but he really liked it," Crewe says.

The company has worked with churches that have large congregations and musical groups and needed sound systems installed. "Churches don't have technicians, so we set them up so they can operate the system themselves, and we'll train them, too," Crewe explains.

Crewestone also did a live broadcast of the Christmas parade in Hampton for the city on local station WVEC TV-13. "We produced it and bought the time for the city," Crewe notes. "They loved it because we provided a full turnkey service."

Crewe claims that whatever the request, Crewestone "can do it faster, better, cheaper." According to NASA, he isn't exaggerating. "In government business, you often have to deal with people who are more interested in getting the bid than developing the project," says Dr. Thomas Pinelli, who manages NASA's Langley Center for Distance Learning. "Larry represents a company that delivers what they promise, on time and on budget, and it's a quality product. Sometimes in the marketplace with government, one of those three things will be compromised. Not with Crewestone. They are quite different."

The Crewestone Visual Media Group is a full-service film, video, and multimedia production enterprise. The Visual Media Group offers an award-winning staff of writers, producers, editors, and videographers with in-depth experience in helping commercial and government clients communicate their message and educate their constituencies.

The Visual Media Group's talented staff of creative and technical personnel has garnered more than a dozen Emmys™, numerous Tellys and international film festival awards. The Group's areas of expertise include visual media production for business communications with a focus on scientific and technical topics.

The Crewestone Strategic Marketing Group works with clients to develop media

campaigns for issue advocacy, motivation, training, and public relations. The firm's producers have designed campaigns at the highest level for such clients as the Department of Defense, the City of Hampton, and NASA.

The Crewestone Systems Engineering Group specializes in design and integration of broadcast production, audiovisual conference and custom design of multimedia systems for commercial and government clients. The Systems Engineering Group offers consulting, equipment, systems installation and on-site maintenance.

The Systems Engineering Group provides facilities management services and currently manages visual media requirements for NASA Langley Research Center and the Veterans Medical Center of Hampton.

Crewestone's outstanding government and commercial media communications services have resulted in more than fifty major national awards over a five-year period. The awards include fifteen Emmys, the Telly Award, the Scientific and Technical award, the New York Film Festivals Award, the Communicator Award, the Chris Award, Japan Prize for Educational Programming, an the Axiem Award.

In addition to winning NASA's "Videographer of the Year Award" for 2004, Crewestone Technologies won NASA's award for "Minority Subcontractor of the Year" marking the first time a service contractor—not a research or IT company—won the honor. Crewestone was awarded a proclamation from the City of Hampton in honor of receiving the distinguished award. Larry Crewe was recently named one of *Minority Business Enterprise* magazine's "Fifty Influential Minorities in Business," and the Crewestone founders earned the Virginia Peninsula Chamber of Commerce's "Small Business Person of the Year" for 2005.

Crewestone's service and support of several civic and professional organizations in the community included memberships in the Virginia Peninsula Chamber of Commerce, the Virginia Minority Supplier Development Council, and as a speaker. Larry and his wife, Jennifer, have been members of New Life Church in Hampton for more than twenty-five years.

Crewestone's corporate headquarters is located at 1919 Commerce Drive, Suite 420 in Hampton. Crewestone also has offices in Richmond and the Washington, D.C. area. The firm is located on the Internet at www.crewestone.com.

⚓

Above: The founders of Crewestone were the recipients of the Virginia Peninsula Chamber of Commerce's 2005 "Small Business Person of the Year" Award.

Below: Crewestone Technologies is a recipient of Telly Awards for video production.

LIEBHERR

The T 282 B is not only the worlds biggest diesel-electric truck on two axels and six wheels, it is the biggest AC drive truck. This is undoubtedly the most advantageous drive for a mining haul truck today.

Liebherr-International AG, headquartered in Bulle, Switzerland, is one of the world's largest family owned businesses and is composed of more than ninety companies, four of which are located in Newport News, Virginia. The Liebherr Group employs in excess of twenty-two thousand people worldwide. Given the range of industries that the Liebherr Group of companies is involved in, it's hard to believe Liebherr started with a single man and his exceptionally bright idea.

In Germany in 1949, Dr. Hans Liebherr invented the first mobile, affordable, and easy-to-assemble tower crane, which revolutionized the building industry. This invention served as the cornerstone on which the company and future companies would be built. From that small beginning, Liebherr-International AG has grown to offer hundreds of products and services in several industry sectors, including Earthmoving and Mining, Mobile Cranes, Construction Cranes and Concrete Mixing Technology, Maritime Cranes, Machine Tool and Material Flow Technology, Component Manufacturing, Domestic Appliances and Aerospace and Transport Technology.

Dr. Liebherr's instinct for successful products and market diversification proved extremely effective and within ten years new products such as hydraulic excavators, concrete mixers, gear-cutting machines and refrigerators were added, with new factories built in Europe to manufacture them.

The consistent interest in developing new technologically innovative products has continued through the years, supported and defined by the second generation of the Liebherr family. The decentrally organized Liebherr Group is divided into company units of manageable size, operating autonomously. This ensures close proximity to the customer and the ability to respond flexibly to market signals in global competition. The Liebherr Groups holding companies are owned entirely by members of the Liebherr family.

The year 1970 marked the beginning of Liebherr's North American venture with the construction in Newport News, Virginia of two 300,000-square-foot production facilities to manufacture excavators and cranes. A four-story office building was added shortly

thereafter. In 1972, Liebherr started designing and building specialty cranes such as the 120/25-ton Polar Crane (cranes that operate in a circle) and the 150-ton Turbine Crane, which were delivered to a nuclear power station in Kuosheng, Taiwan. Other Polar Cranes were sold to the Tennessee Valley Authority Bellefonte Nuclear Plant in Alabama.

Also during these early years, Liebherr designed and manufactured fifty-ton Polar Cranes for the U.S. Navy for Mare Island, California and Bangor, Washington. In 1978, Liebherr built one of the world's largest tower cranes, model 1800C. Steel construction work was also done on some standard tower cranes, model 200 HC and 88 HC, in Newport News, while the mechanical parts came from a Liebherr factory in Germany. Overhead cranes, fuel-handling cranes for nuclear power plants and special missile handling cranes for the U.S. Navy were also built in Newport News. After the production of a Container Crane for the Port of Wilmington, North Carolina in 1984, Liebherr decided to build all future cranes at their European factories in Germany and Ireland.

Several sizes of general construction and specialty excavators were designed, sold, manufactured and delivered from the Newport News plant during the 1970s and 1980s. An estimated 1,500 of these early day excavators were built, most for general construction usage, but some different specialty units were built for the scrap, logging and aggregates industries. One unique machine built for the logging industry was equipped with a Liebherr-designed-and-built cutting shear capable of cutting trees up to twenty-four inches in diameter. Several of these first North American manufactured excavators are still in operation today.

The design and manufacturing facilities at Newport News were converted to the production of Liebherr's range of diesel electric mining trucks in 1998 and remain so today. The plant location is particularly suited to serving not only the domestic mining truck market but shipping to international markets due to the close proximity of excellent port facilities.

Thirty-five years after Dr. Liebherr made his momentous decision to build the North American factory, four Liebherr companies are now located at the Newport News manufacturing complex: Liebherr Cranes Inc. (LCI), Liebherr Concrete Technology Co. (LCT), Liebherr Construction Equipment Co. (LCE), and Liebherr Mining Equipment Co. (LME). Both LCE and LME are a part of Liebherr's EMtech or Earthmoving Technologies group.

Liebherr Cranes, Inc., (LCI) newly founded in 2004, is responsible for the sales, service and parts activities for Liebherr all-terrain (mobile) and large crawler cranes ranging in size from four hundred tons to as much as 1,320 tons in the United States. Its operations include a new repair facility in Houston as well as sales and service offices in Newport News. From Houston, Liebherr Nenzing Crane Co. provides sales and services for large crawler cranes ranging in size from fifty tons to as much as three hundred tons of operating weight, as well as piling and drilling machinery. Maritime cranes and port equipment are supported by a base location in Medley, Florida.

Liebherr LTM mobile cranes are fast-moving units designed for use both on and off road. There are twenty-four Liebherr models available with load capacities ranging between 40 to 1,000 U.S. tons. State-of-the-art data-bus technology ensures a high level of efficiency and safety in use. These fast all-terrain cranes, compact and mobile construction cranes and heavy duty lattice boom cranes are used worldwide and have both power and reliable performance records in all kinds of lifting operations. From assisting with the installation of air conditioning units on high-rise buildings to heavy lifting operations in open-pit mines, to lifting the Concorde aircraft for transport to a museum display location, Liebherr mobile cranes have the "muscle" to get the job done.

For North America's concrete industry, Liebherr Concrete Technology Co. (LCT) made its U.S. debut in 2002, introducing to the U.S. concrete market machinery and equipment for the "Ready-Mix Concrete, Block, Pipe, Precast, and Prestress" production industries, with additional emphasis on intermediate storage, transport of concrete and allied materials. LCT core products include ring-pan mixers, twin-shaft mixers, concrete reclaimers and loading buffers, truck conveyors as well as portable, mobile and stationary batch plants. Depending on the individual jobsite requirements, stationary or mobile systems with production capacities ranging from 65 cubic yards per hundred to 365 cubic yards per hundred of set concrete are available. LCT has the personnel and experience to provide custom-designed batch plants and material handling systems. LCT's ability to offer on-job, site-specific equipment has resulted in exceptional reception for Liebherr products. Major components are stocked locally for rapid turnaround.

Liebherr-Mischtechnik GmbH, Bad Schussenried, Germany, the European concrete technology group, has been active in the concrete industry since 1954, and in the international mixing technology market segment for quite some time prior to Liebherr expanding the concrete-mixing technology into North America.

Liebherr Construction Equipment Co. (LCE), began manufacturing products in North

America in 1972 and has the responsibility for marketing Liebherr construction products throughout the U.S. dealer network. While Liebherr primarily goes to market thru independently owned dealers, our goal is to ensure Liebherr customers receive the product support they are entitled to as Liebherr owners. In 2003, Liebherr Equipment Source was established to provide company-owned dealerships in areas where Liebherr representation was lost due to dealership consolidation or change of ownership. Today company owned "Liebherr Equipment Source" dealerships, are located in Baltimore, Maryland, Manassas, Virginia, and Raleigh, North Carolina. All U.S. construction products that LCE distributes are now manufactured in Europe. LCE marketed products include crawler and wheeled excavators, wheel loaders, hydrostatic crawler loaders and crawler tractors. Two unique LCE products are the A 974, the "World's Largest Wheeled Material Handler" and Liebherr's L 580—"World's Largest Hydrostatic Wheel Loader."

Liebherr's U.S. Litronic hydraulic excavator line, well-known for machine stability and undercarriage construction, ranges in size from 35,000 pounds of operating weight to the rugged R 984 C with an operating weight of 276,600 pounds, a machine for either heavy construction or aggregate production. The term "Litronic" refers to the operating management system that all Liebherr construction and mining excavators feature, which controls and regulates all electronic and hydraulic functions to provide the most comprehensive machine performance.

Liebherr pioneered the hydrostatic transmission for their line of crawler tractors and loaders. The advantages of this system are maximum power transmission with stepless speed control and permanent drive to both tracks even when cornering. The Liebherr wheel loader products are extremely fuel efficient and, as with the crawler loaders and crawler tractors, utilize hydrostatic transmissions. The wheel loaders are adaptable to several industry job applications, general construction, and aggregates and with specially designed attachments, scrap and logging job sites. These products, which have had great success in Europe, made their U.S. debut in 2003.

The Liebherr material handling excavator line, available in wheeled, track or pedestal-mounted, plays a dominant role in the U.S. scrap/recycling market. These machines, specifically designed to handle tough jobsite conditions, provide reliable, continued high lifetime performance. Liebherr material handlers are also operating in mill yards and paper mills as well as port handling operations throughout the U.S.

Manufacturer of the largest diesel electric mining trucks utilized by the mining industry, Liebherr Mining Equipment Co. (LME) has grown significantly within a short period of time. Sales and service-management personnel for the large trucks and for Liebherr's Litronic hydraulic mining excavators sold in the U.S. are also located at the LME plant facility. Regional service locations where large fleets of trucks are located in the U.S. are in Gillette, Wyoming and Elko, Nevada. Major international service locations have been established to provide service for foreign mining operations.

Liebherr's diesel/electric mining-truck product line ranges in payload capacity from 200 short tons to the "World's Largest Diesel Electric, AC Drive Haul Truck," the T 282 B at 400 short tons of payload capacity. The T 282 B, carrying a full load of material, commands attention as it drives down a mine-haul road just by its immense size—47 feet, 6 inches long; 28 feet, 10 inches wide; and 24 feet, 3 inches tall. Dwarfing other manufacturer's trucks with the amount of material the truck can carry—the T 282 B occupies the top place in LME's range of haul trucks. Most people are extremely impressed with the truck's size when standing by one of the trucks' thirteen-foot-tall tires. The low maintenance electric drive technology incorporated in the truck, in conjunction with the world's most powerful commercial engine available, allows for reliable performance of these giant mining trucks hour after hour, day after day, and year after year. Top speed of this gigantic truck is forty miles per hour.

Liebherr mining trucks operate in diversified worldwide mining applications, coal mines, gold mines, the Canadian Oil Sands and at the world's largest copper mine, Chuquicamata, Chile, where temperatures vary as much as sixty-eight degrees daily. LME Service personnel travel to destinations such as Australia, Chile, Canada, Spain, Indonesia, South Africa and Venezuela, as well as domestic locations, to provide experienced guidance on maintenance issues and assist with operator training. Noted for their state-of-the-art technology, reliability, and durability, Liebherr mining trucks have established lifetime records of more than 100,000 hours or ten years of consistent use before being retired.

Litronic hydraulic mining excavators manufactured at Liebherr's Colmar, France, plant, sold and serviced in North America through LME, have operating weights from 500,000 pounds to as much as 1,473,000 pounds. Throughout the U.S., these reliable machines dig their way through coal mines, granite, limestone and other aggregate quarries with efficiency to obtain the raw materials to provide electricity to our homes and to manufacture many of the day-to-day products we use. Large Liebherr Litronic excavators are also utilized to mine the U.S. waterways. From U.S. harbor or channel deepening to excavations of canals, and reservoirs, LME has large Litronic barge-mounted excavators operating, each matched closely to the customer's individual requirements. It is not unusual to see Liebherr barge-mounted excavators operating in harbors against the skylines of major U.S. cities such as New York and Boston, easily performing their assigned tasks in the harshest of environments.

Liebherr Group products operate in a multitude of worldwide industries. These products have established benchmarks that are exceptional in General Construction,

Mining and Concrete Technology, as well as other industries—a tradition that began with Dr. Liebherr's original tower crane.

Looking at some of the more recent Liebherr historical benchmarks and product achievements, it would be difficult to select one over another as being the most outstanding. They all demonstrate Liebherr's vast experience in designing and manufacturing a variety of outstanding products. The Liebherr dynasty all began with Dr. Liebherr's invention of the tower crane and through continued product expansion and growth, Liebherr has evolved into an internationally recognized versatile conglomerate.

As Liebherr in Newport News celebrated its thirty-fifth year in America in 2005, it became evident that Liebherr has grown substantially in North America since 1970. Local employment and career opportunities as a result of Liebherr's active presence in the Hampton Roads area have expanded considerably, especially in the last few years, and the expansion is anticipated to continue. The design, manufacturing production, sales and service of new, technologically advanced products remains an inherent part of the Newport News, Virginia, Liebherr Group of Companies and will continue to be a central focus as the future unfolds.

Mobile cranes lift the Concorde.

CAPTAIN GEORGE'S SEAFOOD RESTAURANT

The Captain George's story is one of family tradition, hard work, and determination, a story that truly exemplifies the American dream.

George Pitsilides was born of Cypriot parents in Hampton in 1953. His father, Chris, immigrated from a small village in Cyprus and arrived at Ellis Island filled with hopes and dreams and thankful for his chance in "the land of opportunity."

After acquiring some restaurant experience in Manhattan, Chris and a cousin headed for Miami, Florida, to open their own restaurant. As fate would have it, they never quite made it to Florida.

Their first stop on the trip south was in Norfolk where Chris was so impressed with the bustling military activity that he decided to open his first restaurant in the area. In 1950, Chris and his cousin opened the Acropole restaurant in Hampton, serving breakfast, lunch and dinner. This meant the men worked eighteen hours a day, seven days a week, but the restaurant was a huge success and Chris could not have been happier.

In 1952, Chris married a young lady named Mary from the village of Lefcara, Cyprus and, in 1962; Chris and Mary opened the C&M Cafeteria in Hampton.

Meanwhile, the Pitsilides family was growing. George was born in 1954, soon followed by two sisters and a brother. George was attracted to the family business at an early age, bussing tables, working in the kitchen and serving as cashier. His passion, however, was in food preparation and recipe engineering.

George married his high school sweetheart, Sherry Breen, in 1974 and, in 1977, Chris retired and the C&M Cafeteria was sold. It was the beginning of a new era for George and Sherry.

They opened The Hampton House, a full-service restaurant serving breakfast, lunch, and dinner, in 1975 and the establishment became a huge success. The Hampton House metamorphosed eventually into the first Captain George's Seafood Restaurant, which seated 350 diners.

In 1977, George and Sherry joined forces with Sherry's parents, who were accomplished restaurant entrepreneurs in their own right, and opened the first of two Fisherman's Wharf restaurants. The restaurants were owned by the Breens but operated by George and Sherry in a partnership, which flourished for years.

Fisherman's Wharf, with a beautiful view of Hampton Creek, was initially an a-la'carte, dinner-only restaurant. But its success encouraged George and Sherry to experiment with a buffet format for special occasions such as Thanksgiving and, eventually, on weekends. In 1980 the restaurant became a full-service gourmet buffet, offering upscale linen service. The buffet restaurant proved so popular that patrons often lined up outside and waited hours to be seated. The Fisherman's Wharf closed in 1998 following the untimely death of Carl Edward Breen who was the mentor and guiding hand for his daughter and son-in-law.

George and Sherry opened their first Captain George's in 1979 in Hampton, Virginia. The second location was opened in 1982 on Laskin Road in Virginia Beach and seated more than seven hundred. Following the now-established seafood buffet format, Captain George's was open for dinner Monday through Saturday and for lunch and dinner on Sundays.

The first Captain George's enjoyed unsurpassed acclaim, not only for the high quality of its food and service but also for its unique décor, which includes the world's largest stained glass dome within the roof of a single restaurant. Sherry's sense of aesthetics and front-of-the-house skills, coupled with George's back-of-the-house engineering, purchasing skill and culinary arts resulted in a marvelous restaurant know by tourists from throughout the nation.

Captain George's Pungo, also in Virginia Beach, opened in 1984. Its location along the intercoastal waterway provided incredible views and a private beach. The Pungo location closed in 2005 after twenty-one years of success.

Captain George's Williamsburg opened in 1985 and has been another spectacular success with its own separate dinner theater and a magnificent décor that includes indoor waterfalls, bridges across running streams, and antique clipper ships as architectural elements. The site also includes outdoor fountains and beautiful, colonial inspired landscaping. The location is famous with tourists and local residents alike and the restaurant's capacity of nine hundred is usually filled.

George and Sherry embarked on their most ambitious adventure to date in 1999, building and designing a gorgeous state-of-the-art restaurant with more than eight hundred seats in Myrtle Beach, South Carolina. This restaurant is the crowning jewel and testament to the efforts and sacrifices of Chris Pitsilides and Carl Breen, both of whom left so much to their families.

George and Sherry have been married more than thirty-three years and have five children, all of whom are involved in the restaurants. The eldest, Kristina, graduated with a degree in Finance from Virginia Tech and is heavily involved in operations. Her husband, Tim Chastain, earned a degree in Culinary Arts from Johnson and Wales University and is now executive chef for all operations. The oldest son, Matthew, is currently pursuing his interest in culinary arts and restaurant management. George and Sherry's second daughter, Nicole, is also heavily involved in restaurant operations along with her husband, Mike, who is on the managerial staff at the Laskin Road location. The youngest boys, Adam and Aaron, are involved in various trade schools and organizations and work part-time at the restaurants.

Held closely together by history, tradition, and wonderful parents, grandparents and great-grandparents, this family will continue to write its successful story for generations to come.

HSBC

HSBC North America Holdings Inc., the holding company for all of HSBC's U.S. and Canadian businesses, including the former Household International businesses, is one of the top ten financial services organizations in the U. S. with assets approaching $300 billion. The company's 53,000 U.S. employees serve more than sixty million customers in five key areas: personal financial services, consumer finance, commercial banking, private banking, and corporate investment banking and markets. Financial products and services are offered under the HSBC, HFC and Beneficial brands.

HSBC, established in 1865 to finance the growing trade between Europe, India and China, is one of the largest banking and financial services organizations in the world. The company ranked as the fifth largest in the world by *Forbes Magazine* in March 2005. HSBC's international network encompasses more than 9,800 offices in seventy-seven countries and territories in Europe, the Asia-Pacific region, the Americas, the Middle East and Africa. HSBC utilizes an international network linked by advanced technology, including a rapidly growing e-commerce capability to provide a comprehensive range of financial services.

HSBC and its employees are committed to five core business principles: outstanding customer service, effective and efficient operations, strong capital and liquidity,

conservative lending policy and strict expense discipline.

Citing an exceptional quality of life in the Hampton Roads area, along with an available workforce and reasonable cost of living, HSBC chose Hampton Roads to build facilities that would serve as the home to three subsidiaries in 1989, creating 1,900 jobs for the Hampton Roads area.

The first subsidiary is Consumer Lending, which offers a wide variety of personal and real estate secured loans under the company's HFC and Beneficial brands, two of the oldest and most widely recognized names in consumer lending. HSBC built its business by providing a personalized solution for its customers' financial needs— whether the customer prefers to visit them at one of its neighborhood branch offices, correspond over the phone, or on the Internet at www.us.hsbc.com.

The Card Services subsidiary also has a facility in Hampton Roads. HSBC's Card Services unit was ranked as the sixth largest issuer of MasterCard® and Visa™ credit cards in the United States as of January 31, 2005. Principal programs in the U.S. are The GM Card® and the Union Plus® card program. The GM Card enables customers to earn discounts on the purchase or lease of a new General Motors vehicle while the Union Plus program provides benefits and services to members of more than sixty labor unions affiliated with the AFL-CIO. Under the company's HSBC®, Household Bank® and Orchard Bank® brands, HSBC also offers specialized credit cards to consumers across the credit spectrum.

Retail Services rounds out the three subsidiaries in Hampton Roads. HSBC's

Retail Services unit is the second-largest issuer of private-label credit cards in the United States. For more than twenty-five years, Retail Services has partnered with leading retailers to offer valuable programs to their customers. The company offers its partners a broad set of products, flexible programs and strong customer relationship management capabilities. The company issues numerous private label credit cards including the Best Buy Card. HSBC provides instant credit lines and customer financing terms for its merchants for both revolving and closed-end accounts and accepts applications for credit online, in-store and over the phone, managing relationships with more than sixty merchants including Costco, Kmart, Levitz, Liz Claiborne, Saks, Sony, Gateway, Guitar Center, hpshopping.com, Kawasaki, IKEA, Microsoft, Mitsubishi, Rhodes, QVC, uBid and Yamaha.

HSBC has earned a reputation as an employer of choice. In 2003 and 2004, the company was named one of the "Top 25 Places to Work in Hampton Roads." Additionally, in 2004, HSBC was named one of the "Best in Chesapeake" by *The Virginian-Pilot*. The company has also been recognized by a variety of magazines including *Working Mother, Training* and *Computerworld*.

Throughout the years, HSBC has recognized that its greatest asset has always been its employees and the core principles for which they, and the corporation, stand. By treating the customers fairly and ethically, listening to them, and adhering to the highest ethical standards, the employee forms a bond with the customer that cannot be broken.

HSBC aims to build stronger, safer, more prosperous communities by investing human, financial and in-kind contributions in projects and programs that make a lasting impact by promoting self sufficiency in three areas: Education, Housing and Community Enrichment, including the Environment.

Each employee is also committed to exceptional corporate citizenship through active community involvement in several different forms. HSBC and its employees contributed more than $30 million to nonprofit organizations in the United States. Locally, HSBC participates in many United Way activities, Paint Your Heart Out, Chamber of Commerce initiatives, Relay for Life, Junior Achievement and many other civic/community programs. The company has also been a major sponsor of the AAU Junior Olympic Games since 2001 as well sponsoring the Senior Games since 2003.

By encouraging community volunteerism among its employees, HSBC is committed to improving the quality of life in Hampton Road and the surrounding areas.

With a rich history of success behind it and an eye toward the future, HSBC plans to continue growing its business and serving the borrowing needs of consumers around the world.

THE OLD POINT NATIONAL BANK

In today's climate of bank mergers and consolidations, it is rare for a financial institution to remain independent for more than eighty years, much less retain its original name.

The Old Point National Bank was organized in 1922 when a group of businessmen in the Elizabeth City County township of Phoebus organized a bank to serve the needs of local businesses. Old Point National Bank has grown to assets of more than $750 million but has managed to retain the personal touch provided by a small, hometown bank.

A key factor in the longevity and success of Old Point is its stability. For example, the company has elected only forty-four board members since its founding, including the fifteen who serve today, and has had only four chief executive officers. Old Point currently has thirty-six officers and employees who have been with the bank for more than twenty years. Five senior managers have been with the company an average of more than twenty-five years.

Although there were a few lean years, Old Point has survived depressions, recessions and wars with tenacity and nerve.

The town of Phoebus consolidated with Hampton in the 1950s and the bank opened its first branch in 1963. The seventies and eighties were major expansion years for the bank, coupled with exceptional

growth and profits. The bank added and then expanded a new main office and opened a number of branches throughout the Peninsula.

Old Point opened its seventeenth office in the New Town area of Williamsburg and its eighteenth in Virginia Beach in 2005. The nineteenth branch, Eagle Harbor, opened in Isle of Wight County in 2006.

A two-bank holding company, Old Point Financial Corporation is comprised of Old Point National Bank and Old Point Trust and Financial Services. Through the Trust arm of the company, Old Point provides many hands-on, personalized wealth management services to individuals, families and businesses.

"We are a Hampton Roads bank and we intend to remain one," asserts Robert F. Shuford, president, chairman and CEO of Old Point Financial Corporation, the bank's parent company. His comment reflects a market-loyal objective that is an anomaly in today's world of interstate, nationwide, and even global banking ventures.

Old Point remains small enough to provide the highest level of individual attention, but is large enough to provide all the modern services, including on-line banking and bill pay.

Old Point has long been regarded as a bank that works particularly well with

business and is sincerely interested in the success of its commercial customers. Bank officers who deal with business customers have the authority and the willingness to make decisions about their accounts, and as a result, many long-term relationships have developed. The bank serves a wide range of business clients, from small "mom-and-pop" operations to large corporations.

"Many of our longtime clients are professionals who have been with us since the earliest days of their practices," says Shuford. "We take care of their personal and business needs, including real estate concerns and trust and wealth management issues."

"Our reputation in wealth management speaks for itself," adds Eugene M. Jordan II, president and CEO of Old Point Trust & Financial Services, N.A., the bank's sister company. "Area families and businesses have relied on our experience for generations."

Because it is locally managed, Old Point offers customers the greatest degree of flexibility. "Because our decisions are made right here in Hampton Roads, we are very nimble," says Louis G. Morris, president and CEO of Old Point National Bank. "And because we know our market, we are ideally positioned to meet our customer's needs and help them achieve their goals."

As a community bank, Old Point National Bank and its more than three hundred employees take great pride in giving back to the community in a variety of ways. Virtually all the officers serve on at least one local community service board and employees are active in a variety of civic and service-oriented organizations. The bank also participates in festivals and events through sponsorships, and partners with local groups and schools to help create a better community.

For more information on Old Point National Bank, visit the website at www.oldpoint.com.

Eugene M. Jordan II, president and CEO, Old Point Trust & Financial Services; Louis G. Morris, president and CEO, Old Point National Bank; Robert F. Shuford, chairman, president and CEO, Old Point Financial Corporation.

HOLIDAY INN OLDE TOWNE PORTSMOUTH

⚓

Above: The Cock Island Bar & Grill.

Holiday Inn Olde Towne Portsmouth is ideally situated to make your stay in the Portsmouth area convenient, comfortable and memorable. The first thing you'll notice upon your arrival is the hotel's ideal location in the heart of Olde Towne Portsmouth directly adjacent to Tidewater Yacht Marina and North Street Ferry Landing.

The hotel overlooks the water and the world's largest shipyard and offers a panoramic view of the Elizabeth River and downtown Norfolk. We're also within easy access of historic downtown Portsmouth and we're a scenic ferry ride from the Norfolk Financial District.

Watch tugboats, aircraft carriers and sailboats cruise past from one of the deluxe Riverfront rooms and you'll immediately begin to feel a sense of relaxation washing over you. Riverview rooms provide a panoramic view of both the Elizabeth River and the busy Tidewater Yacht Marina, which serves more than 4,000 boats each year.

Inside the hotel's 219 guest rooms you'll find an array of amenities designed to make your stay comfortable and trouble free. Each room features either two double beds with an activity table or a king-size bed with an executive desk and chair.

Amenities include AM/FM radio, alarm clock, cable television with remote control, coffeemaker, dataport phones, free morning newspaper delivered to your room, hair dryer, iron and ironing board and modem connection. Other amenities include voicemail, a work desk with lamp, on command pay movies, dry cleaning and laundry, on-site guest laundry, safety deposit box, complimentary

parking and a wide range of business services available through the on-site business center. The center is open daily from 9 a.m. to 5 p.m. Services include copying services, facsimile services and access to personal computers and printers.

Holiday Inn Olde Town is a great place for both leisure and business travelers. Whether you're planning a meeting, wedding, reunion, banquet or any other group event, we have the facilities and the experience to make everything run smoothly. The conference and banquet facilities offer a variety of space and features to accommodate small as well as large groups.

The hotel offers more than 8,000 square feet of banquet and meeting space for groups of 5 to 500. It also offers 2,000 square feet of meeting space and the largest meeting room can accommodate 25 8-by-10-foot exhibit booths.

Equipment and services are available to make your meetings run smoothly. They include secretarial services, microphones, flip charts, lecterns, projectors, LCDs, VCRs, ISDN lines, modem lines, and alternative business services. Special rooms and catering packages are available, too.

You won't have to go far to find a great place to eat. The Island Grill Restaurant offers a casual atmosphere with a breathtaking view of the Elizabeth River. A breakfast buffet is served daily in season and the luncheon buffet featuring two entrees, four vegetables, soup, salad, beverage and dessert is served Monday through Friday.

The dinner menu features a variety of pastas, steaks, and seafood prepared daily. We also offer a great place to unwind after a long day. The Cock Island Bar & Grill offers a relaxing atmosphere for drinks with friends. Live entertainment is offered every Wednesday and Friday or, in the summer months, sit outside on the huge outdoor patio to enjoy the music, weather, and scenery.

You may find your stay here so enjoyable that you're reluctant to leave the hotel's comfortable confines. But for those who wish to explore the Portsmouth area you'll find plenty to do and see. Portsmouth is home to a wide variety of historic districts where you'll find numerous homes boasting a rich diversity of architectural styles.

Be sure to visit one of the many museums, shop at boutiques and galleries along High Street, take a harbor cruise aboard the *Carrie B* and dine in one of many fine restaurants. Take in a movie at the Commodore Theatre, enjoy a self-guided walking tour or a narrated trolley tour through historic Olde Towne or enjoy a leisurely stroll along the famous seawall.

The Children's Museum of Virginia is one of the area's most popular attractions. The state's largest children's museum offers more than eighty hands-on exhibits, temporary rotating exhibits, a sixty-four-seat planetarium and a one million dollar antique toy and model train collection. The nation's military history is commemorated at the naval Shipyard Museum & Lightship Museum, where uniforms, cannon balls, models of ships and a portion of the CSS *Virginia* (the *Merrimac*) are on display.

The *Carrie B* offers daytime and sunset cruises aboard a replica of a nineteenth century Mississippi riverboat. From its deck you can explore the world's largest natural harbor, view the nation's first naval shipyard and cruise the site of the Civil War battle between the *Monitor* and the *Merrimac*.

Riverview Gallery, One High Street, features the work of local and national artists. Works include many handcrafted items at affordable prices. Ask the friendly staff for help in finding an item that's just right to take home or send to a loved one. It's just one of many fine galleries you'll find in the Portsmouth area.

Portsmouth is teeming with historic sites, including the city-owned Cedar Grove Cemetery, established in 1832 and listed on the Virginia and National Registers of Historic

Places. The cemetery is known for its funerary art and the civic, business, maritime, religious, and military leaders buried there. Historic markers placed throughout the cemetery allow for self-guided tours.

You will find much more to do and see on your trip to the Portsmouth area. A wide range of recreational and outdoor activities are available as well as nightlife and fun-filled activities for the kids. And your visit will be especially enjoyable when you stay at the Holiday Inn Olde Towne Portsmouth, just a stone's throw away from the best that Virginia has to offer.

TowneBank

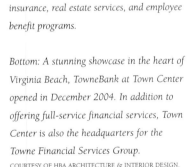

By now, most folks have heard the story. The tale of a community bank started in a garage that achieved profitability in just eleven short months. A community bank that opened three offices in three cities on the same day in April 1999. A community bank that raised more than $49 million in start-up capital from more than four thousand shareholders. It's an amazing story, and it's all true.

To this day, TowneBank enjoys a reputation as the most successful new bank ever chartered in Virginia. As of December 2005, the bank had grown from humble beginnings to a sixteen-branch network with more than $1.8 billion in assets. Spreading the Towne family spirit from Virginia Beach to Williamsburg, the bank now offers a full array of financial services, including insurance, investments, mortgage, title insurance, real estate services, employee benefits and more.

The vision for TowneBank was formed in the spring of 1998. Chairman and CEO Bob Aston and President Scott Morgan were community bankers at heart, having first formed a friendship at Citizens Trust Bank in Portsmouth, Virginia. They teamed up again at Commerce Bank, until acquired by BB&T in 1996. Tired of life in the fast lane, they longed to return to the warmth and family-oriented values of hometown banking.

Talking daily, they met with friends to discuss starting a new community bank. The support was overwhelming. The decision was made to recruit the very best employees. Upscale banking facilities and exquisite customer service would be the hallmarks. And the bank would be a community steward, led by dedicated directors in each city.

The newly formed group made a pilgrimage to the state capital to have a preliminary meeting with the Virginia Banking Commissioner. The vision to open

three offices at the same time had never been done before. The amount of capital needed was high. But the track record of the management team and the directorate was impressive.

An ad for the initial stock offering ran in *The Virginian-Pilot* and the response was overwhelming. The phones rang off the hook with urgent messages from friends seeking assurance that they could invest in this exciting new venture. And the initial team of eleven employees went to work.

There's more to tell, but suffice it to say, things went well. In fact, they went very well. After submitting pounds of paper to the FDIC and the Bureau of Banking, TowneBank received its charter. On April 8, 1999, three new hometown banking offices opened in Hampton Roads—one in Chesapeake, one in Portsmouth, and one in Virginia Beach.

Every year since, there's been something exciting to celebrate. The TowneBank "Beetles," a unique business courier service, debuted in year one. Years two and three had the bank joining forces with Kellam-Eaton-Huey, a well-known and prestigious insurance agency, and welcoming the talented mortgage team from Hampton Roads Funding. In 2004, longtime friends from the Wren investment team came on board to form Towne Investment Group. That same year, TowneBank expanded to the Peninsula, welcoming Harbor Bank, a community bank with a hometown approach. And, most recently, GSH Residential Real Estate joined the Towne family. It's all part of the master plan to build a wonderful association of friends who are eager to serve the financial needs of all the bank's members.

TowneBank also has a charitable arm, the TowneBank Foundation, which provides grants to numerous organizations throughout the Hampton Roads community. Through annual fundraising events, plus an annual contribution of TowneBank's profits, the Foundation's endowment will provide contributions to many deserving organizations for generations to come.

"When we formed TowneBank in 1999, we knew we wanted to get back to the basics of banking," shares Chairman Bob Aston. "To us, it's all about friendships and relationships. Every loan we make benefits our community. Every dollar we contribute serves the families and children in our hometown. Together, we are building a great community asset. It's a terrific feeling to be a part of a team that is so giving, in both volunteer time and dollars, to make Hampton Roads a better place to live. We're proud to be such a special part of our hometown."

TowneBank has several locations throughout the Hampton Roads area. To find a branch location or automatic teller machine near you, please visit TowneBank on the Internet at www.townebankonline.com.

Above: TowneBank's Member Service Center, located at The Riverfront in HarbourView in Suffolk, Virginia, opened in July 2003. Situated on seven acres, this sixty-thousand-square-foot facility houses the bank's primary operational functions. The Member Service Center is host to the annual TowneBank Foundation Golf Tournament, the Fall Extravaganza, and many other bank and community events.

Below: In May 2005, TowneBank opened its first office in Norfolk, Virginia, the financial headquarters of Hampton Roads. The Norfolk office is located at 109 East Main Street in a 100-year old historic building that has been beautifully restored.

MARTY'S LOBSTER HOUSE

Many area residents still have fond memories of Marty's Lobster House, one of the first upscale restaurants in the Virginia Beach area. It was the sort of restaurant where the men were expected to wear a dress coat and it wasn't uncommon to find one of the owners, Johnny and Della Paphites, joining you for dinner.

Johnny and Della owned and operated Marty's Lobster House from 1952 until 1977 and they turned it into one of the hottest spots on the beach. The restaurant attracted local residents, as well as tourists, with its prime location, elegance and incredible dinners. All of the customers had one thing in common; they would return for another great meal.

Johnny grew up in Cyprus and came to the United States after working for a couple of years in swank clubs and restaurants in England. He arrived in America at the age of eighteen just in time to be drafted into the U.S. Army during World War II. By the end of the war, he had been promoted to Staff Sergeant and was in charge of feeding 3,500 German POW's daily.

Johnny had married a small-town girl from North Carolina, Della Mae Davis, and the couple settled in Norfolk following the war. They opened their first club, Windsor House, on Hampton Boulevard, then a restaurant called the Victory, which was located at Ward's Corner. The Windsor was noted for its popular dance floor and the live big band radio broadcasts that originated there. They also owned and operated the popular Court Café across from the police station and courthouse in downtown Norfolk

Johnny and Della took over Marty's Lobster House at Thirty-third and Atlantic in 1952. At the time, Marty's was the only building on the beach for blocks and blocks but it soon attracted a loyal following.

Marty's Lobster House became a landmark because of a giant sign on the roof. The sign featured a huge neon lobster that appeared to be pulling up a woman's skirt that extended into the night sky. The clever logo caught the attention of many passing celebrities including the McGuire Sisters, bandleaders Xavier Cugat and Guy Lombardo, and famed singer Rudy Valee.

Marty's was famous for its signature dishes such as lobster, snapper and Delmonico steaks. Della drove to the airport each morning to pick up the fresh lobsters and Johnny ordered all his steaks from Evans and Van Cleef, a supplier of gourmet foods in Washington, DC.

Johnny insisted that his lobsters were the best on the beach and that one of his lobsters "was worth ten

at any other restaurant." For customers who didn't want lobster, Johnny recommended his Red Snapper or Pompano, which he got fresh from Florida. No other restaurateur at the beach offered genuine Florida Snapper, filling orders instead with less tasty Japanese fish.

Johnny also praised his steaks, noting that each one was marbled exactly so that the flavorful juices came out in the broiling.

Although the Paphites' would share their recipes with anyone who asked, few could get the dishes to come out the same way. Johnny once told a newspaper reporter, "I have no secrets. I give all my recipes away and tell them exactly what to do—but they never do it right. They keep calling me back and telling me I left something out. But I tell them everything. Then I even tell them that if they want to cook like me, then they have to spend forty-eight years in the restaurant business."

Part of Johnny's secret was insisting on separate chefs for salads, frying and broiling. Each was a specialist at his task. A chef at heart, Johnny considered every dish on the menu the culmination of his life experiences.

Johnny and Della's sons, Tassos and Chris, grew up in the business and started working at the restaurant as soon as they were tall enough to look over the tables. They continued working at Marty's during summers while they were in college and are now partners in a fast-food franchise.

Johnny became a mentor to many of his employees and encouraged several of his chefs to open their own restaurants. He was always eager to teach them the fine points of the restaurant business.

Marty's Lobster House customers, even summer vacationers, returned often and Johnny and Della became close friends with many of them. Lots of people met their future husband or wife at Marty's and Johnny and Della became known

as matchmakers, even serving as godparents for some of the children.

Johnny retired in 1977 after operating Marty's for twenty-five years. He passed away December 19, 1996 at the age of eighty-five. Della still lives in Virginia Beach, along with her two sons, their wives, and seven grandchildren.

Although Marty's Lobster House is gone, it still lives on in the memories of the thousands who dined there over the years. And the taste of Marty's still lingers in his recipe for Lobster Princess:

A basic cream sauce
Two-ounces Spanish pimentos
One-ounce crème sherry wine
Three-ounces sliced mushrooms
Six-ounces fresh lobster meat
Romano cheese
Butter
Paprika

Prepare cream sauce and add the wine. Sauté the lobster meat in small amount of butter. Blend together all the ingredients except the cheese and paprika. Place in casserole dish. Sprinkle with Romano cheese and paprika. Bake at 400 degrees for five minutes. Serves one.

Marty's Lobster House was always a family business. Pictured are John Paphites, his wife, Della, and their sons Tassos (left) and Chris

NAE FEDERAL CREDIT UNION

NAE Federal Credit Union got its start in April 1965 when ten employees at the nearby Ford Motor Company plant put up $5 each to purchase a federal charter to start the non-profit financial institution.

The idea began with a friend of Palmer and Katy Stillman, who had belonged to a credit union in western Virginia. The friend raved about how the credit union treated its members and how credit unions charged smaller fees than banks and made money available to members who needed loans.

Palmer, who graduated from Old Dominion University with a bachelor's degree in business administration, conducted some research and decided it would be a good thing to open a credit union serving Ford employees.

The Norfolk Assembly Employees Credit Union, as it was originally called, opened for business in the two hundred square-foot enclosed porch on the back of the Stillmans' house in Indian River. Palmer was elected to the board of directors and appointed treasurer/manager, a position he has held ever since.

In the early days, Katy would drive to the plant once a day to drop off the checks for loans and withdrawals prepared the previous night. After a full day's work at the Ford plant, Palmer would gather daily deposits, approve loan and membership applications and requests for withdrawals and he and Katy would prepare for the next day's delivery.

The credit union operated this way until 1978 when it opened a 4,200-square-foot office on Indian River Road. A second office opened in 1994 on Battlefield Boulevard across from Chesapeake General Hospital, and in 2003, a third office opened in the Western Branch area of Chesapeake.

Palmer retired from Ford in January 1983, giving him the opportunity to run the credit union on a full-time basis. Although the credit union was formed to serve Ford employees, the National Credit Union Administration has granted it a community charter which allows it to serve persons who live, work (or regularly conduct business in), worship, volunteer, or go to school in, and businesses and other legal entities in Isle of Wight and Southampton Counties, including the cities of Franklin, Chesapeake, Norfolk, Portsmouth, Suffolk, and Virginia Beach. Palmer currently serves as president and CEO, while Katy serves as vice president.

The credit union that began with $50 and ten members has grown to $100 million in assets and 15,000 members. It employs more than fifty people at its three offices and works hard to attract and retain members by providing responsive, creative solutions to their financial needs.

It does this by providing quality products of value, effective, targeted marketing, superior member service, highly efficient operations and sound fiscal policies. But the reasons for its success go beyond finances. From the beginning, guided by a strong and stable board of directors with an average of

twenty-one years of volunteer service, the Stillmans have operated NAE Federal Credit Union by the following three principles:

- Treat others the way you want to be treated;
- You're not old until you stop learning, and;
- Try not to get above the level of the person you're trying to serve.

These principles, along with great employees, have made NAE Federal Credit Union successful. Giving members great service is the foundation on which the credit union's success is built. But NAE Federal Credit Union not only gives great service to its members, it also looks after them and cares about their welfare.

A perfect example of this took place in the late 1970s when Ford decided to stop making cars at its Norfolk plant and make trucks only. In the changeover, the company laid off four hundred people who had loans with the credit union.

The last thing the members needed at a time like this was pressure from a financial institution threatening them to pay up or else. The credit union did not pressure people to pay beyond their means and eventually everything worked out. Members appreciate that kind of loyalty and have reciprocated with loyalty of their own.

Several key strategies implemented by NAE Federal Credit Union have proven successful throughout the years and have contributed to ongoing financial success. These strategies include:

- Maintaining a managed loan-to-share ratio that meets member needs;
- Maintaining a strong net worth ratio;
- Consistently posting strong earnings;
- Maintaining a solid reputation among members;
- Establishing itself as the primary lending source for members, and;

- Continually meeting the needs of low-income members.

NAE Federal Credit Union has also demonstrated its loyalty to the community through its participation in the annual Make-A-Wish Foundation fund drive and its support for Habitat for Humanity. The credit union has supported this charity by donating a house.

NAE Federal Credit Union owes much of its success to the Stillmans, who in recent years have built a framework for the transition that will take place once they move on. No matter who runs the credit union in the coming years, you can rely on it to continue offering top-notch customer service to its members in an atmosphere built on kindness and respect.

For more information on what NAE Federal Credit Union has to offer you, please visit www.naefcu.org.

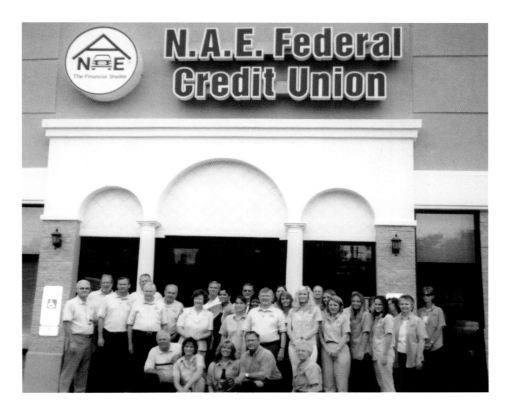

EQUIDATA

The organization known today as Equidata started business in 1905 with only one employee, stacks of index cards and a new-fangled invention called the telephone. The company has changed names and mission several times over the century and is known today as Equidata, a nationwide credit reporting and collection agency.

The Peninsula Grocer's Association, Equidata's original name, was formed by a group of area grocers as a way of exchanging ideas and promoting the grocery business. Since a major problem was customers who failed to pay their bills, the association soon evolved into a credit bureau. Files of credit experience were developed on individuals who were slow to pay their bills and these files were shared with association members.

The credit bureau was so successful that retailers of furniture, jewelry and soft goods asked to become members and the association's name was changed to the Newport News Retail Merchants Association. The association now focused its efforts on representing the credit reporting needs of all retailers.

Credit restrictions imposed by the government during World Wars I and II, along with the economic upheaval of the Great Depression, slowed the credit bureau's progress. Prosperity returned following World War II, however, and the credit bureau began a sustained period of diversification and growth. Although the growth was slowed some by the

Above: Chairman of the Board and CEO Grady M. Blaylock and Vice Chairman of the Board and Assistant CEO Loretta K. Zeitz, 2005.

Below: The building fondly referred to as the "Thirty-Second Street Office." The Peninsula Retail Merchants Association, now known as Equidata, was located in several downtown Newport News locations, including the above Thirty-Second Street office until moving to its present location in 1983.

wars in Korea and Vietnam, merchants were finding that it was good business to extend credit to worthy customers. The credit bureau's role was to help merchants investigate credit worthiness and report on credit histories.

A milestone in the credit reporting industry came in 1971 when the Fair Credit Reporting Act (FCRA) became law. The FCRA law created uniformity in the credit reporting industry by establishing specific guidelines and permissible purposes for the use of credit reports, as well as providing basic rights for consumers.

The FCRA provided the first legislation for the industry and has been amended seventeen times since its enactment with the most recent being the passage of the Fair and Accurate Credit Transactions Act in 2003. With credit becoming more commonplace, additional federal and state laws were enacted that govern other aspects of the credit reporting and collection industry. These include the Equal Credit Opportunity Act, Fair Debt Collection Practices Act and the Credit Repair Organizations Act.

A merger with the Hampton Retail Merchants Association and its credit bureau in 1970 and the purchase of the Credit Bureau of Williamsburg in 1972 helped build the company into a needed single repository for all credit and collection information in the area. To reflect the change, the organization's name was changed to Peninsula Retail Merchants Association following the consolidation of all credit bureaus from Toano to Hampton Roads.

Until 1974, credit bureau records were maintained manually on mechanized rotating files, a very labor-intensive system.

Computerization of credit bureau files opened up a new era in credit reporting, allowing subscribers to receive data from a terminal in their offices instead of by telephone or by mail.

The association relocated in 1983 from downtown Newport News to its current thirty-thousand-square-foot facility on three acres in the Oyster Point Business Park in Newport News. This move reflected the shift in the business community and allowed the credit bureau to be more accessible to customers in the Williamsburg area.

On May 31, 1989, Peninsula Retail Merchants Association became Commonwealth Information Services, Inc., a privately held stock company. Growth since then has been phenomenal and the company now has customers from coast-to-coast, in addition to the Virginia Peninsula.

Today, the firm is known as Equidata and operates three profit centers: credit bureau services, accounts receivable management services, and mortgage credit reporting services.

The credit bureau provides products and services to businesses from all three of the national credit reporting agencies, including credit scoring, fraud prevention tools, skip tracing services, employment screening and commercial credit reports. Other services include criminal history checks, eviction reports, tax return verification reports and driving records.

The credit bureau also provides direct-to-consumer credit reports and scores, credit monitoring and consumer credit resolution services.

The Mortgage Credit Reporting Division provides specialized credit reporting services to mortgage lenders and the Accounts Receivable Management Services Division provides collection services to commercial, retail, medical and utility markets for consumer and commercial accounts.

Equidata is headed by Chairman of the Board and CEO Grady M. Blaylock CCCE, CCBE, and Vice Chairman of the Board and Assistant CEO Loretta K. Zeitz.

Blaylock joined the company in 1974 as executive vice president, became president in 1987 and chairman of the board in 2002.

Zeitz began her career with the company as a part-time credit bureau employee in 1974 and is involved in all phases of the organization today.

Led by Blaylock's entrepreneurial style, Equidata is one of the few remaining credit bureaus in the country and the only one in Virginia that provides credit reports from all three major credit-reporting companies.

Equidata's motto, "People Who Know People," best describes the organization's key characteristic. Equidata is known as a highly respected and innovative company that strives to provide customers with the best credit reporting and collection services available. Equidata is constantly upgrading its services and expanding its product line to stay on the leading edge of technology. Equidata employees pride themselves on their professionalism and world-class customer service.

Equidata is located at 724 Thimble Shoals Boulevard in Newport News, Virginia 23606. You may reach Equidata by calling 757-873-0519 or toll-free 800-288-9809 or on the Internet at www.equidata.com.

⚓

Above: The Honorable Joe S. Frank, Mayor City of Newport News and pictured on right, presents a proclamation to Equidata and its Peninsula Credit Bureau for celebrating 100 years of continuous business in 2005 to Grady M. Blaylock and Loretta K. Zeitz.

Below: Equidata's current location in the Oyster Point Business Park.

Bank of the Commonwealth

Above: Bank of the Commonwealth's Main Office is located at 403 Boush Street in Norfolk.

Below: Bank of the Commonwealth Chairman of the Board, President, and CEO E.J. Woodard, Jr., CLBB.

Every community should be served by at least one locally owned and operated independent financial institution. This objective, advanced by a group of civic leaders in 1970, has flourished into our present-day Bank of the Commonwealth. The related conviction that residents could best be served by their friends and neighbors has endured throughout the bank's thirty-five year history and is the key to its success.

The bank was chartered on March 10, 1970, and its doors were opened to customers and shareholders for the first time on April 14, 1971,

as the only independent state-chartered bank serving citizens of Norfolk, Virginia, at the time. Under the guidance of our president and board of directors, bank staff began its long-standing commitment to meet the financial needs of individuals, businesses, churches, synagogues, and nonprofit organizations throughout our community. We also began pledging resources in association with local, state and federal governments to revive depressed or blighted neighborhoods.

We believe the economic health of our community depends upon individual success. That is why throughout our history we have listened and responded to thousands of customers, small business owners and civic group leaders who have relied on our encouragement and support. To guide our customers and investors toward achieving their goals, we patiently let those we lead build confidence in their vision. We understand their dreams and exhibit the strength of character to serve as an example for them to follow.

The bank works with small- and medium-size businesses, offering financial counseling and a broad range of depository and credit services. The bank understands that each customer is an individual who operates under a unique set of circumstances. The bank attempts to learn as much as possible about its customers' businesses and use that knowledge to align the business' objectives as well as the individual customer's wants and needs with the best strategy for the bank's participation in their success.

At Bank of the Commonwealth, it is the bank's mission to provide value-driven services that embody product selection, price, convenience and quality. Its products and services are designed to meet the changing economic demands that its customers face daily. It provides customers with products and services ranging from consumer checking accounts, commercial loans and trust services to mortgages, wealth management services and a vast array of insurance products.

In keeping with the times, the bank offers high-tech services such as twenty-four hour telephone banking, VISA check cards, and

online banking services for business and home use. No matter how high-tech its services may become, the foundation on which the service is built will always be the warm smiles and friendly handshakes that customers have appreciated since 1971.

The bank's people—the directorate, senior management and staff—continue to be its most valuable assets. Bank of the Commonwealth employees are innovative, creative, and have a strong desire to serve, always going the extra measure to ensure their customers' satisfaction.

Continuing their positive work outside of the bank, the bank's people allow it to fulfill one of its most important missions—community investment. By volunteering their time and resources to civic, charitable, and social organizations, Bank of the Commonwealth and its employees are the proud recipients of numerous community recognition awards like the United Way Achievers Award.

The bank is a supporter of the Greater Norfolk Corporation, the Heart Association, the Diabetes Foundation, the Norfolk SPCA, the Arthritis Foundation, the Tidewater Business Financing Corporation and more than fifty community boards and committees.

This spirit of compassion and volunteerism at Bank of the Commonwealth begins at the top with the bank's current Chairman, President, and CEO E. J. Woodard, Jr. A native of the Tidewater community, Woodard is a graduate of Woodrow Wilson High School in Portsmouth, Virginia. He continued his education at Frederick College, Old Dominion University and the American Institute of Banking. Married since 1967, he and his wife have one son. He is an active member of Talbot Park Baptist Church and has served on many civic and charitable organizations, committees and boards.

Woodard joined Bank of the Commonwealth in February 1972. He quickly rose to become the youngest individual elected to the position of bank president in the United States in 1973. He continues to guide

Bank of the Commonwealth's success by providing secure employment and career advancement for the benefit of bank staff and diligently pursues increased profitability and growth for the benefit of its shareholders.

The proof of his, and concurrently the bank's, success is perhaps best measured by the number of customers who have banked with Bank of the Commonwealth for decades and whose children and grandchildren have come to the bank to meet their financial needs. Faithful customers come to Bank of the Commonwealth—and stay with Bank of the Commonwealth—because they appreciate the difference the bank makes in their lives and the communities it serves.

The bank's vision for the future includes establishing itself as the premier community bank serving individuals and businesses in Hampton Roads. Although it continues to grow and reach out to new communities, it is still a local bank and its commitment to the Hampton Roads community will always reflect its special appreciation for the trust its customers and shareholders have placed in Bank of the Commonwealth.

Bank of the Commonwealth will always be the bank where you can bank with your neighbors. It welcomes the opportunity to count you among its customers, shareholders, and friends.

⚓

Above: Bank of the Commonwealth Executive Vice President and Chief Financial Officer Cynthia A. Sabol, CPA.

Below: Under the "Paint Your Heart Out Norfolk!" program sponsored by local Rotary Clubs, bank employees paint and repair the exteriors of homes for elderly, handicapped and low-income residents.

1ST ADVANTAGE FEDERAL CREDIT UNION

⚓

Above: Kiln Creek Branch features ample parking, six drive-thrus, two ATMs and video drive-thru displays.

Below: 1st Advantage Federal Credit Union offers seminars on checking accounts, retirement planning and much more all without a charge.

1st Advantage Federal Credit Union is a community chartered credit union providing financial services to the Hampton Roads community for over fifty years. Any member of the community that lives, works, worships or attends school in the Greater Virginia Peninsula area, including Hampton, Newport News, Williamsburg, Poquoson, York County, James City County, and Gloucester County, is eligible for membership.

In the past three years, 1st Advantage has experienced a fifty percent growth in assets in conjunction with opening membership eligibility to the entire community. To keep up with the rapid growth, they have opened three new branches in the past year, including a new headquarters located in York County and branch locations in Williamsburg and Gloucester County.

In order to support their mission, "To enhance the value of membership," 1st Advantage Federal Credit Union has made a commitment to educate the neighborhoods they serve. They accomplish this by offering a series of free seminars on topics such as the basics of checking, estate planning, identity theft, retirement planning and the principles of general financial health. Seminars are held regularly and are open to everyone in the community without charge.

The past year has not only brought additional branch locations, but 1st Advantage has adopted a new look as well. Branches have been renovated into state-of-the-art facilities providing faster, more efficient products and services including Coffee Cafes and Tech Kiosks with secure Internet access to their Homebanking and Bill Pay site.

1st Advantage supports the community through involvement with many charitable organizations including Habitat for Humanity, Relay for Life, Make-A-Wish, Center for Child and Family Services and sponsors several Bloodmobile drives each year. In addition, 1st Advantage colleagues and community members came together to raise over $80,000 for the Tsunami Relief and over $200,000 for the Hurricane Katrina Relief. Their colleagues also donate over thirty-five hundred hours of community service per year to participate in these and other worthwhile events.

1st Advantage, formerly known as Fort Eustis Federal Credit Union, has come a long way since their doors opened September 20, 1951. The credit union currently serves over 60,000 members located in all fifty states as well as overseas. Its assets are rapidly approaching $500 million and as of 2006, 1st Advantage Federal Credit Union will have nine branch locations spread across the Peninsula to serve its members.

Original organizers and charter members of the credit union were Charles D. Wary, Virginia S. Crawford, Benny L. Lacks, Margaret C. Tabb, E. M. Stevens, Eulalia G. Powell, Jean Fagley, R. E. Smith, Lynwood M. Perkins, and L. B. Epps.

As the story of their beginning goes, it all started on a hot August afternoon in 1951 when a small group of civilian employees at Fort Eustis were steamed, not so much by the heat but by the high interest rates charged by the 'loan sharks' that preyed on the employees.

As the discussion proceeded, someone asked, "How can we start a credit union?" The employees investigated the question, made application to the proper authorities, and on September 20, 1951, charter number 7448 was issued to the Fort Eustis Federal Credit Union.

The elected treasurer collected five hundred dollars from the charter members and carried the money around in a cigar box, along with a ledger showing who owed what. In those days, loans were made to any civilian employee of Fort Eustis without a credit check. The money was loaned solely on trust, epitomizing the credit union's motto, "People Helping People."

For more information, including branch or automatic teller machine locations, investment services, or even discount tickets, please call 1st Advantage Federal Credit Union at 757-877-2444 or toll free at 800-359-7650, or visit www.1stadvantage.org.

1st Advantage supports its community, here volunteers from 1st Advantage help build a home fot Habitat for Humanity.

GRAY'S PHARMACY

In no small measure, the history of Gray's Pharmacy is intertwined with the life and personality of its founder, Duryea DeBaun "Doc" Gray. He was born in 1892 in South Norfolk where his parents, William Frederick Gray and Theodosia Mary DeBaun, resided at Poindexter and D Streets.

In 1910, Gray graduated from Norfolk Academy, which was located on Bank Street prior to 1916. In 1912, he graduated from the Medical College of Virginia as a fully trained pharmacist.

R. L. Walkers Pharmacy in Brambleton employed Gray from 1914 to 1918. In 1916, he had married Sarah Elizabeth "Sadie" Morse of West Thirty-eighth Street in Norfolk. Two years later (in 1918) he bought Mac McNichols Confectionary at Forty-fourth and Myers Avenue. The business was renamed Gray's Pharmacy and Gray, his wife, and year-old son moved into the apartment above the store. Some years later, Myers Avenue was renamed Hampton Boulevard and Forty-fourth Street became Forty-eighth.

In the early days the store had three employees: one each at the front counter and the soda fountain, along with a delivery boy. In 1918, this staff, along with Gray himself, realized gross sales, on a good day, of $25. By 1968, the payroll had increased to a total of twenty-four people and the daily gross averaged $1,000.

Gray also had a strong desire to keep up-to-the-moment with industry trends that he felt would be of benefit to his operation but, at the same time, pay homage to the past. His was among the first pharmacies to make an extensive effort to provide delivery service over an area that was extremely wide considering the size of his operation. At the beginning, deliveries were made on Gray's personal 1912 Harley-Davidson V-Twin. Later, bicycle and an automobile supplemented this and, eventually, deliveries were made entirely by automobile. Another innovation was the opening of Post Office Substation #1. This was the first such facility in Virginia and continued operation, offering full postal services, until July 2005,

Duryea DeBaun "Doc" Gray, founder of Gray's Pharmacy.

when the U.S. Postal Service closed most of these facilities nationwide.

Gray also had a good size collection of memorabilia in the stockroom, which included typewriters dating from the teens through the thirties. There was also a "penny slot" machine left from the days of McNichols Confectionary. The machine remained in use until slots were outlawed. For the risk of only a penny, a customer had a chance to win a five-cent token good only for merchandise within the store. The penny scale inside the front doors today was also part of the 1918 purchase and still provides one's weight and fortune. There were a good number of period bottles, cans, and cardboard tubes containing such arcane as "Zanzibar Cloves," "Powdered Elm Bark," and a quarter-ounce bottle of "Gold Chlorie." From time to time Doc would get a phone call asking how some of these compounds were used and he would always have an answer.

Gray's business sense was of two kinds. In the earlier days, he would buy up smaller competitors as they came on the market and transfer their prescriptions to his main location. At the end of the lease, the smaller store would be closed down. He also had an uncanny ability to know intuitively what—and how many—

seasonal specialty items he could sell, thus avoiding carryover of stock that could be out of fashion by the next year. The decisions to buy out competitors, of course, were based on careful calculation. Although unerringly accurate, buying Christmas goods in August was entirely a matter of gut feeling.

There was other family participation in the store in later years. Gray's son, D. D. Gray, Jr., worked in the store during high school and summers while attending MCV. Upon his graduation in 1939 he went to work in the business full time until his death in 1959 due to complications following heart surgery. In the late 1940s and mid-'50s, he served several terms on the State Board of Pharmacy, one of which was as its president. Following World War II, Doc's son-in-law, B. J. Luhring, joined the operation until the business was sold. Doc's two grandsons—D. D. Gray III and William T.

Gray—also worked for the family business in the 1950s and '60s.

There were numerous long-term employees whose major contributions to making Gray's Pharmacy what it was—and is today—were beyond value. Each is a story in its own right. When Doc decided that fifty-one years was enough, he felt extremely fortunate that A. R. "Boots" Culler was in a position to take over the maintenance of the tradition in 1969 and, indeed, he did a fine job.

Doc died in April 1984. The business was sold to David J. Halla in 1989 in a deal partially brokered by Doc's family, which had hopes that it would be a seamless transition. From the beginning, Halla has done everything possible to retain the atmosphere of the past. He has, however, failed to develop a taste for Hava-Tampa, New Jewel cigars that had perfumed the back counter during Doc's tenure.

The evolution of Gray's Pharmacy through the years.

GEICO

GEICO takes pride in being one of the nation's fastest growing auto insurance companies and we are equally proud of the work we do outside our office walls. Part of GEICO's corporate mission is to encourage active, involved citizenship. GEICO associates read, build, mentor, walk, run, coach—we do whatever it takes to help organizations and people in need.

GEICO's Virginia Beach regional office is no exception. Associates in the region have been helping make the Hampton Roads community a better place through their efforts with both local and national organizations.

GEICO takes a leading role in the safety arena by promoting and improving highway safety to reduce traffic deaths and injuries. GEICO's "Real Teen Driving" video is included as a mandatory component in the Drive Safe Hampton Roads' "Get It Together" seat belt campaign, adopted by approximately forty area high schools. GEICO's Real Teen Driving program went on to earn the John T. Hanna Award for "Traffic Safety Excellence" and the Governor's Award for Youth Traffic Safety.

GEICO's Virginia Beach associates are involved in numerous volunteer and fundraising efforts:

- GEICO associates take an active role in Relay For Life, the American Cancer Society's signature event that raises money for research, education, advocacy, and patient services. This event is neither a race nor an athletic event, but a community gathering with something for everyone. GEICO entered over 30 teams and raised nearly $60,000 during Relay For Life 2005.

- Through the 2005 United Way Campaign, GEICO associates raised a total of $255,000. They were also the presenting sponsors of the first-ever United Way telethon of South Hampton Roads in February 2006.

- More than four hundred Virginia Beach associates volunteered to help many worthwhile organizations in 2005, as part of the GEICO Corporate Community Citizens (GCCC).

Each year, GEICO's Virginia Beach regional office recognizes its associates' volunteer contributions to the community and presents GEICO Volunteer Services Awards to recognize those who volunteer.

On the corporate level, GEICO sponsors neighborhood and educational programs and holds company-wide fundraisers in support of worthy causes. GEICO also supports its associates by matching their contributions to charitable organizations (up to $500) and to colleges and universities (up to $2,500).

As individuals and as a corporate citizen, we know the only way to build stronger communities for tomorrow is to invest our time and energy today. We're proud of the many ways we contribute. We call it our insurance plan for the future.

Below: GEICO's Virginia Beach office.

Bottom: GEICO's 2005 Relay for Life team at Oceana Park in Virginia Beach.

With a history scanning more than 135 years, SunTrust Bank has roots deep in Virginia history. Its predecessor institutions, Farmer's Bank of Virginia and Planter's National Bank, played pivotal roles in many of the Commonwealth's major events, including the rebuilding of Richmond following the Civil War.

SunTrust has served the banking needs of Eastern Virginia since the mid 1800s. Its Norfolk affiliate was established in 1867 and in Williamsburg, Gloucester and the Eastern Shore, SunTrust is the oldest bank in the market.

Along the way, Planter's National Bank became United Virginia Bank, changed its name to Crestar in the mid-eighties and merged with SunTrust Bank on December 21, 1998.

Although SunTrust Bank is justly proud of its rich heritage; its focus is on the future. The institution is deeply involved in improving the economic wellbeing of the region. This respect for the community is evident in a number of ways—from providing seed financing for the $300 million MacArthur Center, the City of Norfolk's downtown retail complex, to driving nails and helping build a Habitat for Humanity home.

"Our clients and their businesses are enmeshed with the identity of the region," comments Bill Butler, SunTrust, Hampton Roads president and CEO. "This has become increasingly rare in today's world of mega mergers," he said, citing such examples as being the lead bank for many of the region's top businesses and a primary financier for the peanut industry in Suffolk.

Local autonomy and decision making, which helps build personal relationships, means that most loan requests are approved within the region with many approvals on the same day.

SunTrust combines a "small-town" approach to banking with leading-edge capabilities that include products and services such as sophisticated treasury management; municipal financing; short and long-term investment capabilities; electronic data exchange with customers; and international capabilities. The bank's Internet-based products and services include websites offering secure on-line trading capabilities.

SunTrust also believes in being a good citizen of the communities it serves. In addition to the more than $750,000, which SunTrust contributes annually to charities in Hampton Roads, employees participate in such activities as Paint Your Heart Out, Relay for Life, Muscular Dystrophy Telethon and countless other volunteer events.

SunTrust Banks, Inc., headquartered in Atlanta, is one of the nation's largest banking organizations, serving a broad range of consumer, commercial, corporate and institutional clients. As of September 30, 2005, SunTrust had total assets of $172.4 billion and total deposits of $113.7 billion. The company operates an extensive branch and ATM network throughout the high growth Southeast and Mid-Atlantic markets and a full array of technology-based, twenty-four hour delivery channels. The company also serves customers in selected markets nationally. Its primary businesses include deposit, credit, and trust and investment services. Through various subsidiaries, the company provides credit cards, mortgage banking, insurance, brokerage, equipment leasing and capital markets services. SunTrust's Internet address is www.suntrust.com.

SUNTRUST BANK

SunTrust Hampton Roads moved their local headquarters to 150 West Main Street in downtown Norfolk in 2003.

LIPTON TEA

Above: Thomas J. Lipton.

Below: Lipton Tea's facility in Suffolk.

Businessman and philanthropist Thomas J. Lipton founded the first Lipton Tea Shop in Glasgow, Scotland in 1871. The Suffolk tea plant did not come along until 1955 but in the past fifty years, the community that marked the life of Sir Thomas Lipton has known the plant for hard work, innovation and dedication.

Over the years, production at the Suffolk plant has expanded from a single product, Flo-Thru Tea Bag, to a variety of regular, naturally decaffeinated teas, instant teas, food service teas and a wide array of specialty tea lines. In 2006, organic tea and pyramid-shaped tea bags were introduced.

Lipton's tea production facility in Suffolk is a blend of traditional and modern. While the plant culture continues to reflect the heritage of its founder, employees are constantly creating a dynamic contemporary environment built on principles of continuous improvement.

Lipton currently operates a four-shift, 7-day, 24-hour operation with a staff of more than 300 employees. The longevity of the plant can be attributed to the innovative spirit and dedication of these employees.

The Suffolk operation is devoted exclusively to tea production. The staff can be given almost any challenging request to modify or fabricate equipment to meet customer demands and they always come up with a solution.

The 15 production lines with 120 Constanta tea-packaging machines make up 69 percent of Lipton's Suffolk plant business. Lipton's talented operators run several tea machines, perform quality inspections, and assist the mechanics in maintaining the machines. Lipton's mechanics are responsible for maintaining tea machines at the expected efficiency rate, making sure at the same time that a quality product is produced. The machines are linked to a computerized system that alerts an operator or mechanic of any problem before it reaches the customer.

Lipton employees demonstrate the kindheartedness and generosity exemplified by the company founder, who became a noted philanthropist as well as one of the world's most successful businessmen.

A few of the community outreach programs conducted by the Suffolk plant include donations to a wide range of health, arts, cultural, and educational organizations. Active employee volunteerism includes a School-Business Partnership with Suffolk's Kilby Shores Elementary School. Employees participate in an extensive recycling program in which seventy percent of the plant's environmental waste is recycled or reused.

Other community outreach programs include participation in the Nansemond-Suffolk Volunteer Rescue Squad, the March of Dimes, and the American Cancer Society's Relay for Life.

The Suffolk facility celebrated its fiftieth year in 2005, and is proud that it remains the only Lipton leaf tea producer in the United States. Lipton Tea appreciates the support of its neighbors, the local and state governments, and its dedicated customers and suppliers and, most of all, its highly committed employees.

HOLLY POINT APARTMENTS

Holly Point Apartments, located at 2410 Holly Point Boulevard in Chesapeake, are custom designed for exclusive residential living. With extraordinary amenities, quality construction and a spectacular landscape, Holly Point offers everything you would expect in fine apartment living. No wonder Holly Point is known as "The Hideaway Next Door."

At Holly Point, you'll find one, two, or three bedroom apartments—ranging from 850 to 1,890 square feet—in addition to townhomes and furnished corporate apartments.

Holly Point is professionally managed by Drucker & Falk, LLC, one of the nation's oldest and most prestigious investment real estate firms. Drucker & Falk, LLC, now manages more than twenty-eight thousand residential units, including Holly Point Apartments in Chesapeake.

You may lease a beautiful home at Holly Point with confidence because of Drucker & Falk's long history of quality and integrity. Residents may choose from among sixteen floor plans, some with porches and water views. Features include private entrances, patios and balconies, large kitchens with utility rooms, bay windows, ceiling fans, spacious closets, and monitored alarm systems.

Among the many community features are gated entrances, impeccable landscaping, saunas and whirlpool, Olympic size swimming pool, twenty-four-hour fitness center, two tennis courts, two playgrounds, putting green, dog run and car care area.

Other amenities include a twenty-four-hour resident business center, the Holly Point Club Room for private parties and resident activities each month. There's even a Holly Point Senior Club.

With all it has to offer, it is no surprise that Holly Point has won the Tidewater Multi-family Housing Council's Award of Excellence for several years in a row.

One Holly Point resident comments, "I cannot believe the customer service I have received at Holly Point. If I had to sum it up in one word I'd say 'outstanding'!"

Another resident commented, "Location-wise, this is one of the best and largest apartments I have ever seen. Thank you for that."

Drucker & Falk, LLC was founded on solid business values, including honesty, integrity and respect for all clients, customers and employees. Those values still drive the organization today.

Above: Holly Point Apartments is located at 2410 Holly Point Boulevard in Chesapeake.

Below: Beautifully landscaped yards await you at Holly Point.

NEWPORT NEWS SHIPBUILDING EMPLOYEES' CREDIT UNION

⚓

Above: Original board of directors, May 1928. Standing, left to right: R.P. Lentz, G.A. Jernigan, J.K.H. Houston, A.N. Shankland, Sr. Seated left to right: J. Cargill Johnson, treasurer; G. Guy Via, secretary; S.S. Archibald, president; T.H. Blair, first vice president; F.W. Wright, second vice president. Not pictured: G.S. Buchanan, A.T. Wiatt and E.T. Goodwin.

Bottom: Corporate office is located at 3711 Huntington Avenue in Newport News, Virginia.

Newport News Shipbuilding Employees' Credit Union was organized in April 1928 to encourage thrift and make loans at a reasonable rate of interest to employees of Newport News Shipbuilding and Dry Dock Company.

The Commonwealth of Virginia chartered the new credit union, which was organized and managed entirely by employees of Newport News Shipbuilding.

During its first month of operation, the credit union collected $972.95 in shares and made loans to members totaling $250. By the end of the first year, the institution had more than 530 members and assets of $15,065. The credit union reached its first million in assets in 1952 and $100 million in assets in 1984, the same year the 100,000th member account was opened.

By 2005, with membership exceeding 80,000, the assets of Newport News Shipbuilding Employees' Credit Union approached $1 billion. The credit union offers a full range of financial services such as loans, mortgages, checking accounts, credit cards, share certificates, money market accounts, individual retirement accounts, and brokerage services.

The Credit Union operated out of the shipyard for the first thirty-five years of its existence before establishing its own downtown facility in 1963. The organization now boasts branches throughout the Hampton Roads community.

Three outstanding individuals—A.T. Wiatt, Frank Beard and Edward Bennett—were instrumental in the organization and growth of the credit union.

A.T. Wiatt, an employee of the shipyard from 1912 until 1954, was a member of the special committee that first organized the credit union. He was elected a member of the original Board of Directors and served faithfully for forty years and nine months. Wiatt was a strong advocate of the credit union movement's motto: "Not for profit, not for charity, but for service."

Known throughout Virginia as "Mr. Credit Union," Frank Beard was labor relations manager for the shipyard and served as credit union president from 1964 until his death in 1970. He also served as president of the Virginia Credit Union League and organized the Hampton Roads Chapter of Credit Unions.

Edward Bennett was employed by the credit union for forty-one years and served on the Board of Directors from 1964 until 1989. He was also a director of the Board of the Virginia Credit Union League and was instrumental in the organization of the Hampton Roads and Tidewater Chapters. In 1982, Bennett became the first credit union official to become president of the Virginia's Automated Clearinghouse Association.

NNSECU members and employees are deeply involved in the community and support dozens of worthwhile organizations, including the American Red Cross, the American Cancer Society, Boy Scouts of America, Children's Miracle Network, Juvenile Diabetes Research Foundation, Peninsula Food Bank and many others.

For additional information or for a branch near you, visit the website at www.nnsecu.org.

After 22 years and 10 moves with Fortune 500 companies, Forrest and Linda Bassett were faced with yet another move. While on a cruise to celebrate their anniversary, Forrest and Linda decided it was time to take control of what they wanted to do and where they wanted to live.

On returning from the cruise, they began a five-month investigation of the franchise industry that resulted in their opening a Signs By Tomorrow store at 11712 Jefferson Avenue in Newport News.

"Making the decision to let go of corporate life at age forty-two was a bit scary with two college-bound young adults," says Forrest. "However, our past careers and life experiences prepared Linda and me to more than maintain our lifestyle and take control of our destiny while enjoying every day."

The Newport News Signs By Tomorrow, founded in 1998, provides signs and visual communications to retail and business customers. The store utilizes state-of-the-art computers and technology to provide a wide variety of exterior and interior signs and banners, competitively priced with rapid turnaround.

The Newport News location grew rapidly and in March 2002, the Bassett's daughter, Lacy, and her fiancé, Jason Kuller, came home from college to help move to a larger location. Before they returned to James Madison University, however, they informed her parents they wanted to transfer to a local school, Christopher Newport University, and learn the business so they could open a Signs By Tomorrow franchise after graduation.

The *Newport News Daily Press* in a 2006 feature article spotlighted the success of this inherited entrepreneurial spirit. As the article reports, "After three years of working with the Bassetts, the two decided to venture out on their own. The Kullers, by now husband-and-wife, approached the Bassetts about opening another location, an idea that had been in the back of their minds since they began working there."

The second Bassett/Kuller family-owned Signs By Tomorrow franchise opened in January 2005 at 1036 Volvo Parkway in Chesapeake.

The newspaper article went on to say, "While each of the family members share an entrepreneurial spirit, the Kullers' younger

perspective blends with the Bassetts' developed business sense and background in marketing."

The Bassetts have played a key role in the development of the Signs By Tomorrow franchise marketing and development program and Forrest has served more than five years on the Franchise Advisory Council, including a term as chairman. In addition, Forrest and Linda were awarded the "2003 Small Business Person of the Year" award by the Virginia Peninsula Chamber of Commerce.

"As owners of two stores, our family loves and enjoys the industry and Signs By Tomorrow," says Forrest. "In fact, we have referred three close friends who have become franchisees through the Signs By Tomorrow Partners in Progress Program."

SIGNS BY TOMORROW

⚓

Below: Forrest and Linda Bassett, Newport News, Virginia.

Bottom: Lacy and Jason Kuller with Kalyx Kuller, "Top Dog of Public Relations," Chesapeake, Virginia.

THE BARTER AUTHORITY

The ancient system of barter—the exchange of goods and services of equal value—was the only form of commerce in the early colonial era in Hampton Roads. The old barter format of the colonial times has been modernized for today's economy thanks to development of on-line computer programs that are just as sophisticated as the ones used by the country's largest banks.

Since banks were not formed in America until 1791, early settlers had to rely on barter arrangements to conduct business. In Hampton Roads, most crops, but particularly tobacco, became the most barter-able products of all. Tobacco became the currency of the Hampton Roads region in those early colonial times. Barter became a form of credit, in that farmers would purchase much needed supplies on credit during the planting season, on the promise to deliver an equal amount of their crops as payment when their harvests came in. Tobacco was used as wages for the soldiers and clergy, to purchase indentured servants, and amazingly—in some cases—to even purchase wives!

Today, hundreds of thousands of businesses, ranging from doctors, lawyers, restaurants, and printers to household names like Xerox and Pepsi conduct millions of dollars worth of barter transactions annually. Businesses today view barter as an excellent tool to increase their sales, preserve their cash flows and maximize their operational capacity.

The premise for today's resurgence of barter is a simple one; most all businesses are looking to grow their revenues while minimizing their costs for attracting new business.

Today's organized barter exchanges like The Barter Authority provide regional businesses with an attractive alternative marketplace to capture more business without incurring any major costs. Barter exchanges focus on bringing their participating business members new customers that they would have never had, but for their involvement in the barter program.

Bartering has come a long way from the Jamestown days in Hampton Roads. But the basic principles that made barter work four hundred years ago holds true today. Commerce must thrive for communities to succeed, and currencies must be established to facilitate that commerce, whether they be the "coin of the realm" or complementary currencies like barter. And, just like the good old colonial times, The Barter Authority does have access to tobacco products on barter, but in this day and age they can't barter to get you a husband or wife!

The Barter Authority is located at 4126 Granby Street in Norfolk. To learn more about the advantages of membership, please call 757-622-4242, or visit www.thebarterauthority.com.

Peter Decker is proof positive that the American dream still lives.

The seventh child of first-generation Lebanese parents, Peter G. Decker, Jr. was born in Norfolk, graduated from Maury High School, served in the U.S. Army and was given an honorable discharge. Determined to succeed, he received a "Poor Man's Scholarship" to attend Old Dominion University and received his law degree from the Marshall Wythe School of Law at The College of William & Mary in 1960.

A talented musician, Decker helped pay his way through school by performing as a singer, as a bass fiddle player and by emceeing many events around the area. He continues to sing and emcee as a hobby and many of his old friends still come to hear him.

A dynamic and passionate man with a larger-than-life personality, Decker began his career as a one-attorney firm forty-five years ago. The firm prospered because of his dedication to helping people and, today, Decker, Cardon, Thomas, Weintraub & Neskis has thirty employees, including eight attorneys and is one of the most respected law firms in the area.

The firm's attorneys include Peter G. Decker, Lawrence M. Cardon, Martin A. Thomas, H. Joel Weintraub, George A. Neskis, Richard W. Ratajczak, Peter G. Decker III, and Michelle R. Parker.

From the very beginning, Decker insisted that the number one priority for the firm would be helping people. The firm specializes in personal injury law, criminal defense, traffic offenses, probation and parole cases, estate law and business law.

Decker's generosity and commitment to helping people has led him to serve on numerous local, regional and national boards and commissions. He is a dedicated supporter of St. Jude Children's Research Hospital and has served as a member of the hospital's Board of Governors and Directors for more than thirty-five years. In addition, he is a former national executive vice president in charge of fundraising for St. Jude Children's Research Hospital and was named director emeritus of the hospital in 1999.

Decker is also deeply involved in community affairs and serves as chairman of the Advisory Board of the National Maritime Center (Nauticus) and as chairman of the Board of

Commissioners of the Norfolk International Airport Authority. In addition, Decker served thirty years on the Board of SCOPE, the Civic Facilities Commission of Norfolk, and for many years with the Downtown Norfolk Council. In fact, Decker chaired the effort to bring ambassadors to Downtown Norfolk through the Business Improvement District and it has proven to be a most beneficial program to the merchants and visitors alike in Norfolk.

Decker was on the powerful Virginia State Board of Corrections for twelve years and served as chairman of corrections for seven of those years. Decker also served for four years on the Virginia State Board of Education.

Decker has a deep love for his hometown of Norfolk. He and his wife, Bess, introduced "Mermaids on Parade" to Norfolk in 2000. Now, when you walk around Norfolk's neighborhoods, you are greeted by colorful, life-size mermaid statues. The program has generated hundreds of thousands of dollars for area arts organizations, and the mermaid is a widely recognized symbol of Norfolk. Among the many awards Decker has received, one of the most distinguished was the award he received from the prestigious Cosmopolitan Club as "First Citizen of the City of Norfolk" in 1999.

According to Decker, the benchmarks by which his firm measures success are not what some observers might expect. For nearly a half-century, the firm has measured victory against defeat by whether or not it got the best possible result for its clients.

When all is said and done, Decker believes the firm's interests are served only by serving the interests of the people who have turned to him for help.

DECKER, CARDON, THOMAS, WEINTRAUB & NESKIS, P.C.

Front row (from left to right): H. Joel Weintraub, Peter G. Decker, Jr., and Peter G. Decker III. Middle row: Martin A. Thomas and George A. Neskis. Back row: Richard W. Ratajczak, Lawrence M. Cardon, and Michelle R. Parker.

CROSSROADS FUEL SERVICE

Crossroads Fuel Service Inc. began in 1960 when John W. Keffer decided it would be a natural extension of the plumbing and heating contracting business in which he worked. A neighbor, Merlin Miller, agreed to invest in Keffer's venture and the two men began Miller & Keffer Oil Company.

They made supply arrangements with Phillips Petroleum and recorded first-year sales of $10,000. Five years later, Keffer purchased a gas station and small store at Mount Pleasant Road and Centerville Turnpike, becoming the first service station serviced by Miller & Keffer. The station has gone through several additions and renovations through the years, but it remains one of Crossroad Fuel's best gasoline accounts.

In 1967, Keffer bought Miller's half of the partnership and, changed the name to Crossroads Fuel Service. He took the name from the intersection of Mount Pleasant Road and Centerville Turnpike. Sales that year reached $250,000.

The company continued to grow slowly with Keffer working full time at the Ford plant and operating the oil company on the side. He had help from part-time employees, including his son, Alan. In 1971, Keffer incorporated as Crossroads Fuel Service Inc. and, a year later, left the Ford plant to devote his full attention to the business.

The business expanded to Elizabeth City, North Carolina in 1973 with the purchase of a small Phillips 66 jobbership and a Citgo jobbership that, together, nearly doubled the company's size. The oil shortage of the early 1970s presented unforeseen challenges to the oil industry. Crossroads not only survived this period, it prospered. It did so through hard work and the fact that the company had developed a good relationship with both Phillips and Citgo. Business increased another twenty-five percent at a time when many small oil jobbers were going out of business.

In 1981 the company purchased Reid Fuel Oil Service in Suffolk, Virginia, adding the third branch office to the Crossroads family. Crossroads also purchased Gulf Oil, Amoco and Unocal 76 jobberships to further expand its business. The company dropped the Citgo brand, Gulf became BP and Phillips pulled out of Virginia and northeastern North Carolina in the 1980s.

But Crossroads continued to grow at a steady rate. In 1992 the company expanded into the propane business, beginning much the same as it had in the oil business more than three decades earlier. With a used delivery truck, a few customers, a dream and a firm determination, the company set out to win the confidence and the business of propane customers.

Throughout the next several years, propane operations expanded to each of the company's four locations, which now included Sunbury, North Carolina, a site Crossroads added in 1991 when it purchased Byrum Oil Company.

All ten of Keffer's children worked in the business at one time or another. Some worked for very short periods of time, while others made the business their full time careers. Lynn Keffer, the eighth child and fourth boy, serves as president, while Marilyn, the fifth child and second girl, serves as secretary and treasurer.

Keffer passed away in 1996, leaving a legacy of hard work and generosity. Under Lynn and Marilyn Keffer's leadership, Crossroads has continued to expand. The company now has office and storage facilities in Chesapeake and Franklin, Virginia, and Hertford, Sunbury, and Columbia, North Carolina. Crossroads offers BP/Amoco, Sunoco and Pure branded gasoline to its forty-five retail gasoline station/store accounts.

The company sells and delivers more than 25 million gallons of petroleum products using its fleet of 40 delivery trucks. Crossroads employs 50 and has sales of more than $40 million.

Crossroads Fuel Service Inc. continues to provide old-fashioned customer service and quality products. And although much about the company will no doubt change in the future, its old-fashioned commitment to service and quality will never waver.

One of the delights of living in Hampton Roads is having the wonders of the Chesapeake Bay at your doorstep. With a wide range of services and amenities, Salt Ponds Marina is ready to help residents and visitors alike take full advantage of the area's many attractions.

Voted "Best Marina" on the lower Chesapeake Bay for many years by the *Chesapeake Bay Magazine* reader survey, Salt Ponds Marina offers a number of advantages for all types of boaters.

The marina provides 254 slips accommodating boats up to 110 feet in length, state-of-the-art floating docks, and dockside pedestals with electrical and water hookups. Annual and transient slips are available. You'll find a fuel dock with gas, diesel and sewage pump-out, four strategically located shower facilities and two coin laundries. A professionally trained staff is ready to help meet your needs.

You'll enjoy the facilities at Salt Ponds Marina whether you're an experienced boater or someone who just likes to hang out around the water. The marina offers a full-service waterfront restaurant with a banquet facility, cabana bar and pool. On-site, are also a marine service, a marine broker, a boat club, and a ship store with gifts, clothing, snacks and sodas. There is also a family pool for the kids.

You can go for a walk on the beach or take a day trip from Salt Ponds Marina to Busch Gardens or the historic sites of Colonial Williamsburg, Jamestown, and Yorktown, which are within twenty-five minutes of the marina. You can fish in the bay or venture to the Atlantic for deep-sea fishing on one of the charter boats that dock at the marina. Salt Ponds is only fifty-three miles from the Norfolk Canyon and three-and-a-half hours from the Gulf Stream.

There is a wide array of fish in the bay including, flounder, rockfish, cobia, and speckled trout or you can head to sea and land a trophy size tuna, marlin, or dolphin. Catches can be brought into the marina for official weighing or to use one of our cleaning stations.

If you're coming by sea, Salt Ponds is located halfway between Hampton Roads Channel and Back River Channel, 332 degrees from Thimble Shoals Light. Visitors coming by land will find easy access from I-64. Take the Mallory Street exit (268) north on Mallory to Pembroke Avenue, right to the bay, and take a left onto First Street and go three-quarters of a mile to the entrance of Salt Ponds.

FRANKIE'S PLACE FOR RIBS

One of the best restaurants for barbeque ribs and chicken in Virginia Beach can be found at the corner of Kempsville and Providence Roads in the Fairfield Shopping Center. The restaurant is called Frankie's Place for Ribs and it has been voted the "Best of the Beach" by *The Virginian-Pilot* newspaper for a dozen years.

The secret to Frankie's popularity, according to owner Mike Daniel, is quality. "We look for quality to begin with," he says. "That means the best baby back ribs we can find, not the cheapest."

Then, the tender, meaty ribs are smoked and marinated in Frankie's secret BBQ sauce and charcoal grilled to produce a delicious hickory-smoked flavor.

If you're not in the mood for ribs, Frankie's Certified Angus Beef steaks and all the other menu items are equally delicious.

Frankie's is open seven days a week for lunch and dinner. The restaurant also offers pick-up or home delivery within the area. You can also have Frankie's ribs shipped to your home, no matter where you live. They will arrive fully cooked and frozen; all you have to do is warm them up.

The staff at Frankie's Place for Ribs is professional and friendly and several have been working at the restaurant since it opened sixteen years ago. Frankie's is a friendly place to visit and kids are always welcome.

Right: Historical interpreters fire muskets at Yorktown Victory Center's recreated Continental Army Encampment.

COURTESY OF THE YORKTOWN VICTORY CENTER

Opposite: The Daughters of Durand-Ruel *by Pierre Auguste Renoir. The painting is part of the collection at the Chrysler Museum of Art in Norfolk.*

COURTESY OF THE CHRYSLER MUSEUM OF ART.

Great Bridge Lock.

PHOTO BY PAUL CLANCY

BUILDING A GREATER HAMPTON ROADS

Hampton Roads' real estate, construction companies, and manufacturing industries shape the county's future and provide fuel for the state

SPECIAL THANKS TO

Ferguson

R. D. Lambert & Son, Inc., General Contractor

Stock Building Supply

COLDWELL BANKER PROFESSIONAL, REALTORS®

A century of outstanding success. A complete range of services. A vital part of every community it serves. Offices throughout the United States to meet the needs of your every move and help you make your dreams come true. That's what happens when good becomes great. And that's what happens every day at Coldwell Banker Professional, Realtors®, your perfect partner in real estate. At Coldwell Banker Professional, Realtors®, we're with you all the way home.

This is the story of the growth and development of the Coldwell Banker company and of Coldwell Banker Professional, Realtors® in Hampton Roads, one of the most unique franchise groups ever developed upon the sound practices and innovative thinking at the company's roots.

What began as one man's desire to provide honorable, ethical and professional real estate services to consumers has come to set the standards in the real estate industry. Colbert Coldwell's dedication to his profession is the underlying strength for Coldwell Banker's continuing success. From the time Benjamin Banker joined the firm in 1913, the values the two men shared never wavered. Expansion and innovation have always been integral to Coldwell Banker's success. In 1981, Coldwell Banker Residential Affiliates, Inc., began franchising real estate brokerage offices. By 1991 there were locations in all

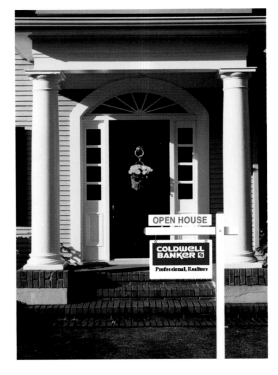

fifty states. International expansion began in the mid-1990s.

Today Coldwell Banker Real Estate Corporation franchises operate over thirty nine hundred offices worldwide. Approximately one in ten of all United States home sales that use a real estate agent involve a Coldwell Banker sales associate.

In 2001, in response to the changing real estate market, six of the best local minds in the business came together. Their reputations and level of success placed them at the top of their industry. Tommy Thompson, Tim Gifford, Dorcas Helfant-Browning, Rick West, and Bill Shelton, along with Williamsburg's John Wilson set out to create a business plan unlike anything that had gone before. Egos, and even the names of their agencies, were set aside as they took pride in their diversity, and united the best in Hampton Roads under one umbrella. That umbrella would be a new organization—Coldwell Banker Professional, Realtors®.

In 2002, two additional brokers, Parker Neff with Cooke and Neff, Inc., and Fella Rhodes with Rhodes Realty of Chesapeake, joined as branch partners in the firm. Allen Pyle of Pyle Realty joined as a branch partner in 2006 bringing the total number of offices, serving Eastern Virginia from North

❦

Above: Your Perfect Partner® in real estate!

Below: Superior customer service is Coldwell Banker's main priority. Its highly trained agents thoroughly explain the buying and selling process from beginning to end.

Carolina to Richmond, to fourteen. Managing partners include:

- Dorcas Helfant-Browning, Helfant Realty Virginia Beach (757-463-1212). Helfant-Browning, the new organization's general managing partner, established Helfant Realty in 1976. This industry trailblazer and workplace dynamo has been in the business for three decades. She served as the Virginia Association of Realtors®' (VAR) first woman president, first woman president of the one-million strong National Association of Realtors® (NAR) and holds professional designations CRB, CRS, CIPS, and LTG. Both NAR and VAR have recognized her with the prestigious "Realtor of the Year" award.

- Tim Gifford, Gifford Realty, Norfolk (757-583-1000). Gifford Realty, founded by Joan Gifford in 1955, and one of the first Norfolk businesses owned by a woman. Tim Gifford, the firm's managing broker, with over thirty-five years of real estate experience, learned at the knee of his entrepreneurial mother. Before joining Gifford in 1974, Tim joined the U.S. Army and served in the Vietnam War earning three Bronze Stars and three Purple Hearts for his service.

- Bill Shelton, Harbor Realty, Portsmouth (757-484-4400). Harbor Realty was established by Bill Shelton in 1986. With over 30 years of real estate experience, twenty-three of those as a broker, Shelton was on the commercial side for ten years, and was chosen 1991 "Realtor® of the Year." A past president of the Portsmouth Area Board of Realtors®, he was instrumental in laying the groundwork for the Portsmouth/ Chesapeake Realtors® Association, serving as its president in 1993.

- Tommy Thompson, Harrison & Lear, Hampton (757-838-1111). Thompson leads Harrison & Lear Realty, founded in 1952. A man of many hats—chairman of Kikotan Company, real estate broker and developer, and owner of Willow Oak Farm—Thompson has been in real estate for over forty-three years. After serving in Korea, he joined the real estate business. He

twice served as president of the Peninsula Homebuilders Association and was honored as "Builder of the Year." He was named as a National Association of Home Builders life director.

- Rick West, Suburban Realty, Poquoson (757-868-0000). After graduating from Virginia Tech, West entered real estate. In 1986, he established Suburban Realty, which became a Coldwell Banker in 1989. West is a builder and developer, managing partner with Suburban Building since 1986, and active in the Virginia Peninsula

Above: Allow Rusty to help you "retrieve" your next home.

Below: As part of a national initiative celebrating its hundredth birthday, Coldwell Banker is building one hundred homes in cooperation with Habitat for Humanity.

Association of Realtors as a director and policy committee chairperson.

- John Wilson, Brooks Realty, Williamsburg (757-229-9595). Brooks Real Estate was founded in Williamsburg in 1885. In his sixteen years in real estate, Wilson served as president of the Williamsburg Area Association of Realtors (WAAR) and WMLS.

The sole two-time recipient of the WAAR "Realtor® of the Year," he is the youngest Realtor® to receive the Williamsburg Area Lifetime Achievement Award.

Community Outreach is an integral part of Coldwell Banker Professional, Realtors®. In celebration of its hundredth year, Coldwell Banker centers its community concerns on Habitat for Humanity, a fitting focus, by building one hundred homes nationally. Funds are being raised locally to build a Habitat house in Hampton Roads. Both

as individuals and members of the Coldwell Banker family, its partners are committed to the health and well being of their communities.

They have served their country in Korea and Vietnam, and as members of the Army National Guard. They are members of the American Legion. They have been deeply involved with the growth and development of their communities, serving with the Hampton Roads Chamber of Commerce and the business and community associations in their cities, as volunteers with the March of Dimes, shelters for battered women, the American Heart Association, the Boy Scouts, Sertoma and Ruritan Clubs, and with Little League. At the state level, they work to protect vital interests on the Governor's Commission on Base Retention and the Virginia Assembly's Joint Commission on Taxation.

There are always some good moving stories in the works at Coldwell Banker Professional, Realtors. One is about the frazzling confrontation you face when faced with picking up your entire home life and moving it from one place, cross-country, to another. That's a big down-side for individuals confronted with it. The equally big upside? Your Coldwell Banker expert relocation specialist, armed with just the right tools and

technical know-how along with an exclusive concierge program—the one that spruces up your home quickly. This fully-trained, extremely knowledgeable individual takes the ropes Coldwell Banker knows so well, and makes the whole operation, and your peace of mind, a whole lot easier.

Another is the selling story. Want real exposure for your home? Of course you do. The kind that brings results. The next step? A call to your Coldwell Banker Professional, Realtors® office where home-selling experts have the tools, systems, technical know-how and full real estate services to sell your home fast, and offer you the comfort of expert advice. With the support of Coldwell Banker's national network and backed by a full century of experience, your Hampton Roads Coldwell Banker Sales Associate offers you a world of difference. And Coldwell Banker is just a convenient click or call away: www.cb-pro.com or 1-866-757-4968. It is ready when you're ready to get movin'!

As first time buyers explore their options, and baby boomers spread out the search for second, and even third, homes, your Coldwell Banker agent is here to answer your questions and meet every need. With the latest in todays complex technologies backing them up, Coldwell Banker's team has already stepped firmly into the future. As closings become paperless, and can be accomplished across thousands of miles, as Coldwell Banker's LeadRouter service instantly and seamlessly connects you with a Coldwell Banker agent, the future promises to be an amazing place, and the buying or selling of your next home a very rewarding experience. Coldwell Banker has been here in the past and will continue to serve in the future.

Above: Cross country crisis? Coldwell Banker Professional, Realtors®, with you all the way home.

Below: Coldwell Banker Professional, Realtors® turns dreams into realities.

CMSS
Architects, PC

Since its founding in 1982 by architects Burrell Saunders and John Crouse, CMSS Architects has played a vital role in the twenty-first century growth and development of Hampton Roads. From its participation in the revitalization of downtown Norfolk, to the design of new downtowns for the cities of Virginia Beach and Newport News, CMSS' work reflects the grace, hospitality and charm of Hampton Roads' traditional neighborhoods and downtowns and provides a backdrop for social interaction, commerce and celebration.

CMSS was founded on the belief that people have the ability to create positive change in their communities. Beginning in Virginia Beach, the company set out to be a catalyst for proactive community design and development. In the decades that followed, co-founders Crouse and Saunders held to the belief that as architects, planners, and advisors, it was their responsibility to create designs that would instill a sense of excitement, hope and empowerment.

As the firm reaches its twenty-fifth year in 2007, CMSS has established itself as a preeminent planning and design firm, serving local, regional, national and international clients, with a staff of more than one hundred and offices in Virginia Beach, Reston and Richmond. The firm has received more than seventy-five national, state and local design awards from organizations such as the American Institute of Architects, the American Society of Landscape Architects and the American Society of Interior Designers. The company's growth and success has not affected CMSS' steadfast dedication to Hampton Roads, however, and the firm has secured its position as an important stakeholder in the region's history and future.

Built on progressive business principles and a unique repertoire of talent, CMSS' success stems from an integrated, holistic approach that recognizes the impact of the

Summer 2007 will see the opening the Sandler Center for the Performing Arts, a twelve-hundred-seat theater slated to become the City's premier arts venue attracting regional and national talent.

Town Center's success can be measured by its increasing momentum and influence on surrounding developments. As other urban-style developments begin to replace nearby strip malls and "big box" stores, Town Center's most enduring legacy will be its impact on the future growth of Virginia Beach and the region.

City Center at Oyster Point, Newport News is a 52-acre, $300-million, mixed-use development located within the Oyster Point business park, the City's central business district. Named 2002's "Most Significant Commercial Real Estate Project in Virginia" by *Virginia Business Magazine* and CCIM, City Center is geared towards the transformation of suburban sprawl patterns into a high-end, urban development.

As the urban designer and town architect, CMSS devised a plan to realign the city's emerging central commercial district with the

⚓

Left: A 17-block, $400-million public/private endeavor, Town Center of Virginia Beach is a new urban district that offers a full complement of integrated uses including office space, retail shops, restaurants, entertainment, hospitality, and upscale apartments, as well as a beautiful public plaza and a state-of-the-art 1,200-seat performing arts center.
PHOTOGRAPH BY STEVE BUDMAN.

Below: Town Center's Fountain Square Plaza and Retail district were designed to enhance the urban identity of the Town Center, and to create an inviting, versatile, pedestrian-friendly environment.

built environment on individuals and communities. From the renovation of small, individual spaces to the planning of urban centers and traditional neighborhoods, CMSS creates imaginative solutions that instill unity, create identity and ignite enthusiasm.

Decades after the founding of the City of Virginia Beach, a community-based initiative was established to develop a true downtown within the once quiet oceanfront resort. Led by a group of local business leaders, in partnership with the City of Virginia Beach and CMSS Architects, this initiative would repackage the city's commercial corridor and create a modern mixed-use urban core, and the new downtown Virginia Beach.

The 17-acre site was selected in the city's designated 340-acre Central Business District for its development potential, interstate access, and location within the City's main commercial corridor. A $400-million public/private endeavor, Town Center of Virginia Beach offers commercial office space, retail shops, hotels, restaurants, entertainment, and upscale apartments.

Above: Designed to realign the city's downtown with the shifting population core, City Center at Oyster Point is a $400-million, mixed-use development located on 52 acres within the Oyster Point business park, Newport News' central business district and the emerging commercial center for the entire Virginia Peninsula.
PHOTOGRAPH BY STEVE BUDMAN.

Below: Located adjacent to the historic Freemason District, overlooking the scenic Elizabeth River, PierPointe Condominiums has knitted together neighborhoods in and around Freemason with the downtown area by infilling previously under-utilized land.

shifting population core. By placing the development in the center of a suburban office park, city officials hoped to initiate the successful evolution of its central business district from suburban office to a mixed-use, high-density, urban environment. Upon completion, City Center at Oyster Point will include one million square feet of "Class A" office space in 12 buildings; 600 residential units; a 250,000-square-foot main street shopping, dining, and entertainment district; street and structured parking for 4,700 cars; and the 256-room, 204,000-square-foot Marriott hotel and conference center. The centerpiece of the development is a five-acre fountain lake surrounded by landscaped walkways and an eight-acre waterfront park. As it expands, the development will weave together the area's disparate components and establish City Center as a regional focal point.

In the 1980s, the City of Norfolk embarked on a massive revitalization plan that would transform its downtown—then a

deserted neighborhood of vacant buildings and scattered office spaces—into a livable, reinvigorated mixed-use community. In the late 1990s, city leaders began focusing on the repair of the historic downtown and created a plan to return the district to a flourishing urban core. CMSS Architects has been an active leader in the revival efforts since the mid-1990s. As architect for the Heritage at Freemason Harbor, the city's first new residential project in more than two decades, CMSS helped pioneer the efforts to bring the downtown back to life. As the first community of its kind for the city, Freemason Harbor established a new standard for Norfolk development. Located within walking distance of a variety of cultural attractions, restaurants, and shopping, the development fully utilizes its context and location to reach a residential market previously not addressed within the city.

The project served as a catalyst for several other CMSS residential infill projects including PierPointe Condominiums (completed in 2000), and 388 Boush Street (completed in 2006), and Tazewell Place (to be completed in 2007). CMSS also provided planning and design for several high-rise buildings that have helped transform Norfolk's financial district. The 150 West Main tower is a testament to the success of the city's revitalization efforts. As a gateway to downtown, the twenty-story building is a strong expression of prosperity and growth. Other projects include the One Bank Street Tower, and the twenty-story Trader Square, scheduled to be completed in 2006. For several years, the firm has also engaged in a series of adaptive reuse and renovation projects on several historic buildings along downtown's

Granby Street and Monticello Avenue corridors. Among these is the renovation of the NorVa Theater, a vaudeville theater and movie house built in 1913, now returned to its original function—with a concert hall, restaurant and administrative spaces added.

In 2005, CMSS began working with developers Intracoastal Investors, LLC on the design and planning of Culpepper Landing, a new 488-acre Traditional Neighborhood Development (TND) near historic Deep Creek and the Dismal Swamp Canal in Chesapeake. Culpepper Landing will include more than 1,000 homes, and 20,000 square feet of retail and commercial space. Plans also include an eco-lodge and conference center, and a small marina allowing access to the Intracoastal Waterway—all in an integrated setting on the edge of the Great Dismal Swamp National Wildlife refuge. Designed to reflect a respect for nature and love of community, and built on the traditions set forth by the America's colonial forefathers, Culpepper Landing will be a village with enduring value for the region.

Outside the Hampton Roads area, CMSS has teamed with developers, environmental agencies and local officials in Richmond to create The Village of Rocketts Landing, a $250-million, mixed-use urban village on a once neglected brownfield along the banks of the James River. In Northern Virginia, CMSS is helping to develop a holistic town center that preserves the historical heritage of the Old Town District in Fairfax, while allowing smart development that will bring new life to the downtown area. Internationally, CMSS is continuing its work with the U.S. State Department, designing embassy complexes in Europe, Africa, and Asia. CMSS Architects' dedication to creating environments that improve lives extends to green design. The firm is a member of United States Green Building Council. Several members of the firm, including co-founder Crouse, are certified by LEED (Leadership in Energy and Environmental Design), which administers a voluntary, consensus-based national standard for developing high-performance, sustainable buildings. CMSS sees each project as a collaborative process—involving the client, the community and the design team—the goal of which is to shape environments that enhance, reflect and inspire our society.

CMSS Architects, PC, is headquartered in the Town Center of Virginia Beach at 4505 Columbus Street, Suite 100. Please visit www.cmssarchitects.com for more information.

Left: Utilizing a variety of influences, from nineteenth-century industrial warehouses to traditional European plazas, CMSS creates unique and robust shopping and dining environments, which cater to a wide spectrum of diverse tastes.
PHOTOGRAPH BY STEVE BUDMAN.

Below: Culpepper Landing, a 488-acre traditional neighborhood development located in the Deep Creek district of Chesapeake, will create more than 1,000 homes and 20,000 square feet of retail in a village setting along the edge of one of Virginia's most majestic natural settings, the Great Dismal Swamp.

ROSELAND PROPERTY COMPANY

Roseland Property Company is a full service real estate organization involved in the development and construction of urban infill, residential and mixed-use properties throughout the Northeastern and Mid-Atlantic United States. The corporate office is located in Short Hills, New Jersey; regional offices are located in Portsmouth, Virginia, and Boston, Massachusetts. With strong historical expertise in land use, construction and property management, Roseland is positioned to maximize the value of its real estate portfolio of more than fifty properties including institutional grade multifamily rental communities, townhome and single-family for-sale communities, mixed-use master planned and urban infill communities, as well as its portfolio of more than fifteen thousand developable residential land units.

The company's flagship endeavor is the development and construction of Port Imperial, a multibillion mixed-use, master-planned waterfront development, which spans two miles directly across the Hudson River from Midtown Manhattan. This development helped pioneer an industry-wide interest in the untapped potential of New Jersey's last great land resource, its "Gold Coast" riverfront facing Manhattan, where fifteen million square feet of institutional grade commercial and residential

projects are under development or have recently been completed.

A key element of the success of Roseland as one of the nation's premier urban infill developers is its strategic relationships with its institutional partners.

In the fall of 2003, Roseland Property Company was pleased to open a regional office in Portsmouth, Virginia, which is part of the dynamic Hampton Roads area. Since that time, the company has announced several very significant projects in the region.

The first Roseland development in Hampton Roads was The Myrtles at Olde Towne. These apartment homes were built at the entrances of Portsmouth Naval Medical Center. The Myrtles represents the highest standards of quality in apartment home living. The buildings are architecturally significant and capture the historical architecture of two of Portsmouth's neighborhoods, Olde Towne and Parkview. The buildings are constructed with the finest building materials and, like the city they are located in, they will stand the test of time. This property like all of Roseland's properties represents the Roseland commitment to a quality lifestyle through state-of-the-art service and amenities.

The Myrtles at Olde Towne, which opened in the summer of 2005, includes a clubhouse, pool house, six apartment buildings,

including a total of 246 apartment homes, and 12 six-bay garage buildings. The one and two-bedroom apartment homes have security systems, surround sound systems, high-speed Internet connections and nine-foot ceilings. Some apartment homes include dens. The six main buildings have interior hallways and monumental central lobbies with elevators. Exterior heat pump condensers are hidden in rooftop wells to provide increased eye appeal.

At the heart of the complex is the six-thousand-square-foot clubhouse, which provides residents with amenities unique to the area. The clubhouse offers a fountain pool, state-of-the-art exercise facility, billiard room with bar, and home theater with a large projection screen, surround sound and oversized seating.

Adding to the appeal of The Myrtles is its proximity to the Portsmouth Naval Medical Center, the nation's first naval hospital. The

apartments are also within walking distance of the Elizabeth River ferry, which travels to Waterside in Norfolk.

Soon after its opening, The Myrtles at Olde Towne received the First Honor Award for "Best Multi-Family" project in the 2005 Excellence in Development competition sponsored by the *Hampton Roads Business Journal*.

In presenting the award, the *Business Journal* said, "Design-wise, the new apartments complement the older neighborhoods' traditional architecture. The most important part of the planning process was to ensure the neighborhood was pedestrian friendly. To help achieve this, units are equipped with street-level porches, which promote neighborly mingling and enhance the urban character of the development."

While The Myrtles was under construction, Roseland Property Company purchased The Heights at Olde Towne, two nearby thirty-year old, eight-story apartment buildings, and transformed them with a multimillion dollar renovation. Roseland bought the buildings in November 2003 and the project was completed in the spring of 2005. Within two months, the two buildings achieved one hundred percent occupancy by modernizing every feature of this building and backing it up with Roseland Management.

In 2006, Roseland Property Company will break ground on one of the largest private developments in all of Hampton Roads, which is "High Street" in Williamsburg, Virginia. Roseland was selected by the City of Williamsburg to develop this strategically located fifty-three acre site in the center of this very special city. High Street will represent a development cost of approximately $200 million, and be a wonderful compilation of shops and housing, designed by some of the nation's foremost architects.

The Myrtles at Olde Towne, The Heights at Olde Towne, and High Street do not represent the total scope of Roseland's development activity in the Hampton Roads area, but they are representative of the Roseland commitment to quality. Roseland will continue to believe in the future of Hampton Roads for years to come. Roseland Property Company is pleased to be an active member of the Hampton Roads community. Its commitment to the markets it serves is to build buildings and communities, like time-honored places such as Jamestown, Williamsburg, Portsmouth, and Norfolk, which have stood the test of generations and served our nation well. The company's success is based on its people who believe passionately in its stewardship as developers and managers.

Lambert's Point Docks has served shippers, manufacturers and brokers for more than sixty-five years, handling their import and export needs from one of the East Coast's finest natural, deepwater harbors.

As Virginia's largest break-bulk marine terminal, Lambert's Point Docks moves more than a half-million tons of cargo annually. Three piers provide berthing space for as many as six ships simultaneously with water depths of 32 to 36 feet at the berths. The docks cover 117 acres and offer more than 1.2 million square feet of warehouse storage.

As a subsidiary of Norfolk Southern Corporation, Lambert's Point Docks features direct rail access to the Norfolk Southern Railway system, which operates in twenty-two states and Canada, with links to all other major railroads. In addition, the docks are conveniently located within two miles of key Interstate highway interchanges, affording customers the power of choice in transportation. Lambert's Point Docks' strategic location in Norfolk is within a day's travel of nearly half of the nation's industrial and business centers.

Lambert's Point Docks further extends its customer's power of choice through its affiliation with MODALGISTICS, Norfolk Southern Corporation's logistics business unit. MODALGISTICS partners with the customer to provide complete supply chain management through Lambert's Point Docks.

At Lambert's Point Docks, transloading service for special project cargos is performance driven. Performance driven transloading is safe, efficient, and focused on the customer's cargo-handling requirements. Lambert's Point Docks employees are experienced in handling a wide variety of project cargo, including turbines, transformers, generators, locomotives and other heavy and outsized equipment. The terminal features specialized heavy loading/unloading equipment, mobile ramps and other equipment to move project cargo safely and efficiently.

Situated on one of the East Coast's finest deepwater harbors, with a channel depth of forty-five feet, Lambert's Point Docks is ideally positioned to serve world markets. The harbor offers protection against severe weather, and vessels encounter no bridges between the docks and the open sea. The docks feature two finger piers with a minimum depth of 32 to 36 feet at berths, which can accommodate up to four panamax vessels simultaneously.

Lambert's Point Docks also offers lay berth rentals, warehouse storage space and outdoor storage for lease.

Security is always a primary concern at Lambert's Point Docks and twenty-four-hour security personnel compliant with federal and maritime regulations protect the enclosed facility.

Lambert's Point Docks is considered the finest mid-Atlantic gateway for transloading, particularly for such commodities as rubber, wood products, machinery/special projects cargo, and most break-bulk cargo. Scales and tugboats are available on premises and refrigeration is available. Other equipment includes mobile ramps for off-loading and two articulated fifty-ton gantry cranes with automatic spreader bars.

Lambert's Point Docks is your Mid-Atlantic gateway for break-bulk transloading.

INSTANT TECHNOLOGIES, INC.
BY GERARD T. RAMSEY, PH.D.

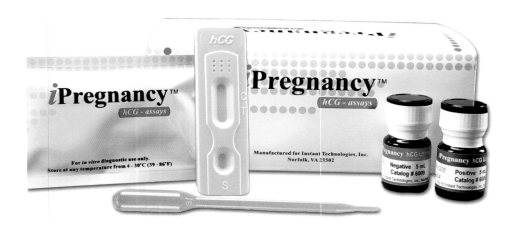

Since 1997, Instant Technologies has been serving clients with the highest quality instant testing products at competitive prices while offering superior product training and customer care. Everything has a beginning and while its beginning was humble at the onset, its eyes, its vision has always been set on the horizon; though it looks to the past as well, lest it fails to learn from what has gone before.

People are a critical variable in the company's continuing success. A closely held family business, Instant Technologies has grown its family to include an extended family whose members are characterized by intelligence, critical thinking, ingenuity and the ability to work smart.

In the very beginning, there was James Ramsey, now CEO and navigator of Instant Technologies. Incorporating the talent of family and friends, Ramsey built a brain trust of sorts, garnering experience and education from psychology to medicine as well as a host of degrees from the school of hard knocks.

While impossible to name all the names, Instant Technologies continues to add talent including such industry insiders as Jeff Konecke, the new director of business development, formerly president of ABI. And while each name is important, Instant Technologies has become more than a sum of its parts, standing on its own, functioning with success as a legitimate entity in itself.

Instant Technologies has a host of customers across industry, government, military, schools, employment, and healthcare. It is the satisfied customer, however, that accounts for the company's continuing success. A major strength across time has been the company's willingness to listen to and attend to the needs, real and perceived, of its customers. Instant Technologies' product offerings and marketing/ educational support is a direct response to what its customers have to say.

State-of-the-art training, DVD and CD videos provide the company's customers and distributors with essential support and education. Its interactive website, www.tryi.com, is specifically designed to provide education and product information in a relevant user-friendly format. The company believes its success is a reflection of how its customers perceive its products and services.

In recent years the company's annual organic growth has exceeded forty percent. In response to customer and market demands, Instant Technologies has provided a continual flow of new products and services with a particular emphasis on exclusivity and intellectual property innovations.

The flow of new products has accompanied a successful program of market branding, making the Instant Technologies brand a dominant name in the quick test industry. The company's year upon year growth has provided it with economies of scale allowing it favorable manufacturing strength and enabling it to maintain enviable inventory levels and same day shipping ninety-eight percent of the time. Such superior fulfillment capabilities and competent consumer service has coupled with the other factors to enable the company to maintain growth in revenues and profits. Quality and efficiency in people, products and fulfillment are integral aspects of Instant Technologies' success.

To accentuate the phenomenal organic growth Instant Technologies has enjoyed, a series of strategic acquisitions and partnerships have been set into play. To expand its product presence to the over-the-counter marketplace, Instant Technologies acquired Accu-Stat Diagnostics, Inc. of Lake Forest, California, on February 2, 2006. Accu-Stat's FDA 510K clearances to sell home testing products across the counter provides an exciting new market for drugs of abuse, breath alcohol, cholesterol, and fecal occult blood testing

Since its inception in 1997, Instant Technologies has grown organically and through strategic acqui-sitions to become a leading force in the development and distribution of rapid test devices. More recently, Instant Technologies has moved aggressively into the European marketplace extending its vision to include the United Kingdom and beyond. It is anticipated that strategic acquisitions will continue in the coming months and years.

Instant Technologies' philosophy of quality, customer service and pro-duct innovation continues to support its expanding line of products and services. Continual attention to the needs of its many customers

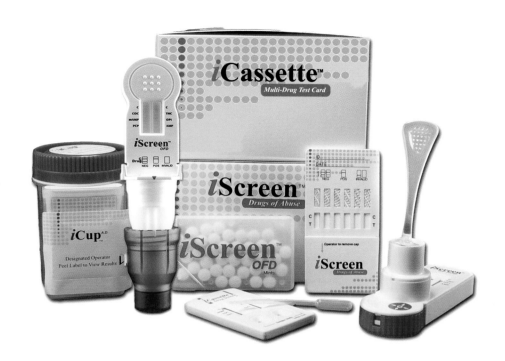

as well as the maintenance of a positive work environment makes possible the synergy that is the headline in Instant Technologies' success story.

For more information about Instant Technologies, please contact Director of Business Development Jeff Konecke at 800-340-4029, 888-340-4029, or by email at jkonecke@tryi.com.

HyVal
Industries,
Incorporated

Clockwise from top left:

The HyVal Industries, Incorporated home office.

Machine shop facilities.

The machine shop computerized milling machine.

The hydraulic hose manufacturing shop.

Another part of the hydraulic hose manufacturing shop.

The year was 1978 and William P. Tinder was unhappy with his job because he didn't like the way the company was being directed and organized. He became so dissatisfied that he resigned, found a partner, Alice P. Bailey, and organized HyVal Industries, Incorporated.

The objective of the new business was to provide hydraulic repairs and service primarily to shipyards having master ship repair contracts with the government for repairs to Navy and Military Sealift Command ships.

HyVal was organized on May 1, 1978, with the two partners, a secretary, a hydraulic technician, an inside machinist, and an outside machinist on the payroll.

The partners were well versed and experienced in both the government and civilian side of master ship repair contracts and they soon received their first purchase order: steering gear repairs on the USS *Yosemite*, which was docked in Charleston, South Carolina. The HyVal crew worked long hours to complete the scheduled repairs by the date specified in the government contract.

Business grew steadily for HyVal and the number of employees increased eventually to around sixty-five. The partners recognized the need to expand the business so they would be responsible for all types of repairs, not just hydraulic. These included electrical, mechanical, structural, pipefitting, welding, brazing, and final testing of the system. This approach gave HyVal complete control in fixing any problems it found.

A change in business philosophy in 1982 led to a decision to downsize the business by two-thirds. The owners decided that instead of trying to perform all the work on regular time pay (eight hours/day, forty hours/week); they would keep a downsized crew and add premium pay (more than eight hours/day and on Saturday/Sunday) in order to complete tasks on time. This way, employees were compensated at time-and-a-half or double-time for their additional efforts and their take home pay increased substantially.

This approach has worked so well that HyVal continues the policy today.

HyVal's original business philosophy of "do the best repair possible within the limits of the contract, at a reasonable price, in the least amount of time possible" has been refined over the years and still holds true today.

If additional adverse conditions are found in the course of repairs, the customer is always notified so that the additional needed repairs may be incorporated into the existing contract at the customer's discretion. This helps provide better service for the customer by eliminating future repairs and allows any problems to be corrected at a lower cost. This approach has led to an enviable record of customer satisfaction.

HyVal's business philosophy is well stated in the firm's Mission Statement: "HyVal Industries, Incorporated, will continuously strive to achieve improved customer satisfaction by meeting or exceeding customer requirements through innovation, competitive pricing, superior quality, on-time contract completion, and strong, solid teamwork."

HyVal feels good word of mouth is the best form of advertising possible and the company's positive word of mouth has resulted in every business owners dream situation—to have sole source contract business with a customer. For example, good customer satisfaction on the part of HyVal's government customers has resulted in a "basic ordering agreement" with the Navy Department for the repair and testing of nearly all the "broken but refurbishable" hydraulic pumps, motors, and valves used in the fleet today.

The broken units are shipped to HyVal's facility where they are overhauled and tested, then distributed to the designated naval installation.

Clockwise from top, right:

Hydraulic test stands.

A close-up of a hydraulic test stand #1.

A close-up of a hydraulic test stand #2.

A repaired hydraulic pump ready for shipment back to Naval Inventory Control.

A tear down of a hydraulic pump.

According to HyVal President William P. Tinder, such sources of long-term income are what every business owner desires because it provides the business growth needed to support the required additional effort.

HyVal Industries, Incorporated is headquartered at 898 Widgeon Road in Norfolk.

THE DRAGAS COMPANIES

By promoting quality as the fundamental element of true value, The Dragas Companies has become one of Hampton Roads' largest housing providers by creating quality homes in neighborhoods of enduring beauty.

The Dragas Companies are rooted in a strong tradition of excellence that began in 1968 when George Dragas established the Dragas Mortgage Company. Shortly thereafter, George and his brother, Mark, teamed up to expand the business into development and construction. Today, CEO Helen E. Dragas, President Philip A. Shucet, and Chief Operating Officer John C. "Buck" Buckley III, share those same family values.

Together, Helen, Philip and Buck and the entire Dragas Companies' family continue that same hallmark of excellence as it heads toward the fourth decade of bringing customers the home and lifestyle they deserve.

Although Dragas constructed single-family homes in the seventies, the company decided eventually to concentrate on development of condominium projects. Dragas' first condominium development, Birdneck North in Virginia Beach, opened more than twenty-five years ago.

The Dragas Companies also develops apartment and office properties and provides property management, real estate brokerage and mortgage lending services.

Dragas Realty has in-house counselors selling exclusively for Dragas. Homebuyers are offered a combination of design, location, lifestyle, quality construction, and value, backed by one, two, and ten-year warranties.

The family business is now in its second generation and is headed by Helen E. Dragas, the daughter of George Dragas. Helen grew up in the business, starting as a teenager conducting door-to-door market research. She later served as marketing director and sales manager for the The Dragas Companies.

She received her undergraduate and MBA degrees from the

Above: Helen E. Dragas, CEO.

Below: Mark and George Dragas.

University of Virginia and became president of Dragas Mortgage Companies in 1988. She became president and CEO of the building operation in 1996.

"We're residential homebuilders who specialize in creating a community atmosphere," says Helen. "We focus on condominiums and multifamily developments and we have a track record of excellence."

The Dragas Companies received the coveted Lee Evans Award of Excellence from the National Association of Home Builders and *Builders Magazine* in 1999. The award, given annually to a single builder in the United States, recognizes overall achievement in housing.

A panel of industry experts selected The Dragas Companies for the award,

based on performance in customer service and quality, design and construction, community and industry service, finance and operations, and marketing.

The organization has received dozens of other awards for quality and excellence, including multiple Awards of Excellence from the Tidewater Home Builders Association/Tidewater Multifamily Council for Columbus Station Apartments and Certificates of Merit for "Outstanding Residential Development" from the City of Virginia Beach Planning Commission for Development of Southampton at Salem Springs, Red Mill Village, and Cromwell Park at Salem.

Other Dragas Communities include Birdneck North, Fairfield Gardens, Harbour Point Condominiums, Columbus Station Condominiums, Knell's Ridge Condominiums, Great Neck Grove, The Gables at Kempsville Greens, Lake Smith Condominiums, Wellington at Dam Neck, Asbury at Plantation Woods, Camden Village, Brenneman Farm, The Gables at Bellamy, Lesner Pointe & Lesner Point East, Tarleton Oaks at Tallwood, North Trail at the Arboretum, The Hampshires at Greenbrier, and Ridgely Manor at Lake Smith, which includes five condominium communities: Farrcroft, Belmeade, Westbriar, Grace Hill, and Southmoor Village.

The Dragas philosophy is best captured in its Builders Story, which is displayed in every sales office. "Because of our commitment to our customers, as well as our relentless commitment to quality and value, we've won the trust of more than three thousand owners and families who call our communities home, people who share a common vision to live in a home of lasting quality that creates lasting value. We firmly believe that without quality, there is no true value.

"Our behavior day after day reinforces our commitment. All our employees are keenly focused on creating neighborhoods of enduring beauty. We work hard to deliver a well-planned balance between home and community design, construction practices, convenient locations, competitive prices and true customer service. We will not disappear after you move in. Our full-time customer care representatives will remain committed to your satisfaction."

According to Chief Operating Officer John C. Buckley, III, "The biggest competitive edge we have is the overall quality of the homes we deliver. We really supervise the process."

Helen adds, "Our tradition of excellence has a foundation in the dedication of our valued employees. They deserve the credit for making our homes superior and our company successful."

The Dragas Companies commitment to the community at large includes creation of a charitable foundation to which the company contributes between five and ten percent of its earnings each year. The primary focus of the charitable endeavors is education.

The Dragas Companies is headquartered at 4538 Bonney Road in Virginia Beach. The company website is www.dragas.com.

⚓

The corporate offices of
The Dragas Companies.

BECO

Burt Cutright and Eric Olson founded BECO, which specializes in residential, multifamily and commercial construction, land development, property management and cable broadband services, in 1990.

In 1989, Cutright and Olson, who have partnered in various ventures for more than twenty years, had the opportunity to purchase an apartment building together. That small apartment complex became the foundation for the multifaceted corporation known as BECO.

Olson's twenty-two years of experience includes land acquisitions, coordination with local, state and federal governments, and contract administration. He directs and administers all residential construction for the company.

Cutright, an engineering technology graduate of Old Dominion University, has more than twenty-three years of experience in engineering, construction and land development. Land development and construction of multifamily communities are his passion and inspiration.

In the early days, BECO specialized in restoring affordable homes, then expanded and began construction of new homes. By offering several different models and flexible floor plans, BECO has been able to grow and build more homes each year, emerging as a leader in new home construction. Currently, BECO builds more than one hundred homes each year, for an average selling price of $300,000.

BECO's success in home building led naturally to an expansion into land development. Today, BECO acquires the land and financing, and develops and builds on it. BECO's land development started with commercial ventures and expanded into new home communities and multifamily sites.

BECO Asset Management was formed in 2003 to manage all multifamily and commercial properties built by BECO. By managing the properties it owns, BECO can ensure that all its properties are kept to the highest standards.

BECO has provided third-party cable and Internet services to residents of Harbour Breeze Apartments since it was opened in 2002. BECO Cable Broadband, LLC was formed in 2003 and offers cable and Internet services in BECO's Class A apartments, condominiums and select commercial properties.

Since it was organized, BECO has demonstrated sound business practices, built lasting relationships and enjoyed an exceptional track record of fiscal responsibility. BECO ranges from $60 to $70 million per year in construction value, pursuing ventures from Florida to Washington, D.C. The company continues to experience significant expansion, growing twenty-four percent from 2002 to 2003 and forty-nine percent from 2003 to 2004 in home sales alone.

At BECO, planning and communication are the foundation of all construction projects. The construction program originates in the design stage and BECO's production managers are included in the design process to ensure they are aware of the unique construction requirements of each development.

To provide construction of the highest quality, each member of BECO's team of seasoned professionals is hand selected. This has resulted in a staff of loyal people who contribute their time and talents to make every venture a success.

Descended from generations of custom builders, Cutright and Olson have built a company that is known as the leader in Lifestyle Homes, offering families' custom-designed homes that reflect their individual lifestyles. BECO builds more than a hundred new homes each year, totaling from 1,120 to 3,575 square feet.

With flexible designs, custom floor plans and fine craftsmanship, each single-family BECO home reflects a commitment to quality that is unmatched in the region.

While new homes have been BECO's foundation, multifamily communities represent the investment side of the business. The multifamily segment of the business began in 2000 with construction of Silverlake Villas, a ten-unit condominium complex close to the oceanfront off Birdneck Road in Virginia Beach. Priced in the $120s, these condominiums provided beach residents with affordable housing in an attractive setting.

BECO's first luxury apartment complex was Harbour Breeze in Suffolk, one of Hampton Roads fastest growing areas. Harbour Breeze, offering 328 luxury apartments, was voted the Best Apartment Complex in Suffolk for 2003 and 2004 in the "Best of Hampton Roads" competition.

Today the BECO team builds multifamily dwellings strictly for investment purposes. As a result, BECO is well recognized by different municipalities because they know BECO will not only build the project, but also own and maintain it.

BECO's Commercial Division provides an opportunity to invest in communities throughout the region. Currently, the firm builds and manages office/flex space buildings in Chesapeake, Suffolk, and Cape Charles.

Butts Station Commercial Center, built in 1998, was BECO's first commercial property. The office complex on Green Tree Road in Chesapeake includes forty-four thousand square feet of office flex space with dock and grade loading.

Capitalizing on the growing high-tech corridor in the Greenbrier area adjacent to I-64 and I-464, BECO developed a parcel of land and constructed Battlefield Lakes Technology Center, three office/warehouse buildings consisting of 85,000 square feet.

BECO's Harbour Breeze Professional Center in Suffolk was the recipient of the 2004 Award of Merit for "Best Office Building" presented by the Hampton Roads Association for Commercial Real Estate.

BECO is headquartered at 609 Independence Parkway in Chesapeake. The firm also operates a branch office in Cape Charles, Virginia. For additional information, please visit www.becohomes.com.

PRUDENTIAL MCCARDLE REALTY

Kimber and Randy Smith.

For the members of the Smith family of Williamsburg, real estate is part of their DNA. Jodie Smith, now retired, became a real estate agent in the 1960s and his wife, Randy, entered the field in 1974 with the firm she helps run today. Their son, Kimber, began his career with Dun & Bradstreet in Washington, D.C., but moved back to Williamsburg to raise his family and decided real estate offered a great opportunity. He joined the same firm as his mother, McCardle Realty, in 1988 and became sales manager in 1992.

A year later, in 1993, mother and son had an opportunity to purchase the firm and jumped at the chance. They share equal ownership, with Kimber serving as president and Randy as vice president.

Larry McCardle and Barbara Murphy founded Murphy & McCardle Realty in 1970 with an office on Richmond Road in Williamsburg. McCardle purchased Murphy's

share of the company in 1982 and began doing business as McCardle Realty, Inc.

When the Smith's purchased the firm in 1993 it consisted of two offices in Williamsburg, with thirty-six agents and a support staff of eight.

McCardle Realty grew rapidly under the direction of Randy and Kimber. A third office was opened in James City County in 1994, and in 1997, Greensprings Realty, a division of McCardle Realty, was organized to market the communities of Greensprings Plantation and Greensprings West.

In 1999 the firm made the strategic decision to join with the nationwide Prudential Real Estate Affiliates, which boasts over 60,000 agents and 2,000 independently owned and operated offices in North America.

The Prudential affiliation has allowed the company to leverage the local "McCardle" brand with the internationally recognized "Prudential" brand, which is recognized by ninety-eight percent of all consumers in North America. The Prudential network provides national advertising, a broker network of more than sixty thousand agents as a referral source, and an international corporate relocation network as additional sources of business.

In 2002, Prudential McCardle Realty acquired Powell & Associates in Newport News, which provided a base of operations on the Lower Peninsula and much greater coverage for the Prudential franchise, trading as Prudential McCardle-Powell Realty. In 2003 the company acquired Hazelwood Realtors in Norge, Virginia, and continued operations at the firm's office on Richmond Road, trading as Prudential McCardle-Hazelwood Realty.

Today, Prudential McCardle Realty has four offices, including Greensprings Realty, and employs more than a hundred full-time agents, supported by a staff of eighteen.

The firm's closed sales volume has grown from just over $50 million in 1993 to more than $350 million in 2005 and Prudential McCardle Realty is ranked number one among all Williamsburg-headquartered real estate companies, a distinction it has claimed for seventeen consecutive years.

In addition to its real estate brokerage operations, McCardle Realty, Inc. formed a

joint venture mortgage company in 2003 with Charter One Mortgage Corporation, trading as First Charter Mortgage of Williamsburg. In 2004 the Smiths formed a partnership to create a settlement service and title insurance company known as Colonial Virginia Settlement Services, LLC.

Community service is a cornerstone of the McCardle company philosophy. The company believes strongly in giving back to the community and each year the firm donates thousands of dollars to local charities, organizations and foundations. Among the recipients are the Colonial Williamsburg Foundation, The Williamsburg Land Conservancy, the United Way Campaign, Hospice House, Relay for Life, American Heart Association, Avalon, the Heritage Humane Society, Housing Partnerships, Child Development Resources, local youth sports teams, area school projects, and many other organizations and community projects.

Both Randy and Kimber have served as president of the Williamsburg Area Association of Realtors and have been recognized by the industry with numerous awards. Both are committed to retaining the unique historical and environmental areas of Williamsburg, with Kimber serving in leadership roles with the

Williamsburg Land Conservancy, and Randy serving on the boards of the James River Association and the Friends of the National Park Service for Greensprings Plantation.

Randy and Kimber were honored for their outstanding contributions to the real estate industry and the community in 2005 when they were named Williamsburg Chamber of Commerce's "Small Business Persons of the Year."

That same year, Prudential McCardle Realty moved into a new $3-million, 12,250 square-foot office building in New Town next to the Williamsburg/James City County Courthouse. The new headquarters building provides more than six miles of high-speed Internet cable and state-of-the-art equipment, including a voice-over Internet protocol telephone system that integrates phone, voice mail, and e-mail.

Prudential McCardle Realty takes great pride in being the area's largest full service residential and commercial real estate company. The Realtors of Prudential McCardle Realty have won numerous local and national sales awards.

Prudential McCardle is proud of its reputation as "Williamsburg's Home Team." If it is real estate in Williamsburg you seek, Prudential McCardle Realty is the only name you need to remember.

Prudential McCardle Realty's headquarters is located at 4135 Ironbound Road in Williamsburg.

CENTURY CONCRETE

Forty years ago, Preston M. White, Jr., saw a niche in the construction business and a future in concrete. "In 1966 most general contractors still did their own concrete work but I thought there were opportunities for a specialty concrete company," White explains. After he started Century Concrete, White's prediction proved prescient. General contractors began focusing more on managing construction accompanied by an increasing reliance on subcontractors.

The construction industry's shift to using specialists has helped Century Concrete flourish. The Virginia Beach-based firm started with four employees in 1966. It now has 450. Century's first contract was for two outdoor basketball courts costing $12,500. Today, Century relies on twenty-five teams to run a couple of dozen jobs simultaneously. The company pours more than 200,000 cubic yards of concrete annually and generates $60 million a year from projects in Virginia, southern Maryland and northeastern North Carolina.

Century Concrete has weathered the economic downturns of the past four decades by working in the public sector as well as building construction. "If it's made of concrete, we can do it," says White. While the company started out doing primarily flatwork, it has moved into creating sound walls for interstate highways, concrete frames, airfield concrete paving, bridges, marine terminals and parking decks. Century also constructs tilt-wall buildings for warehouses, big box stores and public/institutional projects.

White graduated from Virginia Tech with a degree in building construction and considerable experience working with concrete. During college, the Norfolk native worked summers on the Chesapeake Bay Bridge Tunnel. After graduation, he started with Vanguard Construction, a Norfolk firm whose main focus is bridge-building.

When White decided to start his own company, his brother-in-law James P. Woodard, a University of Virginia graduate, took a two-week vacation from his accounting job to help get Century Concrete going. Woodard never went back, staying on as White's partner until retiring in 1995.

Century Concrete has grown into one of the biggest specialty concrete contractors in Virginia and White credits the company's success to the depth and breadth of its management expertise. Three key people are Michael J. Hauser, vice president of operations and a Virginia Tech graduate in civil engineering; Kenneth M. Bowab, vice president of finance and an Old Dominion University business and accounting graduate; and A. Patrick McLaughlin, vice president of estimating and a University of Florida building construction graduate. Hauser joined the company in 1991, Bowab in 1994, and McLaughlin in 1995.

Above: The Westin Hotel-Condos, Virginia Beach.

Below: Virginia Beach Convention Center.

Recruiting remains a priority in a company that has always planned for the future. Century Concrete also places high value on retaining good employees. The on-going education program demonstrates that commitment by emphasizing classroom and on-the-job training in operating equipment and equipment maintenance, field engineering and management, management supervision and, most important, safety. The company's confidence in the skill and training of its employees is evidenced by their uncommon level of autonomy.

Century Concrete places a premium on experience and the total years in the field is telling. The six members of the project management staff have a combined total of 67 years experience, the 32 on the field supervision staff have 450, the seven on the construction support staff have 15, and the four on the safety team have 40.

While experience and training are pluses, the two traits White values most in new hires are a willingness to work and a positive attitude. "Our employees are responsible for Century Concrete's reputation for aggressive scheduling, safety and quality work."

"Preston has built a wonderful organization of educated, highly-qualified professionals," says John Stanchina, vice president of Rutherford and Century Concrete's bonding agent for many years. "He's invested a lot of time in attracting top graduates in civil engineering and construction management and then molding them into the company. The quality of leadership comes across in the field supervision where every employee has to understand the need for speed, safety and project management."

Growth over the past four decades has averaged 5 to 15 percent every year, the kind of steady, controlled increase White prefers. "We have a reputation for competitive pricing; high-quality, aggressive scheduling; safe workplaces and a high degree of customer satisfaction. We don't want to risk any of those positives by growing too fast," White says.

Currently, the company is constructing the structural frame for Virginia's tallest building, a thirty-eight-story hotel/residential complex in Virginia Beach's Town Center. Concurrent

projects include the Virginia Beach performing arts center, also located at Town Center, the Mount Vernon Orientation Center in Mount Vernon, Virginia, Westminster Canterbury in Richmond, and the Virginia Beach Convention Center. Also under construction is Harbors Edge, a seventeen-story retirement community and adjoining medical facility on the Norfolk waterfront.

"Concrete is a difficult business with a heavy labor component," Stanchina says. "Century Concrete takes the time to pull a job apart and then do it right, with speed and safety."

White sees continued growth and profitability in Century Concrete's future. "We're a financially strong, conservatively managed company," he concludes. "We just need to maintain our operating methods and keep hiring top-notch employees."

Above: The Marriott Hotel and Conference Center in Newport News

Below: The Hampton Roads Convention Center.

T. Parker Host, Incorporated

T. Parker Host, Jr. likes to tell visitors to his shipping firm that "There's been a Host on the waterfront in Hampton Roads for more than a hundred years."

It all began with his grandfather, Lewis C. Host, who was weighmaster at the former C&O coal pier in Newport News from the early 1890s until the mid 1930s. Host recalls that his grandfather was so good at his job he could memorize the scale weight of each rail car as it went over the scales, list each car's weight on a tally sheet and then calculate the tonnage of cargo loaded onboard the vessel!

In 1923, T. Parker Host founded the ship agency and brokerage business that still carries his name. He headed the firm until his death in 1962. A vigorous and farsighted businessman, T. Parker Host was also active in local civic affairs, serving as mayor of Newport News and a commissioner of the Virginia Port Authority.

When the senior Host founded the company, Newport News was the "kingpin of shipping" in Hampton Roads and T. Parker Host, conveniently located on the third floor of the old C&O Terminal building downtown, grew as coal and other cargos increased.

T. Parker Host, Jr., born two years after his father founded the firm, never doubted that he would one day join the family business. He came to work for the company in 1948 after serving in the U.S. Army Air Corps and studying at the University of Virginia. Today he serves as the company chairman.

T. Parker Host, Jr., was born and raised in Newport News and, like his father before him, has been active in local civic affairs. He served on the Newport News City Council from 1966 to 1970 and held leadership positions in the Hampton Roads Maritime Association, which honored him with its "Mr. Hampton Roads Award" in 1981.

He was president of the Newport News Mariners' Museum from 1980-1985, shepherding the facility through an important planning phase for future growth.

His two sons, Thomas P. Host III and David F. Host, also grew up in the business and came aboard at an early age. Tom now serves as senior vice president and David is president and CEO.

During the agency's early years, Hampton Roads and other Virginia ports were primarily involved with bulk and breakbulk cargos. Coal was a major commodity along with wood products, tobacco, grains, scrap, and fertilizers. The company expanded following World War II and became a highly respected port agent for liner services handling general cargo and, in the early 70's, became involved with container ships representing Columbus Line and Maersk Line.

Evolving with the times, T. Parker Host, Inc., now provides professional and competitive services to a wide range of leading shippers and receivers. It continues to handle a variety of import and export commodities throughout the ports, including grains, fertilizers, chemicals, cement, scrap, and clean and heavy oils. T. Parker Host, Inc., has also played a key role in coal exports, a major bulk commodity handled by the port, and is still actively involved in representing breakbulk operators and container lines.

As a shipping agent, T. Parker Host, Inc., serves as the local representative for shipping lines, owners and operators of vessels. The company arranges port calls, coordinates the loading and unloading of cargos, and makes certain vessels under their consignment receive a speedy turn around.

Two events during the 1980s shifted the focus of the shipping business from Newport News to Norfolk: the merger of the Norfolk and Western Railway and Southern Railway, which allowed Norfolk to offer favorable shipping rates; and the consolidation of the ports of Norfolk, Newport News, and Portsmouth into the unified Port of Hampton Roads.

Three Generations of Hosts.

T. Parker Host, Jr., was a key leader of the ports' unification as president of the Hampton Roads Maritime Association, and today remains an avid proponent of port unification. "For us to become a great port, we had to unshackle parochial attitudes and unite under one banner," he says. Leading the fight to overcome those attitudes and unify the ports was probably the major battle of his career. Host was the chairman of the Hampton Roads Maritime Association ad hoc committee, Harbor Deepening Project in the early 1980s, which enabled the ports in Hampton Roads to achieve an outbound fifty foot channel allowing coal vessels to sail with a greater quantity of coal thereby ensuring our success as the leading coal export port on the Atlantic seaboard.

Assistant Secretary of the Army Robert K. Dawson, by his letter of April 6, 1987, praised Host and his committee for its efforts to bring needed improvement to one of the nation's vital ports by recognizing the need to improve and deepen the port's channels to remain competitive in the world's coal market.

This early dredging has greatly enhanced the port's role in serving the large container ships presently calling and will be further enhanced by the completion of the inbound channel to a fifty-foot draft.

The company has also played a major role in the development of The National Maritime Center (Nauticus) as a major cruise terminal on the East Coast. It is presently expanding its facility with a new cruise terminal to serve Norfolk's ever-growing cruise business.

Because of his deep roots in Newport News, Host kept his company headquarters there until port unification dictated a move in 1983 to the World Trade Center overlooking the Elizabeth River. In 2003, T. Parker Host, Inc., moved its offices across the street to the former Haynes building at the corner of Granby and Main Streets, and has just recently moved to 500 Plume Street East.

To meet the needs of a rapidly changing industry, the company now operates offices in Baltimore, Maryland; Wilmington, Delaware; and Philadelphia, Pennsylvania. It also has a partnership with Amelia Maritime Services, which has offices in Jacksonville and Fernandina Beach, Florida; and in Brunswick, Georgia.

As the Host organization moved into the twenty-first century, Tom and David—grandsons of the founder—have ensured a third generation of family leadership for the company whose longevity and expertise has earned the respect of ship owners, terminal operators, and government agencies. T. Parker Host, Inc., is dedicated to providing its principals with quality service to meet their shipping needs.

Above: C&O Merchandise Piers.

Below: Various Terminals on Southern Branch of Elizabeth River.

MALCOLM PIRNIE, INC.

Working in the environmental engineering business for over one hundred years, Malcolm Pirnie is one of the largest consulting firms in the United States concentrating solely on environmental disciplines. From its early focus on drinking water supply and water pollution control, at a time when waterborne disease was a major health concern, the firm has grown and changed with the times. About thirty years ago, Malcolm Pirnie began offering services in solid waste management, and more recently it has expanded its capabilities into the areas of environmental analysis, toxicology, and hazardous waste management. Now its staff of over fifteen hundred engineers, scientists, planners, architects, designers, technicians and support personnel concentrates on environmental areas such as water and wastewater engineering, solid and hazardous waste management, environmental restoration and air pollution control.

Malcolm Pirnie traces its origins in the Hampton Roads area back to 1956, when after studying the water system of Newport News; the firm began work on a broad spectrum of water supply, wastewater treatment and many other environmental projects. As their business grew, in 1971, the firm opened an office in Newport News and began designing the expansion of the Newport News Waterworks.

Hampton Roads, like many other rapidly growing regions in the country, has been particularly vigilant in protecting its valuable

water resources. As the region's population increases, water resource development and protection, water quality management, and the effective treatment of water and wastewater are critical to sustaining the quality of life. Many of their projects in the Hampton Roads area have pioneered the development of sound technical solutions to contemporary environmental problems critical to the region's quality of life. The basis of our success in Hampton Roads rests on close working relationships with long-term clients, whose trust and confidence we gained as we solved their environmental challenges.

The City of Newport News Waterworks supplies drinking water produced at the Lee Hall and Harwood's Mill Water Treatment Plants, to about 350,000 people on the Lower Virginia Peninsula including the cities of Newport News, Hampton, and Poquoson, and portions of James City and York Counties. In 1991 when the Waterworks needed a new way to deal with the naturally occurring, non-toxic, nutrient rich residuals from the incoming raw water, Malcolm Pirnie engineered an innovative residuals disposal approach—land application, an environmentally sound approach to treating, recycling, and disposing of water treatment residuals that involves spreading residuals on the ground on croplands or forests, enabling nineteen hundred dry tons per year of water treatment residuals to be safely assimilated into the City's watershed property. This strategy also integrates well with the Waterworks' forestry management program—with minimal environmental impacts and no effect on groundwater.

Again in 1995, when the Waterworks faced the challenge of modernizing the aging Lee Hall Water Treatment Plant, Malcolm Pirnie was retained to engineer a state-of-the-art, $70-million facility to replace the existing plant. The new Lee Hall Plant will provide Waterworks' customers with safe, reliable drinking water well into the twenty-first century.

In the City of Virginia Beach, when tremendous population growth in the 1970s resulted in a decade-long water shortage, Malcolm Pirnie served as technical consultant

City of Newport News, Lee Hall Water Plant.

for the award-winning Lake Gaston water supply project—at the time, the largest public water supply project in the history of the Commonwealth. A seventy-six mile long raw water pipeline and sixty million gallon per day intake and pumping station on the north side of Lake Gaston in Brunswick County is designed to meet the present and future water needs of the Commonwealth's largest city.

As growth in the Hampton Roads region pushed increasingly westward from the coast, development pressure in the City of Suffolk accelerated. Since 1987, Malcolm Pirnie has provided continuing engineering services to the City to support the expansion of its distribution system and

also to engineer the expansion and improvement of treatment at the G. Robert House, Jr. Water Treatment Facility. Besides helping to develop new, high quality water supply sources, Malcolm Pirnie designed an innovative, award-winning electro dialysis reversal (EDR) drinking water treatment system that will allow the City to comply with current and expected future drinking water regulations. And, as an added benefit, the City will be able to attract a desirable mix of industrial, commercial and residential development in accordance with the City's Comprehensive Plan.

In a unique project, Malcolm Pirnie worked with the Virginia Port Authority to design an award-winning man-made oyster reef near downtown Portsmouth and the Midtown Tunnel—the first time a new oyster reef was designed and built

as mitigation for environmental impacts. This project marks the start of restoration of the marine ecosystem in the Elizabeth River and it is considered a "step in the right direction" and a positive new approach for mitigating impacts to tidal wetlands. Its success has been documented by the Virginia Marine Resources Commission, which recently reported a dense colonization of spat on the constructed reef.

After fifty years and numerous local environmental projects, Malcolm Pirnie is an important member of the Hampton Roads community—and plans to continue providing sound environmental engineering and science services to sustain the region's quality of life for future generations.

Top: City of Virginia Beach—Lake Gaston Pump Station.

Middle: City of Suffolk—G. Robert House, Jr. Water Plant.

Bottom: Virginia Port Authority—Man-made Oyster Reef.

THE FUTURA GROUP

The Futura Group, headed by longtime Virginia Beach builders Rick Payne and Rick Gregor, specializes in develop/build projects throughout southeastern Virginia and North Carolina. From semi-custom and custom homes, condominium projects, remodeling and renovations and commercial development, The Futura Group strives to make each project one the developers would be proud to call home.

Payne and Gregor, who boast more than forty years of combined experience, renamed their building and development company The Futura Group, LLC in 2004. The new name replaced what was Bay Reflections, LLC. The new name reflects The Futura Group's expanded reach to all of Hampton Roads and northeastern North Carolina. The name also takes into account the company's willingness to employ environmentally aware building techniques and use the most recent technology, materials and designs in its structures.

The Futura Group developments include Mill Dam Landing, Bridgett's Landing, and Tranquility by the Bay, Windsor Woods, and Island Estates, a thirty-three-home development spread over twenty-five acres. Island Estates was recognized by the Elizabeth River Project for its environmentally sensitive design.

Other projects currently under construction include Mayberry in Virginia Beach, The Gateway in Portsmouth, and Colonial Village in Edenton, North Carolina.

The Futura Group is also the developer for two of the region's most exciting recent communities; The Spectrum at Willoughby Point and The Sanctuary at False Cape.

The Sanctuary at False Cape is a one-of-a-kind, oceanfront community skillfully built along Virginia's most pristine beach. The Sanctuary is situated on Virginia's Outer Banks, one of the last large untouched tracts of oceanfront beach in the Commonwealth.

The owners of The Futura Group decided early on that the only way to compliment such a location was with an artfully built community offering such luxury amenities as a fitness center, a library, covered parking, three pools, party room with kitchen, game room, green space and an exclusive beach.

The Sanctuary's 248 residences come in a dozen unique floor plans with two, three, and four bedroom configurations, including two-story penthouses. The ninety-nine-units in Phase One closed in June of 2006. Phase Two is scheduled to close in 2007.

To the north of The Sanctuary is the quiet beach community of Sandbridge; to the south are the rolling sand dunes of False Cape State Park and Little Island State Park; to the west are the eight thousand acres of the Back Bay National Wildlife Refuge; and to the east is the wide-open Atlantic Ocean.

❦

Above: Futura Group owners Rick Payne and Rick Gregor.

Below: A Tranquility by the Bay detail.

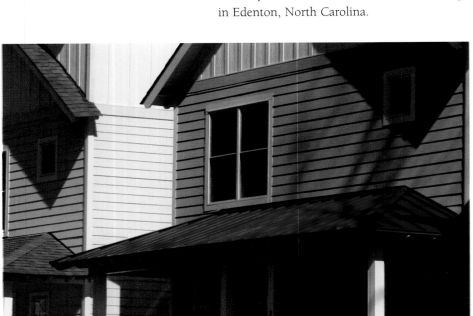

The Futura Group has taken all necessary steps to make The Sanctuary a gentle neighbor to this delicate environment.

While developing The Sanctuary, The Futura Group worked closely with federal, state and local officials to protect the breeding grounds of the ocean sea turtles that nest on area beaches.

Since turtle hatchlings always emerge at night, the flow of traditional outdoor white lights can be a tremendous distraction and prevent the turtles from reaching the ocean during the critical first forty-eight hours of life. To protect the turtles, The Futura Group installed oceanfront lighting with special red casings for use during the turtle-breeding season.

According to the Back Bay Wildlife Refuge, the turtles travel up the eastern seaboard each year, some from as far away as South and Central America, to nest on the Virginia shore. Somehow, the turtles are imprinted at birth to return here and lay their eggs. A wildlife refuge spokesperson says the specialty lighting provided at The Sanctuary by The Futura Group is certain to be a critical component of the ongoing effort to protect and preserve future turtle populations.

Work began in March of 2006 on The Spectrum at Willoughby Point, which will become the new gateway to Norfolk from the west. A hotel, restaurant and warehouses on the site were demolished to make way for The Spectrum, which will continue the revitalization of the Willoughby/Ocean View areas.

The iconic King Neptune statue formerly seen from I-64 is being incorporated into the landscape design for the new resort. When complete, the new landmark community will have 294 condominium residences, thirty town homes and three loft apartments, complemented by 22,000 square feet of retail space and 79 boat slips.

The residences at The Spectrum at Willoughby Point will come in a variety of two, three, and four-bedroom condominiums ranging from approximately 1,300 square feet to more than 3,000 square feet. Deluxe amenities include a pool, clubhouse, fitness center, library and the most spectacular sunset available anywhere in Hampton Roads. With a panoramic view of the Chesapeake Bay and the Elizabeth and James Rivers, right at the mouth of Hampton Roads Harbor, there is simply no other waterfront location like this anywhere.

The partners in The Futura Group, Payne and Gregor, along with Brian K. Holland, are also partners in a variety of other related businesses, including Atlantic Bay Mortgage Group, PortFolio Real Estate Company, and Prestige Title Company.

Headquarters for The Futura Group is located at 116 Landmark Square in Virginia Beach. For additional information, please visit www.thefuturagroup.com.

Above: An artist's rendering of The Sanctuary at False Cape.

Below: An artist's rendering of The Spectrum at Willoughby Point.

ROYSTER-CLARK, INC.

Royster-Clark, Inc. was established in 1992 through a merger of the Royster Company and W. S. Clark & Sons Inc., two firms with roots dating from the late nineteenth century.

Today, Royster-Clark is one of the largest retailers of fertilizer, seed, crop production products and agronomic services in the United States. The firm operates more than 250 retail farm supply and service centers in twenty-one states while distributing to thirty states.

The Royster Company was founded in Tarboro, North Carolina, in 1885 and has been engaged in the fertilizer business throughout its history. In the late 1880s, it moved its corporate headquarters to Norfolk and the "Royster" building is still seen today at the corner of Granby Street and City Hall Avenue. In 1980, Royster was acquired by Universal Leaf Tobacco Company, Inc. and, in 1985, was sold to a Danish concern, Superphos. In 1991, Royster closed its Norfolk headquarters and split headquarters between Florence,

Above: Original Royster building, c. the 1940s.

Below: The Tarboro, North Carolina, factory 1885.

South Carolina for its retail division and Mulberry, Florida for phosphates.

W. S. Clark was organized as a general mercantile business in Tarboro, North Carolina, in 1872. In 1978 it began a disciplined expansion in the fertilizer business and grew to include approximately sixty locations in Virginia, North Carolina and South Carolina.

In 1992 an acquisition group established by The Sterling Group, Inc. of Houston, Texas and James Shirley of Norfolk acquired the farm marketing retail group from Royster. This group serviced a 16-state area through 58 retail service centers, 12 wholesale distribution facilities, and 35 independent commission agents.

An expansion phase began following the merger of the Royster Company and W. S. Clark & Sons in 1992. Francis P. Jenkins, Jr., joined the company in 1994 as Chairman of the Board and, in 1995, assumed the additional role of Chief Executive Officer. Jenkins was joined at that time by G. Kenneth Moshenek, as President and Chief Operating Officer. The expansion, which began in 1996, saw the purchase of Weaver Fertilizer Company, Dixie Guano and Lebanon

Agricorp. In 1999, Royster-Clark acquired IMC Agribusiness, which included 215 retail outlets, the Rainbow division, and two nitrogen-manufacturing plants.

Royster-Clark moved its headquarters from Tarboro back to Norfolk in 1999 in order to maintain a strong east coast presence. Norfolk serves as the operational headquarters and includes finance, marketing, purchasing, logistics and planning departments. To continue a Midwest presence, Collinsville, Illinois is the support office for accounting, information technology, human resources, and environmental health and safety.

The company provides a complete range of agricultural products needed to grow all major crops in the United States. Royster-Clark is recognized as the leader in the fertilizer, seed, crop protection and agronomic services business.

Among Royster-Clark's well-known products are Super Rainbow Fertilizers, Vigoro and Tribute Seeds, TGold Ammonium Sulfate Solution, RoTech, and GloTell.

Royster-Clark believes that U.S. farmers are the original environmentalists and dedicated stewards of our natural resources. Because of this, the company applies an environmental measuring stick to everything it plans and does.

Royster-Clark is recognized as a leader in encouraging and practicing basic conservation farming, precision agriculture, and biotechnology. These practices help to ensure that the integrity of the environment is preserved for future generations. The company is extremely proud to twice be a recipient of the *National Environmental Respect Award*, recognizing its total program for safeguarding the environment. This award cites Royster-Clark's special containment systems at storage facilities, advanced application methods and concern for the safety of employees, customers and community.

Royster-Clark is committed to providing a complete solution for all agricultural crop production needs.

Regardless of what the future brings Royster-Clark will always have a commitment to the agricultural industry because of its rich agricultural heritage, progressive farmers and diversified farm economy. Royster-Clark is committed to providing a complete solution for all agricultural crop production needs.

With more than twenty-five hundred employees, Royster-Clark stays true to its values of honesty, loyalty, integrity and appreciation for its customers. Indeed, the company strives to help make customers more profitable and their lives a little easier.

According to Chairman and CEO Francis P. Jenkins, Jr., Royster-Clark's vision is to be the trusted and recognized leader in the agricultural industry, the resource of first choice for every customer and producer, and a growth company where employees can achieve success and develop to their maximum potential.

Above: President and COO G. Kenneth Moshenek.

Below: CEO Francis P. Jenkins.

MARQUE HOMES BY C. R. McLELLON BUILDER, INC.

Roger McLellon and his wife, Debbie, built their first speculative house in 1984. That home sold quickly and launched a business that has allowed them to build hundreds of custom homes, delight new homeowners across the Peninsula, and make many lifelong friends along the way.

Roger got his start in the building industry by working weekends with his father-in-law, Robert C. Bunting, while working during the week for the government housing industry. He already had background training in architecture and building construction from Thomas Nelson Community College but the time he spent with Bunting was invaluable. "I really learned the nuts and bolts of the industry that way," Roger says.

Debbie is very active in the family business, helping with colors, materials, fixtures, appliances, and selections. "I'm cosmetic, he's construction," she says with a laugh. Debbie decorates a showcase home in each community to show potential buyers what it will feel like to live in that model. It has been quite positive hearing comments from buyers that they feel at home before building their new home.

Also involved in the firm is Debbie's sister, Joan Gummo, who brought twenty years of contracting experience to the company. A design-build firm, Marque Homes will work with plans from other sources or adjust their plans for customers. Roger also builds on client's private lots as well as developments. "We enjoy working with the customer and taking their dreams and making them a reality," he says.

While many facets of the homebuilding process can seem overwhelming and complex to a client, Marque Homes has developed a work ethic that reflects a dedication to a quality product. "We're well known for our follow-through," Roger says. "We stand behind and service our homes."

Roger and Debbie McLellon.

Roger is very responsive to the client's needs. If a client calls with a concern, Roger or someone from the office will contact the client as quickly as possible to address or alleviate their concerns.

Designing speculative and custom design homes allows Roger to work from both fronts of the homebuilding business. Although he admits that speculative homes can be a bit of a gamble, he has a feel for what buyers are looking for. "When you're dealing with real estate, location is everything," he notes. Marque Homes currently builds approximately 60 homes per year, averaging 2,000 to 5,000 square feet.

Coordinating the colors and details of speculative homes usually requires more of Debbie's involvement than that of custom homes. "I coordinate the colors inside and out, paint, vinyl, moldings and cabinets," says Debbie. "I make decisions based on what I think the potential buyer might want and what the market trend is at the time."

When building a home, Roger places emphasis on family areas. Large kitchens with full pantries, useful family rooms and large, well-lighted living areas are hallmarks of Marque Homes. While he specializes in colonial and traditional homes, Roger incorporates many contemporary features such as large closets, full amenities and luxurious master bathrooms into his designs. Marque Homes has participated in thirteen area "Parade of Homes" promotions over the years, winning numerous awards for design and construction.

Roger has seen some significant changes in the industry since he started in business more than two decades ago. "Owners have become more sophisticated and knowledgeable about the building process," he says. "They are demanding top-of-the-line insulation, energy-efficient heating and cooling systems and the finest amenities. With the Internet so accessible, home buyers can fully educate themselves about home products and know exactly what to ask for when customizing their homes."

Marque Homes has built quality homes in a number of Peninsula and Williamsburg communities including Heritage Cove in Poquoson, Running Man in York County, Lakes at Howe Farms in Hampton, Kingsmill,

Governor's Land, and Ford's Colony. The firm is also involved on the cutting edge of Port Warwick in Newport News. Port Warwick is an innovative new-urbanist, mixed-use community in the heart of Newport News. Only two custom homebuilders were selected to build all of the residences in the development.

Marque Homes is also one of the two featured builders in The Settlement at Powhatan Creek, an active adult community located in the heart of Williamsburg's Monticello area. The community will feature over 400 homes and is set on 225 wooded acres in the Powhatan Creek watershed. A luxury clubhouse with amenities such as an indoor/outdoor pool, aerobic and fitness rooms, a grand ballroom, and space for many more amenities will also be available to residents.

Marque Homes by C. R. McLellon Builder Inc. also offers new home quality to remodeling and home improvement projects. Residential projects include new kitchens, baths, room additions, master suites, screened porches and sunrooms. Commercial improvements include projects in medical, professional, retail and restaurant facilities.

Roger is involved in leadership positions with a number of professional organizations. He has been a member of the National Association of Homebuilders Board of Directors and a member of the Peninsula Housing and Builders Association (PHBA) since 1984, serving on its Board of Directors since 1986. Roger was president of PHBA in 1994 and was named its "Builder of the Year" in both 1996 and 2002.

An active member of the community, Roger served as site coordinator for the Poquoson Kids Island project, a member of the building committee for Bethel Baptist Church, a member of the Youth Focus Gathering of Men Board of Directors, and is an annual sponsor of Back River Youth Sports programs. He is also a strong supporter of the International Cooperating Ministries, an organization dedicated to building and nurturing churches worldwide, and Orphan Helpers, which is dedicated to service and ministering to the physical and spiritual needs of orphaned, abandoned and incarcerated children and youth in foreign countries.

Roger and Debbie have three children, Brian, Craig and Carley, and currently reside in

Poquoson, Virginia. Brian is a rising junior attending Hampden Sydney College in Farmville, Virginia. Craig is a senior and Carley is a freshman at Poquoson High School.

Roger and Debbie look forward to the possibility of their children becoming third-generation Marque Homes' builders. "We hope the kids follow their hearts in the careers they choose, but would be honored if one or more of them take over the business someday," says Roger.

Marque Homes by C. R. McLellon Builder Inc. is headquartered at 538G Wythe Creek Road in Poquoson. For additional information, please visit www.marquehomes.net, or call 757-868-9707.

G-U HARDWARE, INC.

G-U Hardware, Inc., which manufactures European-style door and window hardware, began operation in Chuckatuck in 1987. Operating from a small, 1,000-square-foot building in Chuckatuck, G-U Hardware posted first-year sales in excess of $100,000.

Although G-U Hardware's history in the United States is a relatively short one, the company is part of the Gretsch-Unitas Group of companies, which traces its origins to 1907 when Viktor Gretsch began manufacturing "Atlas" pull cord fan-light openers, window stays, and small fittings. The company was located in a small factory in Stuttgart-Feuerbach, Germany. Despite wars and economic upheaval, the company continued to grow and add to its product line, including sliding door fittings, which were patented as early as 1924.

In 1975, Gretch-Unitas began acquiring FERCO, the largest French manufacturer of builders' hardware and in 1983, G-U took over BKS, the most traditional German manufacturer of locking cylinders, locking systems, locks, door closers and anti-panic locks. Storo, Italy's leading handle manufacturer was acquired in 1996. Since 1982, Gretsch-Unitas GmbH has acted as the parent company for the entire group. It initializes research and development within the group and also coordinates marketing activities within those companies.

Gretsch-Unitas remains a family company and the Von Resch family still owns G-U Hardware today.

With its move into the United States in the mid-1980s, G-U soon discovered a ready

market for its top-quality door and window hardware. Leading window manufacturers, such as Pella, became leading customers.

In 1989, G-U Hardware moved into a five-thousand-square-foot facility at Oyster Point Industrial Park. Only a year later an expansion doubled the production space. The year 2000 saw another expansion of the production facility, this time to twenty thousand square feet and establishment of a small assembly workshop in Medford, Wisconsin. Sales in 2000 reached a new record level, an increase of nearly seventy percent in just two years.

G-U West, Inc., a sales and distribution facility, was opened in 2001 in San Juan Capistrano, California. To keep pace with the growing demand for its products, G-U Hardware constructed a thirty-seven-thousand-square-foot sales, distribution, and assembly facility in 2002. This facility is located on nearly five acres of land at 12650 Patrick Henry Drive in Newport News, Virginia. The company now employs thirty people at its Newport News facility. G-U Hardware again recorded

Above: The founding members of the Gretsch-Unitas Group of companies.

Below: The Gretsch-Unitas manufacturing plant in Ditzingen, Germany.

record sales in 2004 and set a vision for quadrupling sales in the next five years.

Kenneth J. Lange was named vice president and general manager of G-U Hardware in 2003, succeeding Kevin McDaniel. Lange previously was general manager of Cooper Bearings, a division of Kaydon Corporation in Virginia Beach.

The success formula for G-U Hardware and the entire Gretsch-Unitas Group is the same today as it was when the company was founded nearly a century ago.

The easy operation of windows and doors has become a matter of course for the company and, since its founding, Gretsch-Unitas has led the market by continually improving its products. The company's guiding principle has always been directed toward making the opening of windows and doors technically better, easier and safer than ever.

Intensive research and development has become a tradition within the Gretsch-Unitas Group of companies. An example of this may be found in builders' hardware and ventilation systems with a high utility value, which are recognized by architects and planners, builders, and

window and door manufacturers alike. Traditional doors and windows reach new heights by being equipped with additional and more sophisticated fittings. The demands and requirements brought forth by architecture, the environment and energy efficiency determine the research and development within the Group.

The production companies within the Gretsch-Unitas Group manufacture a complete assortment of more than 60,000 individual parts in nine countries with approximately 3,500 employees. The sheer variety of the company's product range—from cylinders and master key systems to aluminum and brass designer handles for doors and windows—requires a very particular production technique. A wide variety of materials, such as steel, aluminum, die-cast zinc and plastics, are processed daily.

With a wide product range in the fields of hardware, ventilators, and security fittings, the Gretsch-Unitas Group, including G-U Hardware, offers a convenient one-source solution for meeting the needs of its market.

The Gretsch-Unitas Group of companies stands for only the very top quality. At every stage—from production to supply—motivated and responsible employees work hard each day to maintain high standards. In 1995, Gretsch-Unitas earned certification according to the DIN standards ISO 9001 for its quality control standards.

G-U Hardware and the entire Gretsch-Unitas Group of companies has become a worldwide leader in its field because we are focused on one belief—what is best for its customers.

Above: Stainless steel multipoint door hardware.

Below: G-U Hardware is located at 12650 Patrick Henry Drive in Newport News.

VIRGINIA PORT AUTHORITY

THE PORT OF VIRGINIA

As The Port of Virginia approaches its four hundredth birthday, two decades of rapid growth and upcoming bright prospects have focused all eyes on the future. America's first trading port is positioning itself to become the largest seaport on the East Coast.

On May 14, 1607, 104 Englishmen landed on an island they named Jamestown. Just up the James River from Hampton Roads, the site was selected for its deepwater anchorage and strong defensive position. The colonists struggled mightily. Instead of gold, they discovered hardship. But, led initially by Captain John Smith, they persevered,

established a fledgling economy, and became England's foothold in America.

Although the colonists did not discover raw materials for its sponsor, the Virginia Company of London, they were determined to ship goods back to Europe. The first glassmaking shop in the New World was located at Jamestown. A few years later, the colonists began exporting tobacco, the profitable cash crop that became the backbone of Virginia industry.

The colonists also relied on imports from the homeland to keep them going—sailing ships bearing fresh supplies were always a most welcome sight at Jamestown. As the Virginia colony grew throughout the seventeenth and eighteenth centuries, so did commerce. The cities of Norfolk, Portsmouth and Newport News grew around the waterways of Hampton Roads. In the nineteenth century, Lieutenant Matthew Fontaine Maury, often called "The Father of Oceanography" and author of the classic book The Physical Geography of the Seas, had this to say about the Hampton Roads harbor, "The Civil War interrupted commercial growth at Virginia's seaport and allowed cities such as New York and Charleston to dominate East Coast trade." Today, however, the natural advantages of Hampton Roads' ice-free and centrally located harbor are thrusting The Port of Virginia forward.

Since port unification in the 1970s and early 1980s, when Virginia's three competing marine terminals were consolidated under the control of the Virginia Port Authority, business has skyrocketed. From 1983 to 2005, traffic at the Port of Virginia has increased 576 percent.

More imports and exports now pass through Virginia than through any other U.S. East Coast port except New York and Charleston. And Virginia port officials believe it is only a matter of time until the Port of Virginia becomes the busiest on the Eastern Seaboard.

With international trade expected to double or triple in the next twenty years, four key factors will determine which ports can best accommodate future growth: deeper water to facilitate the jumbo container ships now under construction, intermodal infrastructure to transport goods inland, access to a large customer base, and waterfront property to expand terminal capacity.

Virginia is the only East Coast port with all four attributes, and projects are currently underway to maximize the potential benefit of each.

With current fifty-foot channels and ongoing dredging to deepen the Atlantic channel to fifty-five feet, Virginia boasts the deepest ice-free harbor on the coast. In the coming years these deepwater channels will become prerequisite to growing business as deeper draft ships begin plying the trade lanes.

The Port of Virginia has direct rail access to its terminals, as well as convenient highway connections. Projects, both underway and in the planning phases, will increase the capacity of Virginia infrastructure in the coming years. For example, Norfolk Southern railroad is heightening its tunnels along the route connecting Hampton Roads and Chicago to allow double-stacked intermodal trains direct access to Midwest markets.

The Port of Virginia is located near more markets than any other port. Because of this, companies such as Target and Wal-Mart have chosen to build dozens of large distribution centers in the Commonwealth. This will provide a healthy cargo base as the port grows.

Finally, The Port of Virginia has room to expand. The largest shipline in the world, the A. P. Moller-Maersk Group, is currently building a private terminal in Hampton Roads that will double port capacity. Meanwhile, the

Virginia Port Authority is planning another new marine terminal at Craney Island, as well as renovating its existing facility in Norfolk. These expansion projects will allow Virginia to grow into a hub port in the coming decades, perhaps the largest on the East Coast.

"I think very definitely we will be one of the few hub ports on the East Coast," says Virginia Port Authority Executive Director J. Robert Bray. "I think that's for obvious reasons. We're the only port that is going to have piers deep enough to handle the big ships. We're close to the ocean, we've got great rail service, and I think the future looks pretty bright for us."

COLONNA MARINE RAILWAY

Charles J. Colonna established Colonna Marine Railway, a small shipyard built on the Elizabeth River, in 1875 when times were hard. The Civil War had ended only a decade before and money was still hard to come by as the Old Dominion sought to rebuild from the devastating war.

In spite of the hardships, it was an exciting time for the twenty-six-year-old ship carpenter attempting to build his own business. The nation was reunited after a bloody and costly war and an era of unprecedented growth was slowly getting underway. The port was busy and filled with vessels of all kinds, many of which needed repair. Colonna's new shipyard was well situated in the midst of a thriving seaport and he felt that with hard work the opportunities for success were great.

Nearly all the vessels of the day were wooden and sail powered. They included fish trawlers, oyster boats, barges and bogies, and their construction and repair required the skills of ship carpenters, riggers, sail makers, wood caulkers, painters, and blacksmiths.

Colonna located his shipyard in what was then Norfolk County, on the south bank of the eastern branch of the Elizabeth River, diagonally across the river from downtown Norfolk.

The marine railway had a fifty-ton lifting capacity and was powered by one or two horses as needed, depending on the load being dry-docked. The horses were harnessed to a cross arm attached to a vertical shaft, or "kingpost." While the horses walked in a circle around the kingpost, the cradle on which the vessel rested was pulled out of the water on inclined tracks with steel rollers.

The work sheds and office building were wood framed with a board-and-batten exterior.

A painting of this shipyard was done from written information found in the archives of Colonna's Shipyard, verbal information passed down through the Colonna family, inspection of other old shipyards, and a bit of imagination as to what the facility might have looked like. The imagined parts are, however, based on many years of shipyard experience.

Above: Charles J. Colonna (1849-1920), founder of Colonna's Shipyard.

Below: Colonna Marine Railway, 1875.

COLONNA'S SHIPYARD, INC.

A medium-size full facility ship repair and conversion shipyard employing four hundred people, Colonna's Shipyard, Inc., is one of the state's oldest family-owned businesses. As of 2006, it has been in continuous operation for 131 years.

Colonna's Shipyard, Inc., has grown slowly but steadily from a small boat yard founded by Charles J. Colonna in 1875 to the fifty-five-acre shipyard it is today. The shipyard is located at the confluence of the eastern and southern branches of the Elizabeth River, just across from downtown Norfolk.

The yard services commercial and military vessels from up and down the East Coast and around the world. It is a full-service ship repair and conversion shipyard with three marine railways up to 5,000 tons and two floating drydocks up to 18,000-ton capacity.

The shipyard's workforce includes inside and outside machinists, shipfitters, metal fabricators, welders, pipefitters, electricians, docking crew, laborers, painters, and a gas-free department.

The shipyard and its family of employees are proud of the facility and its highly skilled

and stable workforce. Over the years, Colonna's Shipyard has become known for the very values on which it was founded—hard work, good value, and fairness.

Colonna's Shipyard operates four divisions:
- Steel America specializes in large-scale heavy-duty steel fabrication and machine work. Division head: Ken Mebane.
- Colonna Yachts operates a complete refit and repair facility for megayachts worldwide. Division head: Vance Hull.
- Trade Team provides quality staffing for marine, industrial, and construction. Division head: Ronnie Strange.
- Down River specializes in down river ship repair of all kinds. Division head: Bill Wren.

Colonna Shipyard, Inc.'s, present owner is W. W. Colonna, Jr., chairman of the board and grandson of the founder. Thomas W. Godfrey, Jr., is president and chief executive officer. Other officers include Stephen Walker, vice-president of operations; Richard Sobocinski, vice-president of contracts; Dave DiPersio, chief financial officer; and Ron Jerasa, director of business development.

Above: An aerial view of Colonna's Shipyard, c. 2005.

Left: The SS Argonaut in drydock.

VIRGINIA MARITIME ASSOCIATION

The Virginia Maritime Association (VMA) has promoted, protected and encouraged development of the Port of Hampton Roads since it was founded in 1920. The association is one of the oldest in the nation and plays an increasingly essential role in Virginia's evolution as a "hub" port, and in the success of the many companies whose business relies on the Port's operations.

Through the active involvement of its more than 550 members—representing virtually every industry impacted by the Port—VMA has effectively incorporated a policy of cooperation under which the Port has flourished.

VMA is the "voice of the port" and is actively involved in federal and state legislation protecting the interests of the industry. The association has played an increasingly vital role in continued growth of the Port and will continue to do so in the future.

The Port of Virginia has been a boom to the Commonwealth and the world for nearly four centuries. From the early founding of American's first port at Jamestown in 1607, through the era of the great clipper ships, to the present-day sophistication of computerized intermodal technology, Virginia has been at the forefront of every major change in the shipping industry.

VMA has been a leader and facilitator of change and improvements at the Port for more than eight decades, but none was more important than the unification of the ports in the Hampton Roads harbor.

In 1981, the Virginia General Assembly passed landmark legislation designed to unify the ports under a single agency, the Virginia Port Authority, with a new single operating company, Virginia International Terminals, Inc. In the years preceding unification, ports in the Hampton Roads Harbor were privately operated by competing companies, which caused sporadic growth and splintered marketing efforts. Unification has made the Port of Virginia the fastest growing port complex in the United States.

VMA provides a number of member services to promote shipping interests in throughout the Commonwealth. The Association's goals include:

- Encouraging efficiencies, enhancements and planning through a diversified committee structure;
- Coordinating liaison to the public and all levels of government, promoting commerce as an advocate for the Port;
- Educating the maritime community on Port issues through briefings, publications and other media; and
- Fostering stronger growth of the Port.

With our easy access from the open sea, proximity to two-thirds of our nation's population, and an excellent labor climate, the Port of Virginia is truly on the cusp of greatness.

JOSEPH C. BROWN FAMILY

BUILDERS, GENERAL CONTRACTORS, REAL ESTATE DEVELOPERS

The story of Joseph C. Brown, Sr., is confirmation that the American dream is still alive, that hard work and determination still matter, and that success is still available for those who seek it.

Joe Brown, Sr., grew up on an eastern North Carolina farm and came to Newport News in 1941 after graduating from high school in Plymouth, North Carolina. He had hoped to find a job in the Engineering Department of the Newport News Shipbuilding Company but the nation was soon plunged into World War II and Joe volunteered for the Army.

Joe, Sr., fought with the 86th and 95th Divisions in Germany, including action at the Battle of the Bulge, and was promoted several ranks in the field. His heroism in combat earned him a Bronze Star and Purple Heart.

Following the war, Joe returned to Hampton Roads and married Anne Stassinos, a local girl he had left behind when he joined the Army. Anne worked at home raising a large family, but always found time to be a classroom mom, Little League mom, Scout mom and band mom. She also found time to serve her church and a number of civic organizations.

Joe, Sr. worked during the day for the Corps of Engineers and some of the largest construction firms in the area, and studied engineering at the College of William & Mary extension school at night. He helped lay out the first Elizabeth River tunnel to Portsmouth and worked on the construction of many of the large public housing projects following the war.

Supervising building projects was what Joe, Sr. enjoyed most and he became one of the area's best-known and well-respected project supervisors during the 1950s and 1960s.

During the fast-food restaurant boom of the 1970s, Joe, Sr.—along with his son, Joseph C. Brown, Jr.—built the first Taco Bell, Jack-in-the-Box, Wendy's, Roy Rogers, Western Sizzlin' Steakhouse, and IHOP Restaurants on the east coast, in addition to post offices, shopping centers and office buildings.

Joe, Sr. has served in leadership positions in many professional, civic, veteran, and church associations, and has received the highest commendations.

Today, the family building business is operated by Joe Sr.'s sons, Ronald K. Brown and David S. Brown. They build many commercial projects in the Hampton Roads area. The company, along with partners, has also begun developing, owning and leasing commercial shopping centers throughout the region.

Joe and Anne Brown are the parents of Joe, Jr., Richard, Ronald, and David; and the grandparents of Lauren, David and Nicholas. They celebrated their sixtieth wedding anniversary in July 2005.

J. C. BROWN COMPANY,
Established 1971

WEDGEWOOD BUILDING
ASSOCIATES,
Established 1979

BROWN BUILDING
CORPORATION,
Established 1984

RODA ASSOCIATES,
Established 1986

DRS ASSOCIATES,
Established 1999

ERA ATKINSON REALTY

Frank Atkinson, a Norfolk auto salesman who dabbled in real estate, started Atkinson Realty in 1943. At the time, Frank was selling oceanfront lots for as little as $2,000. After all, who would want to live right on the Atlantic Ocean with all its hazards!

Frank set up shop in a tiny 459 square foot office located on the corner of Fifty-fourth Street and Atlantic Avenue in Virginia Beach. The building had been the original land sales office for the developer of Cape Henry, or "the North End" as it is known today. There was no heat, air-conditioning or even toilet facilities in the office. For that necessity, Frank went next door to a Mr. Lowell's house.

Heating, air conditioning and a bathroom were finally added and the office has served as headquarters for Atkinson Realty for nearly sixty-five years. A second office was opened 1986 and allowed Atkinson Realty to grow from a four-agent operation to a thirty agent, multi-office company.

As Frank sold properties and ocean-side cottages to clients from Norfolk to Richmond, he realized there was also a need to rent those properties to people wishing to vacation at the beach. Since Frank preferred to play golf rather than rent cottages, this duty fell to his secretary, Virginia Butler. Fred and Millie Barham also helped Frank and Virginia grow the business and today Atkinson Realty is the largest rental company in Virginia Beach specializing in vacation homes.

Above: Principal Broker and founder Frank V. Atkinson.

Below: Owner/Broker Betsy Atkinson.

Frank's son, John, began working in the family business in the late 1960s and purchased the firm from his father in the early '70s. He continued the name Frank Atkinson Realty and became a successful broker.

John ran for city treasurer of Virginia Beach in 1978, a position he still holds today. John's wife, Betsy, entered the business when he became treasurer. She bought the company in 1983 and changed the name to Atkinson Realty. Page, Clay, and John, the third generation of Atkinsons, are now active in the business.

Betsy Atkinson has been very involved in professional associations and served eight years as a member of the Virginia Beach Planning Commission, two years as chairman. She was appointed by the Governor to the Board of Visitors of Old Dominion University where she was elected secretary and served on numerous committees.

The firm joined the ERA International franchise system in 1991 and has benefited from the education, training and relocation opportunities provided by ERA.

In addition to sales of oceanfront and waterfront property, Atkinson Realty is the largest resort rental/vacation home rental firm in the area. The company is also involved in the management of condominium associations and time-share resales.

Atkinson Realty has thirty sales agents and three reservationists, as well as administrative staff, in two locations.

For additional information on Atkinson Realty, please go to www.atkinsonrealty.com.

Wayne Harbin, his wife Bonnie, and sons have dedicated themselves to becoming one of the premier homebuilders on the Virginia Peninsula. Thousands of satisfied homeowners attest to the quality of work performed by the Harbins and their team of professionals.

Wayne Harbin began learning about homebuilding soon after graduating from high school. He started his career in 1965, working with a group of Mennonite builders in the Denbigh area. It was a hands-on learning experience because the same crew dug the footings, framed the structure, put on the roofing and siding, and trimmed out the interior.

Wayne and Bonnie established their own firm in Yorktown in 1985, with Bonnie running the office and Wayne supervising site construction. The Harbin's two sons, Doug and Brad, are now managing the firm's offices, with about twenty-five employees.

Homes by Wayne Harbin Builder range in price from the upper $300,000s to more than $800,000. Typical homes include high quality details such as crown moldings, chair railings, hardwood floors, custom-built kitchen cabinets and Andersen® Windows. Staff designers help homeowners select colors, floor coverings and other details to customize their home.

Quality-built homes by Wayne Harbin Builder may be found in the most desirable neighborhoods across the Peninsula and in Gloucester. A new project in Williamsburg targeted at active adults, The Settlement at Powhatan Creek, will begin soon.

Wayne Harbin Builder is the only Peninsula firm to be selected as a *Southern Living* Custom Builder Program member, a prestigious designation awarded to only one hundred homebuilders in the nation. Builders selected for this program must demonstrate the ability to produce classic Southern designs with contemporary living arrangements.

"I'm very proud of our selection by the *Southern Living* Custom Builder Program," says Wayne. "I think it says a great deal about the integrity with which we operate and the reputation we've earned."

Wayne Harbin Builder is dedicated to customer service and ensuring that the home building process will be an enjoyable experience. A project manager serves as liaison with the homeowners to keep them abreast of the construction of their home. A construction scheduling program projects the home's construction from the receipt of permits to final closing, avoiding delays and surprises for the customer.

Wayne Harbin Builder's main office is located at 3630 George Washington Memorial Highway, Suite D, in Yorktown, and the Williamsburg office is located at 3705 Strawberry Plains Road, Suite D. You may contact the firm at 757-867-8307, or view available homes and lots online at www.harbinbuilder.com.

WAYNE HARBIN BUILDER, INC.

Wayne Harbin Builder continues to grow as sons Doug (left) and Brad (right) join their father Wayne in the family business.

COURTESY OF KRISTINA CILIA. ABOVE PHOTOGRAPHS COURTESY OF GEORGE GARDNER

NORTHROP GRUMMAN NEWPORT NEWS

Northrop Grumman Newport News is the nation's sole designer, builder and refueler of nuclear-powered aircraft carriers, and one of only two companies capable of designing and building nuclear powered submarines. The shipyard also provides after-market services for a wide array of naval and commercial vessels.

Northrop Grumman Newport News traces its roots to 1886, when railroad tycoon Collis P. Huntington chartered the Chesapeake Dry Dock & Construction Company. The name was later changed to Newport News Shipbuilding.

Newport News Shipbuilding delivered its first ship; a tugboat named *Dorothy*, in 1891 and, by 1897, NNS had built three warships for the U.S. Navy, the *Nashville*, *Wilmington*, and *Helena*.

Following Huntington's death in 1900, the company issued $5 million in bonds and $6 million in preferred stock to the Huntington family and began the profitable business of building and repairing a large variety of ships.

NNS began building aircraft carriers in the 1930s and the first to be designed from the keel up was the *Ranger*, delivered in 1934. NNS went on to build *Yorktown* and *Enterprise*, two of the most famous fighting ships of World War II.

More than thirty-one thousand employees worked at NNS to deliver ships to the Navy during World War II, and the Navy awarded its prestigious "E" pennant to the company for

Above: Using expertise developed from building 53 attack submarines over four decades, Newport News is constructing the nation's newest attack submarines - the Virginia class, the most advanced submarine in the world.

COURTESY OF NORTHROP GRUMMAN NEWPORT NEWS.

Below: Northrop Grumman Newport News is the nation's sole designer, builder and refueler of nuclear-powered aircraft carriers and is currently building the tenth and final Nimitz-class aircraft carrier, George H. W. Bush (CVN 77).

COURTESY OF NORTHROP GRUMMAN NEWPORT NEWS.

its tremendous contributions and excellence in ship construction. No other shipbuilder delivered such an array of ships or built them faster than Newport News Shipbuilding.

NNS signed a merger agreement with Northrop Grumman Corporation in 2001, creating a $4-billion world-class shipbuilding enterprise with expertise in every class of nuclear and non-nuclear naval ship.

Today, Northrop Grumman Newport News is the sole supplier of U.S. Navy aircraft carriers, and has built twenty-six of the Navy attack submarines in use today. It is the home of the largest dry dock and crane in the Western Hemisphere and the exclusive provider of refueling services for nuclear-powered aircraft carriers.

Northrop Grumman Newport News employs about nineteen thousand people, making it the largest industrial employer in Virginia. Employees make substantial cash and in-kind contributions to hundreds of organizations in the area each year, including Habitat for Humanity, Red Cross blood drives and the United Way.

The vision of Northrop Grumman is to be the most trusted provider of systems and technologies that ensure the security and freedom of our nation and its allies. As the technology leader, we will define the future of defense—from undersea to outer space, as well as cyberspace.

For more information about Northrop Grumman, visit www.northropgrumman.com.

Nearly thirty-five years of dedicated service to clients has earned William E. Wood and Associates, REALTORS® a reputation as "the best in the business."

The firm first opened its doors in 1972 with only three agents and a meager budget. However, Bill and Anne Wood were determined to build a sales force consisting of the very best agents available, backed with exceptional benefits and service.

From the original three agents in the first small office in Virginia Beach, the company has expanded to a sales force of more than seven hundred. William E. Wood and Associates now operates from twenty-one locations serving Williamsburg, Southeast Virginia, Northeast North Carolina and the Outer Banks.

As a company, William E. Wood and Associates has invested heavily in technology in order to stay on the cutting edge and provide its agents with the tools needed for success in today's marketplace. The company website—www.williamewood.com—allows clients to search among thousands of homes in all price ranges. It also provides clients with a free report of today's market value of their home.

The annual sales volume of William E. Wood and Associates has soared in recent years to nearly $3 billion today. This has earned the firm a ranking among the Top Fifty real estate firms

in the nation, including a number ten ranking in closed transactions per agent.

In addition to residential sales offices, the firm operates a New Homes Division, Commercial and Property Management Divisions, as well as training, relocation and marketing services. The company's mission is to serve all the needs of its clients and customers better than anyone else in the business.

William E. Wood and Associates also has a long tradition of giving back to the community. Since its inception, the company has contributed thousands of dollars and countless hours annually to local charities.

The William E. Wood and Associates Foundation will continue that history and strengthen the company's commitment to the community. Originally established as the Wood-Fleming-Frenck Scholarship Fund, community support was provided through educational opportunities to Tidewater Community College and Old Dominion University, nursing schools and other institutes of higher learning. The program was originally funded in large part through the generosity of local builders and contractors who donated their profits from the sale of specially selected scholarship houses.

Today, the largest charitable contribution is made possible through the annual William E. Wood and Associates Charity Golf Classic, which recently raised $45,000 for the William E. Wood and Associates Foundation.

WILLIAM E. WOOD AND ASSOCIATES, REALTORS®

⚓

Above: The corporate offices of William E. Wood and Associates, REALTORS® are located at 1805 Kempsville Road in Virginia Beach.

Below: Shore Drive office in Virginia Beach.

FERGUSON

⚓

Below: Ferguson's professional showroom consultants help customers select products from lighting, to plumbing fixtures, to appliances and accessories.

Bottom: An Associate in Ferguson's Tucson, Arizona, waterworks location pulls fire hydrants to fill an order.

Ferguson, recognized today as the largest distributor of plumbing supplies and pipe, valves and fittings, and the third largest distributor for heating and cooling equipment in the United States, started business in 1953 with $150,000 in starting capital and two locations. With sales exceeding $7 billion, this dynamic organization now employs nearly 21,000 and boasts a coast-to-coast distribution network with approximately 1,300 locations in all 50 states, the District of Columbia, Puerto Rico, and Mexico. Their acquisition by British distribution giant Wolseley plc in 1982 supplied the financial strength for the company's rapid territorial growth and aggressive expansion.

Ferguson focuses on four core businesses— waterworks devoted to supplying water and wastewater products to municipalities and contractors, commercial industrial focused on commercial and mechanical contractors, specialty and industrial businesses, and pipe, valves and fittings; HVAC dealing with heating, ventilation and air conditioning; and the residential business group, which works with builder supplies, showrooms, appliances and lighting.

Plumbing, mechanical and waterworks contractors, kitchen and bath dealers, builders, large industrial businesses, manufacturers, and municipalities all look to Ferguson as an invaluable resource. With an inventory investment of more than $1 billion and a master product file containing 1.6 million products, Ferguson is uniquely positioned to meet the needs of their vast customer base. Their aggressive logistics platform supports cutting edge technology and distribution excellence within nine strategically located distribution centers. More than four thousand fleet vehicles move material across the country to ensure quick, efficient delivery of products.

Ferguson is proud of their strong tradition of giving back to the communities in which they do business—through financial support and volunteerism. Associates are encouraged to participate in community boards, volunteer service and philanthropic events, all of which is part of being good corporate citizens. For 2006, Ferguson has elected to focus charitable efforts on two national organizations. Ferguson has been involved with Habitat for Humanity for many years and will continue as a corporate partner on the 2006 Habitat Builders' Blitz to construct one thousand homes during the first week of June. The other organization, United Way, supports local agencies that provide services to infants, families, school children, and senior citizens in communities across the United States.

In 2005, Wolseley plc announced the exciting development of a North American management team to bring together in the marketplace the exceptional talents and capabilities of all three of their North American operations. Ferguson, Stock Building Supply headquartered in Raleigh, North Carolina, and Wolseley Canada headquartered in Ontario, were aligned to maximize the strengths and resources of the three operating companies.

NORFOLK SOUTHERN CORP.

The story of Norfolk Southern stretches back to the earliest days of American railroading. It is a history of hundreds of combinations, reorganizations and consolidations.

The railroad became an integral part of the Commonwealth in 1837 with the building of the nine-mile long City Point Railroad from Petersburg, Virginia, to Hopewell on the James River, where deep-water vessels unloaded freight and passengers. A decisive point in the history of Virginia rail and Hampton Roads came when Virginia Military Institute graduate and Civil War General William Mahone engineered an innovative roadbed across the Dismal Swamp. He employed a log foundation laid at right angles beneath the surface of the swamp. Although jeered at in the 1850s, Mahone's radical "corduroy road" roadbed still carries immense tonnages of twenty-first century freight in and out of Hampton Roads.

Coal reached Norfolk in 1883 from the newly discovered Pocahontas coalfields in West Virginia. Norfolk Southern's Norfolk and Petersburg predecessor, charted in 1851, opened Pier 1 at Lamberts Point to transload coal to oceangoing vessels. By 1900, Norfolk was the East Coast leader in coal export.

In 1902 the first railroad to carry the name "Norfolk Southern" expanded its route to Virginia Beach and became popular with beachgoers. In the 1930s, the Pennsylvania Railroad connected Norfolk to the North by railroad car ferry floats crossing the Chesapeake Bay to the Delmarva Peninsula. Potatoes, peaches and produce moved north, manufactured goods moved south.

Today, Norfolk Southern continues its legacy as a premier transportation provider linking customers with the marketplaces of the world. Carrying more than seven million rail carload shipments a year, NS operates approximately 21,200 route miles in 22 states,

the District of Columbia and Ontario, Canada, serves every major container port in the eastern United States and provides connections to western rail carriers. Every day some 1,000 trains and 190,000 freight cars are active among customers' locations across the United States. Norfolk Southern's thirty thousand employees have been consistently recognized as safest in the rail industry.

One intermodal train pulled by two locomotives can haul the equivalent of three hundred trucks on the highway. Norfolk Southern operates the most extensive intermodal network in the East and intermodal traffic is a fast-growing business segment.

As North America's largest rail carrier of automotive parts and finished vehicles, NS transports seventy percent of the nation's new cars and trucks. The railroad's Pier 6 at Lamberts Point is one of the largest and fastest coal transloading facility in North America, making it an important logistics link for the railroad, Hampton Roads, and the world.

With an annual throughput capacity of forty-eight million tons, the two shiploaders at Norfolk Southern's Pier 6 permit the facility to load two vessels simultaenously.

R. D. LAMBERT & SON, INC., GENERAL CONTRACTOR

Above: R. D. Lambert in the early days.

Top, right: The TowneBank, Greenbrier banking facility in Chesapeake, Virginia.
COURTESY OF HBA ARCHITECTURE AND INTERIOR DESIGN.

R. D. Lambert Construction Company was founded in 1944 after a previous owner decided his construction company conflicted with his other business interests.

As the story goes, in late 1943 the owner of Hofheimer Construction Company, Henry Hofheimer, purchased a large ready-mix concrete company located in Norfolk. Since he viewed his new company as a conflict of interest with his construction company, he called in several key employees, including R. D. Lambert, and suggested they start their own construction firms. Three construction firms and a surveying company were established as a result of that meeting and three of the companies are still in business, including R. D. Lambert & Son, Inc.

Today, R. D. Lambert & Son, Inc., a full-service general contracting firm, is located in the Greenbrier section of Chesapeake, Virginia. The firm provides services such as design build new construction, additions and alterations, renovations, pre-construction services, and pre-engineered metal buildings.

R. D. Lambert, who established the firm as a sole proprietorship specializing in concrete work, was the driving force behind the firm's early growth. He was assisted by his wife, Ethel, who worked in the office and by his son, Charles, who learned the business literally from the ground up by digging footings during summers and Saturdays during his school days.

The company grew slowly, continuing to concentrate on concrete work and construction of small commercial buildings.

In 1961, Charles Lambert, who had been a construction engineer for the Corps of Engineers, came to work for the family business as vice president. Miles Nowitzky, who had worked with Charles at the Corps of Engineers, soon joined him. Shortly thereafter, the firm was incorporated as R. D. Lambert & Son, Inc.

Under the leadership of Charles Lambert and Miles Nowitzky, and the oversight of R. D., the firm began a period of dramatic growth in both the size of its projects and overall volume. The company's emphasis moved to commercial buildings instead of concrete work, although the firm continued to provide the concrete work for the buildings it constructed.

For a number of years, about seventy-five percent of R. D. Lambert & Son's work involved government projects. As the market changed, the company switched from government contracts to mostly private projects, a work mixture that continues today.

R. D. Lambert & Son, Inc. projects include churches and church-related projects, hospitals, banks, parks, schools, warehouses, preengineered metal buildings, retail stores, and others.

One of the firm's strengths has been the ability to attract and retain good employees and many of the company's twenty-five employees have been with the company twenty years or longer. Gary Richardson, primary owner, started with the firm as a carpenter apprentice in 1969, and is now the president. Susan Allensworth, who began as a secretary in 1968, is now secretary/treasurer and part owner of the company.

Our mission remains the same as when R. D. Lambert founded the company: To provide a quality construction project to our clients, both new and long term, at a fair price and on a reasonable schedule.

For more information about R. D. Lambert & Son, Inc., please visit www.rdlambert.com.

Globe Iron Construction Company, Inc. of Norfolk has served the construction industry for more than eighty years with diverse fabricated structural and miscellaneous steel.

Sol Mednick, a licensed civil engineer, founded the firm in 1923. The company is still privately owned and operated by his descendants.

Globe Iron employs more than 100 people in its fabrication shop and another 30 in the office.

The company's 350,000-square-foot facility is located on a fifteen-acre site at 1401 Maltby Avenue in Norfolk. The facility includes a fabrication plant, a complete steel products warehouse, a blast cleaning/painting shop and a delivery fleet capable of handling a project of any size. With a vast storage yard, Globe Iron can store fabricated materials at its plant months in advance of delivery needs.

Globe Iron's fabricated steel products are used for industrial structures, office buildings, schools, hospitals, shopping centers, specialty fabrications and government and military facilities.

The firm's main focus includes the eastern United States and its location by one of the east coast's busiest ports provides excellent export capabilities.

The company's strength lies in the fact that it can offer its services to a wide range of clients including the building construction market, bridge construction, NASA, the shipbuilding market or the industrial products market. Globe Iron's quality control standards are among the most stringent in the industry and were recently recertified under the AISC category III-B.

Among Globe Iron's many successful projects are the George Mason University Student Recreation Center in Fairfax, the Virginia Tech Athletic Facility at Blacksburg, Hickory High School in Chesapeake, the Virginia Air and Space Center in Hampton and Nauticus Maritime Museum/Center in Norfolk. Globe Iron received an Award of Excellence from the Washington Building Congress, Inc. for its work on the University of Maryland's Campus Recreation Center.

One of Globe Iron's more unusual projects was an exposed steel frame for Nissan Pavilion at Stone Ridge near Manassas, one of the largest and best-equipped concert facilities on the east coast. The Pavilion's six hundred tons of exposed structural steel inspired a *Washington Post* reviewer to note that the structure's "exciting architectural features made of structural steel with soaring columns, bridge weight girders and a network of trusses supporting the roof...are in refreshing contrast to D.C.'s marble cladding and the rustic veneer of other music sheds."

This ability to provide diverse services and the tenacity of Globe Iron's personnel has kept the company strong while many others have failed. With a strong belief that "A Satisfied Customer is a Repeat Customer," Globe Iron looks forward to a bright and growing future.

GLOBE IRON CONSTRUCTION COMPANY, INC.

JOEL S. SHEPPARD, INC.

Joel S. Sheppard completed his first home in 1954, and more than half a century later is still building homes in the Hampton Roads area long after most people would have retired. An active mind, a restless spirit and dedication to quality in everything he does have been the driving forces behind his success in both business and life.

His primary business, Joel S. Sheppard, Inc., has built quality homes throughout the Hampton Roads area, contributing greatly to the community's development. The company has built high-end homes in Kingsmill, Holly Hills, Landfall at Jamestown, Settler's Mill, and Piney Creek, among others.

The multi award-winning builder is known for his attention to quality in everything he does, starting with land selection and continuing throughout the homebuilding process. Sheppard is involved in every aspect of his homes, and to this day is not above picking up hammer and nails to help out.

Sheppard began building in 1953 shortly after moving to Newport News. The Richmond native built his first home in Newport News and lived in it two years before selling it. Thus began a string of homes built, lived in, and sold.

As owner of a homebuilding company, part owner in a builder's supply company, and part owner in several subdivisions, Sheppard gives much of the credit for his success to his wife. Bonnie Sheppard, along with running their home and raising their two children, ran the administrative part of the business.

His office staff, suppliers and work crews also deserve credit for Sheppard's success. Their commitment to service and dedication to customer satisfaction are among the primary reasons customers are happy with their Joel S. Sheppard homes, and that satisfaction has lead to word-of-mouth referrals that no advertising campaign will ever be able to match.

Sheppard, known by those who know him as "Joe," is grateful for the trust that Hampton Roads residents have bestowed upon him. He and Bonnie have expressed their gratitude for that trust by giving back to the community that has been so generous to them. Both have been actively involved in the community by serving on various boards and commissions and have contributed time to various community events.

Joel S. Sheppard, Inc., has built more than 1,500 homes in the past 50 years. That would be more than enough for most homebuilders. Sheppard, on the other hand, continues to work full time in the business and plans to continue for as long as possible.

Retirement, as Sheppard likes to say, is unthinkable.

⚓

Above: Joel S. Sheppard.

Below: One of over 1,500 homes built by Joel S. Sheppard, Inc., in the past 50 years.

Empire Machinery & Supply Corporation was founded by J. Ross McNeal and began business on Water Street in downtown Norfolk in 1914 as a wholesale distributor of industrial, mill and marine supplies.

In the early days, Empire carried such items as sheet metal, wire rope, roofing supplies, pipe valves and fittings, as well as industrial, MRO and marine supplies. Most of the firm's freight and inventory came to Norfolk by boat or train.

The second-largest fire in Norfolk history destroyed Empire's original building in 1950, but the firm rebuilt on the same waterfront site as the original building. At that time, there were no bridges between Norfolk and Portsmouth, so employees who lived in Portsmouth rode the ferry across the Elizabeth River to and from work each day.

During this period, Empire's customer base consisted of lumber mills, construction, ship-building and ship repair, and the government.

In 1964, during the firm's fiftieth anniversary, Empire moved into a new and modern office and warehouse facility in the Norfolk Industrial Park. This location has expanded over the years and now takes up an entire city block in the industrial park. The 75,000 square foot building contains an inventory of more than $3 million. Thirteen delivery vehicles deliver orders from eastern North Carolina to Richmond.

A store in Hampton includes a 2,052-square-foot showroom, which allows customers to shop a large inventory selection.

The store also includes a very popular "will-call" counter.

In 1980, Empire opened a new Hampton office and warehouse in the Hampton Industrial Park. This branch serves Hampton, Newport News, Yorktown, Gloucester, Williamsburg, and Richmond.

In addition to general-line industrial and MRO supplies, Empire stocks an extensive selection of material handling equipment, ranging from hand trucks to a wide array of hoists.

Empire's interactive online store, www.empiremachinery.com, provides instant pricing, order status, delivery invoice and statement information.

The McNeal family under a trust established by the founder still independently owns Empire Machinery & Supply Corporation. The founder's son, H. P. McNeal, Sr., is chairman of the board and third-generation family member Flip McNeal, Jr., is vice chairman. Hank Turner, Jr., is president of the firm.

"I am often asked how Empire has survived the numerous changes and consolidations within our industry," Turner says. "I always respond that Empire has the best people in the industrial supply business. We listen to our customers and work with them to ensure their satisfaction. Our inventory and service are second to none.

"Our company motto is 'where customer service is a commitment, not a department.' This statement is more than a motto; it's our business philosophy."

SPONSORS

ABOUT THE AUTHOR

PAUL CLANCY

Paul Clancy has been a journalist for more than thirty years for newspapers like *The Charlotte Observer*, *The Washington Star*, *USA Today*, and *The Virginian-Pilot*. He was the editor of *Calypso Log*, the magazine of The Cousteau Society, and has written for *Smithsonian*, *Cruising World*, and *Chesapeake Bay* magazines. He has written biographies of Senator Sam J. Ervin of North Carolina and Speaker Thomas P. O'Neill of Massachusetts. His most recent book is *Ironclad*, the story of the loss and recovery of the USS *Monitor*. He lives in Norfolk.